# MICHEL DE MONTAIGNE

# Modern Critical Views

*Continued at back of book*

*Modern Critical Views*

# MICHEL DE MONTAIGNE

*Edited and with an introduction by*
Harold Bloom
Sterling Professor of the Humanities
Yale University

CHELSEA HOUSE PUBLISHERS ◊ 1987
New York ◊ New Haven ◊ Philadelphia

© 1987 by Chelsea House Publishers, a division
of Chelsea House Educational Communications, Inc.,
  95 Madison Avenue, New York, NY 10016
  345 Whitney Avenue, New Haven, CT 06511
  5014 West Chester Pike, Edgemont, PA 19028

Introduction © 1987 by Harold Bloom

Printed and bound in the United States of America

10  9  8  7  6  5  4  3  2  1

∞ The paper used in this publication meets the minimum
requirements of the American National Standard for Permanence
of Paper for Printed Library Materials, Z39.48–1984.

Library of Congress Cataloging-in-Publication Data
Montaigne.
    (Modern critical views)
    Bibliography: p.
    Includes index.
    Summary: A collection of critical essays on Montaigne and
his works arranged in chronological order of publication.
    1. Montaigne, Michel de, 1533–1592—Criticism and
interpretation. [1. Montaigne, Michel de, 1533–1592—
Criticism and interpretation.   2. French literature—
History and criticism]  I. Bloom, Harold.  II. Series.
PQ1643.M5657  1987      844'.3            87-8012
ISBN 1–55546–285–5 (alk. paper)

# Contents

# Editor's Note

This book brings together a representative selection of what I judge to be the best criticism of Montaigne that has been made available in English from 1953 until the present. The critical essays are reprinted here in the chronological order of their English publication. I am grateful to James Swenson and Chantal McCoy for their erudition in helping me to edit this volume.

My introduction examines Montaigne's stance towards his literary precursors, and argues against both Terence Cave's deconstructionist reading of this stance, and Thomas Greene's Humanist interpretation of Montaigne. In a general overview, Herbert Lüthy agrees with Montaigne that the great essayist wrote primarily for his own sake, out of personal necessity, and needed us "in order to reveal himself to himself." Donald M. Frame, Montaigne's translator and biographer, follows with his account of how Montaigne, in his final phase, gave the term of "humanist" a new and more fully human meaning.

The philosopher Maurice Merleau-Ponty surveys Montaigne's "detour toward himself" as the route that gave him "the secret of being simultaneously ironic and solemn, faithful and free." The instrument of *writing* in Montaigne is analyzed by Louis Marin, after which Terence Cave describes the complex series of problems in reading that Montaigne gives us. Irma S. Majer studies Montaigne's travel journals as a record that "has less to do with the topography of real and historical places than with images formed in history and the unconscious."

In an examination of structure and meaning in "The Apology for Raymond Sebond," Catherine Demure finds the text to have a paradoxical structure. Neither faith nor reason enables us to transcend human limitations, yet our desire for God brings about the miracle of divine intervention. Thomas Greene, arguing against Cave's deconstruction, attempts to restore Montaigne to the vital center of his *Essays*.

Tracing Montaigne's search for the self's identity, Jean Starobinski illuminates the essayist's "reflective acceptance of the phenomenal world, as compiled and represented in works of literature." In this book's final analysis, Jefferson Humphries examines what he terms the "anti-influential model of identity" in Montaigne, giving us a reading that contrasts usefully with the darker view suggested in my introduction.

# *Introduction*

$M$ontaigne, until the advent of Shakespeare, is the great figure of the European Renaissance, comparable in cognitive power and in influence to Freud in our century. His mordant essay "Of Books" is marked by a genial irony that is profoundly skeptical of the Humanist program that ostensibly (and rather off-handedly) is endorsed:

> Let people see in what I borrow whether I have known how to choose what would enhance my theme. For I make others say what I cannot say so well, now through the weakness of my language, now through the weakness of my understanding. I do not count my borrowings, I weigh them. And if I had wanted to have them valued by their number, I should have loaded myself with twice as many. They are all, or very nearly all, from such famous and ancient names that they seem to identify themselves enough without me. In the reasonings and inventions that I transplant into my soil and confound with my own, I have sometimes deliberately not indicated the author, in order to hold in check the temerity of those hasty condemnations that are tossed at all sorts of writings, notably recent writings of men still living, and in the vulgar tongue, which invites everyone to talk about them and seems to convict the conception and design of being likewise vulgar. I want them to give Plutarch a fillip on my nose and get burned insulting Seneca in me. I have to hide my weakness under these great authorities. I will love anyone that can unplume me, I mean by clearness of judgment and by the sole distinction of the force and beauty of the remarks. For I who, for lack of memory, fall short at every turn

1

in picking them out by knowledge of their origin, can very well realize, by measuring my capacity, that my soil is not at all capable of producing certain too rich flowers that I find sown there, and that all the fruits of my own growing could not match them.

This hardly seems a matter of classical courage but rather of cunning, humor, skill, and a deliciously bland disarming of one's critics. It is also rather clearly a knowingly defensive irony, directed against a literary anxiety that Montaigne insists is universal, and not merely individual. Montaigne at this time (1578–80) is well underway to his final stance, where he forsakes the high Humanist doctrine in favor of the common life, so as to affirm the exuberance of natural existence, and the enormous virtue of being the *honnête homme,* thus establishing a new norm against which Pascal would rebel, or perhaps an influence that Pascal could neither escape nor accept. What "Of Books" subverts most audaciously is the Humanist scheme of benign displacement by imitation. When Montaigne writes of his unsavory critics, "I want them to give Plutarch a fillip on my nose and get burned insulting Seneca in me," he not only accurately names his prime precursors, but he asserts his own power of contamination. In contrast, consider Ben Jonson, more truly Thomas Greene's hero of "classical courage":

> The third requisite in our poet or maker is imitation, *imitatio,* to be able to convert the substance or riches of another poet to his own use. To make choice of one excellent man above the rest, and so to follow him till he grow very he, or so like him as the copy may be mistaken for the principal. Not as a creature that swallows what it takes in, crude, raw, or undigested; but that feeds with an appetite, and hath a stomach to concoct, divide, and turn all into nourishment. Not to imitate servilely, as Horace saith, and catch at vices for virtue, but to draw forth out of the best and choicest flowers, with the bee, and turn all into honey, work it into one relish and savour; make our imitation sweet; observe how the best writers have imitated, and follow them: how Virgil and Statius have imitated Homer; how Horace, Archilochus; how Alcæus, and the other lyrics; and so of the rest.

Here one imitates precisely as the precursors imitated, which seems to me an apt reduction of the Humanist argument. It is no surprise that Jonson goes on to say of reading that it "maketh a full man," borrowing from his truest precursor Sir Francis Bacon in the essay "Of Studies." Admirable essayist in his narrow mode, Bacon is about as adequate to compete with Montaigne as Jonson was to challenge Shakespeare. It takes a singular perversity to prefer Bacon's essays to Montaigne's, and yet Jonson could insist persuasively that he was being loyal to the Humanist doctrine of imitation:

> Some that turn over all books, and are equally searching in all papers; that write out of what they presently find or meet, without choice. By which means it happens that what they have discredited and impugned in one week, they have before or after extolled the same in another. Such are all the essayists, even their master Montaigne. These, in all they write, confess still what books they have read last, and therein their own folly so much, that they bring it to the stake raw and undigested; not that the place did need it neither, but that they thought themselves furnished and would vent it.

Bacon's essays certainly do not "confess still what books they have read last," and Montaigne is anything but formalist in his use of quite immediate reading. Thomas Greene is wiser, I think, when he recognizes that ambivalence and the antithetical haunt all imitation, however Humanist:

> The process called imitation was not only a technique or a habit; it was also a field of ambivalence, drawing together manifold, tangled, sometimes antithetical attitudes, hopes, pieties, and reluctances within a concrete locus.

At the heart of Humanism was an ambivalence, even an antithetical will, that perhaps still makes the phrase "Christian Humanist" something of an oxymoron. Most simply, Humanism entailed a love of Greek and Latin wisdom and humane letters, a desire to know qualities uniquely available in antiquity. Christianity, in the early Renaissance, indeed became Greek and Latin in its culture, at a certain cost. The morality of the Christian Bible is scarcely Greek or Latin, and the God of Christianity remained the God of Abraham, Isaac, and Jacob, rather than the gods of Achilles, Odysseus, and Aeneas. Imitation or mimesis, whether of nature or of a precursor, is a Greek notion, rather than an Hebraic postulate. We cannot image an ancient Greek or Latin author confronting the stark text of the Second Commandment.

Erich Auerbach, in his *Mimesis: The Representation of Reality in Western Literature,* finds in Rabelais and Montaigne an early Renaissance

freedom of vision, feeling, and thought produced by a perpetual playing
with things, and hints that this freedom began to decline not so much in
Cervantes as in Shakespeare, the two writers who by paradox may be the
only Western authors since antiquity clearly surpassing the powers of even
Rabelais and Montaigne. As Auerbach emphasizes:

> In Rabelais there is no aesthetic standard; everything goes with
> everything. Ordinary reality is set within the most improbable
> fantasy, the coarsest jobs are filled with erudition, moral and
> philosophical enlightenment flows out of obscene expressions
> and stories.

This extraordinary freedom of representation in Rabelais is matched
by Montaigne in Auerbach's description of his emancipation not only from
the Christian conceptual schema but from the cosmological view of his
precursors Cicero, Seneca, and Plutarch:

> His newly acquired freedom was much more exciting, much
> more of the historical moment, directly connected with the feel-
> ing of insecurity. The disconcerting abundance of phenomena
> which now claimed the attention of men seemed overwhelming.
> The world—both outer world and inner world—seemed im-
> mense, boundless, incomprehensible.

Shakespeare, "more consciously aristocratic than Montaigne" in Auerbach's view, grants the aesthetic dignity of the tragic only to princes,
commanders, and eminent figures in Roman history. To the Humanist heritage Auerbach attributes Shakespeare's sense that there is more than a
temporal gap between contemporary life and the heroic past:

> With the first dawn of humanism, there began to be a sense that
> the events of classical history and legend and also those of the
> Bible were not separated from the present simply by an extent
> of time but also by completely different conditions of life. Hu-
> manism with its program of renewal of antique forms of life
> and expression creates a historical perspective in depth such as
> no previous epoch known to us possessed.

Of Cervantes Auerbach beautifully remarks: "So universal and multi-
layered, so noncritical and nonproblematic a gaiety in the portrayal of everyday reality has not been attempted again in European letters." It is as
though Humanist perspectivism—not yet developed in the rambunctious
Rabelais, a powerful shadow in Shakespeare, forsaken for the common life

by Montaigne—had been set aside by a genial power of acceptance of the mundane in Cervantes. But these in any case are the Renaissance writers as strong as Homer, Dante, and Chaucer. With lesser writers (lesser only as compared with these), the opening to the past carried with it a perspectivism that generated anxieties both of influence and of representation. Paradoxically, humanism both exalted and burdened writers by proclaiming that the vernacular could achieve what the ancients had achieved, by the aid of an antique greatness that carried its own implicit force of inhibition.

## II

The literary criticism of the sixteenth century, since it is so entirely part of what can be called a Humanist manifesto, now demands to be read in a certain spirit of affectionate deidealization. The greatest writers of the century accomplish this deidealization by themselves, and if such an activity be considered criticism (and it is), then Montaigne, rather than Du Bellay or Sidney or Tasso, becomes the great critic of the early Renaissance. To call the *Essays* a vast work of literary criticism is a revisionary act of judgment, but only in the sense of seeing now that Sigmund Freud, who died in 1939, appears in 1987 to have been the crucial critic of the twentieth century. Montaigne's defense of the self is also an analysis of the self, and Montaigne appears now to have been the ancestor not only of Emerson and Nietzsche, both of whom acknowledged him, but also of Freud, who did not.

Returning to Montaigne then, in a wider compass than just the essay "Of Books," is to encounter a poetics of the self that is also a relentless (for all its casual mode) critique of the Humanist, idealized poetics of the self. Petrarch, Du Bellay, even the more pragmatic Sidney, and most of all the tormented Tasso—all of them idealize their stance in relation to vernacular precursors, and also in regard to ancient wisdom. Montaigne, once past his Humanist first phase, and his skeptical transition, does not deceive either himself or others when it comes to the problems of writing:

> I have not had regular dealings with any solid book, except Plutarch and Seneca, from whom I draw like the Danaids, incessantly filling up and pouring out. Some of this sticks to this paper; to myself, little or nothing.

This, from near the start of the 1579–80 essay "Of the Education of Children," is one of the most astonishing sentences even in Montaigne.

Terence Cave, in *The Cornucopian Text,* reads this sentence in the manner of Derrida and Barthes:

> The fullness of two model-texts is here designated, it would seem, as a source; the labour of the Danaides would thus represent the activity of transmission or exchange ("commerce"), by which the textual substance of Plutarch and Seneca is displaced into a discourse bearing the signature "Montaigne." But this sentence is marked from the beginning by a negation. Plutarch and Seneca appear in a concessive phrase made possible only by the absence of any "livre solide": a characteristically Montaignian insistence on the emptiness of discourse (particularly the written discourses of pedagogy) allows provisional access to certain privileged texts whose unsystematic, open-ended form endorses that of the *Essais* themselves. The negation is not, however, limited to the unnamed texts Montaigne claims to have neglected. The Danaides are, after all, not a wholly reassuring figure of plenitude. Rabelais cites them as a counter-example of cornucopian productivity, a sign of despair, and the uselessness of their labours is made explicit in the following sentence: "J'en attache quelque chose à ce papier; à moy, si peu que rien." The *locus* is closed, as it began, in negation. The *moi,* in a place outside discourse, is scarcely touched by the language even of Plutarch and Seneca; its integrity is preserved, as at the beginning of the passage, by a repudiation of books. Alien discourse cannot be "attached" to the self, is external to it. Hence the gesture of transference, endlessly repeated, appears as an empty mime. The only thing to which fragments of another text may be attached is "ce papier," a mediate domain which clearly concerns the *moi* (since the sentences inscribed on it have a habit of beginning with "je"), but is no less clearly different from it. The paper on which the text of the *Essais* appears is, indeed, a place of difference: it allows the rewriting and naturalization of foreign texts; it thereby permits the search for the identity of a *moi* in contra-distinction from what is "other"; but at the same time it defers any final access to the goal of the search, since the self is expressly an entity dissociated from the activity of writing.

If read in that deconstructionist manner, then Montaigne is achieving an awareness that the experiential fullness he seeks outside language, and which he hopes to represent in his own language, is no more a true presence in Plutarch and Seneca than in his own pages, or in his own self. Like the Danaids, all writers are condemned to carry the waters of experience in the sieve of language. But Montaigne (unlike Cave) *does* regard the *Moral Essays* of Plutarch and the *Epistles* of Seneca as "solid books." They are not merely privileged texts or sources, but pragmatically, experientially, they have, *for Montaigne,* a different status than his own writing possesses. They are the fathers, true authors and authorities; they do augment because they do not go back to the foundations, but for Montaigne they *are* the foundations. And some of their reality does stick to Montaigne's manuscript and printed page, even if some does not. Montaigne's self is as formidable as the selves of Plutarch and Seneca; his self repels influences. Yet he does grant priority to the text of the fathers, because his text, as opposed to his self, cannot have authority without some transference from the fathers.

Cave concludes his very useful study of Montaigne by turning to the text of the culminating essay, the magnificent "Of Experience" (1587–88). After observing that there is envy and jealousy between our pleasures, so that they clash and interfere with one another, Montaigne opposes himself to those who therefore would abandon natural pleasures:

> I, who operate only close to the ground, hate that inhuman wisdom that would make us disdainful enemies of the cultivation of the body. I consider it equal injustice to set our heart against natural pleasures and to set our heart too much on them. Xerxes was a fool, who, wrapped in all human pleasures, went and offered a prize to anyone who would find him others. But hardly less of a fool is the man who cuts off those that nature has found for him. We should neither pursue them nor flee them, we should accept them. I accept them with more gusto and with better grace than most, and more willingly let myself follow a natural inclination. We have no need to exaggerate their inanity; it makes itself felt enough and evident enough. Much thanks to our sickly, kill-joy mind, which disgusts us with them as well as with itself. It treats both itself and all that it takes in, whether future or past, according to its insatiable, erratic, and versatile nature.

> Unless the vessel's pure, all you pour in turns sour.
> HORACE

> I, who boast of embracing the pleasures of life so assiduously
> and so particularly, find in them, when I look at them thus min-
> utely, virtually nothing but wind. But what of it? We are all
> wind. And even the wind, more wisely than we, loves to make
> a noise and move about, and is content with its own functions,
> without wishing for stability and solidity, qualities that do not
> belong to it.

Cave deconstructs this:

> Full experience is always absent; presence is unattainable. All
> that the *Essais* can do, with their ineradicable self-conscious-
> ness, is to posit paradigms of wholeness as features of a dis-
> course which, as it pours itself out, celebrates its own inanity.
> The Montaignian text represents the emptying of the cornuco-
> pia by the very gesture of extending itself indefinitely until the
> moment of ultimate *egressio* or elimination: the figures of abun-
> dance play a prominent part in the closing pages of "De l'expe-
> rience." Whatever plenitude seems to have been proper to the
> past, whatever festivity is assigned to these terminal moments,
> Montaigne's writing is both the only place in which they can be
> designated, and a place from which they remain inexhaustibly
> absent.

The plenitude of the textual past, of Plutarch, and of Seneca, and of
Horace, is certainly present here, but so is the pragmatic presence of an
achieved text, a newness caught in its annuciation. If we are all wind, and
Montaigne's *Essays* nothing but wind, why then let us be as wise as the
wind. The text, like ourselves, makes a noise and moves about. Like the
wind, we and our texts ought not to seek for qualities not our own. But
an unstable and fluid text, always metamorphic, can be viewed as positively as a mobile self. If Montaigne declares limitation, he also asserts a
freedom, both for his text and for himself.

Montaigne, like the characters of Shakespeare's plays, changes because he listens to what he himself has said. Reading his own text, he becomes Hamlet's precursor, and represents reality in and by himself. His
power of interpretation over his own text is also a power over the precursors' texts, and so makes of his own belatedness an earliness. What Petrarch and Du Bellay and Tasso longed for vainly, what Sidney urbanely
courted, is what Rabelais first possessed in the Renaissance, and is what
culminates in Montaigne's "Of Experience," before it goes on to triumph

again in Don Quixote, Falstaff, and Hamlet. Call it a Humanist reality rather than a Humanist idealization: an exaltation of the vernacular that authentically carried representation back to its Homeric and biblical strength. In that exaltation, the writer makes us see regions of reality we could not have seen without him. As Wallace Stevens said of the poet, the enterprise of the Renaissance Humanist author:

> tries by a peculiar speech to speak

> The peculiar potency of the general,
> To compound the imagination's Latin with
> The lingua franca et jocundissima.

HERBERT LÜTHY

# Montaigne, or the Art of Being Truthful

Reader, here is a truthful book. It warns you, even as you first enter it, that I have set myself only a familiar and private end. I have taken no thought in it either for your needs or my glory. My powers are not equal to such a task. I wish to be seen in it without art or affectation, but simply and naturally: for it is myself I portray. My faults will be found here as they are; also my plain nature, so far as decorum will allow. Had I lived among those peoples of whom it is said they dwell still under the sweet freedom of nature's first laws, I assure you I would have willingly pictured myself wholly naked. Thus, reader, I myself am the only content of my book; there is no reason for you to employ your leisure on so idle and frivolous a subject. Farewell then! From Montaigne, the first of March, 1580.

This was Montaigne's own foreword to the reader when he first set before the public the book, written "for few people and few years," which has since stood fast against the centuries. What remains to be said after this? Montaigne and his book say frankly everything that they have to say about each other: Montaigne about his book and the book about him; and both go to extraordinary lengths to guard against misunderstanding. "Montaigne is neighbour to us all," and the most openhearted, even gossipy neighbour we could wish for. He hides nothing from us, or nothing essential; and if he, who hardly conceals from us a single peculiarity of

From *The Proper Study: Essays on Western Classics,* edited by Quentin Anderson and Joseph A. Mazzeo. © 1962 by St. Martin's Press, Inc.

his diet or his digestion, forgets to speak of other things—completely of his mother, who survived him by nearly ten years, almost completely of his wife, whose existence he mentions once in passing, and of his children, of whom "two or three" died in childhood—then we can conclude only that these were things that touched him little; and that fact, too, rounds out his portrait.

In the same way, what he has to say about God, the world, and his own times is without shadow or mystery: the absolutely straightforward, unconnected, and changeable opinions of a landed nobleman of middle-class temperament and extraction, opinions born more out of his experience and the common judgement of mankind than of any definite *Weltanschauung*, and quite without pretensions to anything higher or more universal. For he is much less concerned to present the results of his thinking, or even to arrive at results at all, than to follow his thought itself in its playful movement, and to carry us with him. We can, indeed, follow him effortlessly, without breathing heavily, for this thought of his never goes very far, it undertakes only little sauntering strolls and always turns back before getting out of sight. Each one of his essays, like the book itself, begins without a purpose; if he sets an object before his mind it is only to put it in motion, as one throws a stone ahead of a dog, not to have him bring it back but to have him run, and is content if he brings back not the stone but an odd piece of wood or a dead mouse.

So it is possible to leaf through the *Essays,* reading a few pages and turning away at pleasure, as Montaigne himself read, as all his best readers have read him, without fear of losing the thread, for there is none. One learns to know him through his book as one would learn to know one's neighbour in life, through accidental meetings, and the more common the meetings, the more unimportant and unconnected the strokes, the more truthful does the portrait finally become. The best introduction to his book might be simply: Take it and read! or better still: read it and take!—for everyone is free to take what suits him, as Montaigne himself took whatever suited him, in order to make it his own, as, according to his own account, he plucked out of his Plutarch, whenever he picked it up, now a wing and now a leg.

Still, almost everyone who has read Montaigne in this way has mistaken the leg or the wing he brought away for the whole of Montaigne. There have been almost as many different Montaignes as there have been readers of him. For the pious, he was a man of piety, and for the free-thinking, a free-thinker; for the pagan, a pagan, and for Christians, a Christian. For the descendants of the Stoa, he was a Stoic moralist, for Epicureans of the higher or lower variety, he was an Epicurean of their variety; the men of the Enlightenment quoted his judgements on witchcraft and miracles with untiring enthusiasm, their adversaries pointed just as enthusiastically to the long essay called "Apology for Raymond Sebond" and its dethronement of reason. Conservatives found in him a defender of tradition, and the inherited order; the advocates of natural rights saw him as a critic of positive law and of the conventions and veneers of civilisation. The list could be extended endlessly, and just as long a list might be drawn up of what his opponents found to reproach him with.

But, in view of all this, how do things stand with his truthfulness? Is it possible to have so many faces without disguising oneself, and so many truths without being a liar?

Montaigne said everything there was to be said about this too, but it has not helped him much. His foreword to the reader is to be taken quite literally—yet that is exactly what almost no one has done. So that if the *Essays* hardly require an introduction they do perhaps require some advice: not to look in them for what they do not contain—that is, truths about anything or anyone except Michel de Montaigne. His thoughts and opinions may be wrong or right; they are true only insofar as they are *his* thoughts. Their truth does not lie in where they tend, for they tend everywhere, but in the place from which they depart and to which they return. *"Ramener à soi"* is one of the key phrases of the *Essays,* untranslatable in its full range of meaning; it means to draw back on onself, to draw to oneself, to take to oneself, but it contains also the logical meaning of a movement of thought from the object to oneself, and the physical gesture of picking up, holding, or embracing. So Montaigne draws to himself what would escape him: his life, his feelings, his thoughts, his book, his very self; and his reproach against the "licentiousness of thought" is nothing else but that it wishes to pass beyond him and his limitations in order to fix itself in the objective, the absolute, and the unlimited. He, Montaigne, wishes to remain with himself.

For this reason his excursions into the more abstruse matters of philosophy remain, even measured by the standards of his time, scanty and negligent, a mere careless gesture of warding off; he does not care about knowledge of things, only about knowledge of himself. Even when he does for once come to grips with the question of how man can know the truth, as in the "Apology for Raymond Sebond," his epistemology remains a kind of shaking of the head: how can man know anything when he cannot even grasp himself? All his philosophic arguments are such arguments *ad hominem,* as unphilosophic as they can be. What has the objective truth of a philosophic proposition to do with the philosopher who propounds it, his indigestion, his passions, and his personal truthfulness?

These are frivolous arguments for anyone who is seeking knowledge of things. But Montaigne has another purpose, for which he wishes never to lose sight of himself, and another frame of reference, which measures truth not by what is said, but by the sayer—which prefers, in other words, subjective truthfulness to objective truth. Every discipline, from physics to theology, can advance step by step from once-given premises to conclusions that pass far beyond the insight and imaginative power of the investigator, and lose all connection with him. Such knowledge, which cuts itself loose from the knower and cleaves to the object, has nothing more to say to him, Michel de Montaigne; it is of no use for self-knowledge. It is for this reason that the disconnectedness, wilfulness, and apparent purposelessness of his essays, the sauntering, tentative, and unpredictable movement of his thought, are not mere wilfulness or incapacity. A thought or a style which submitted itself to any discipline would cease, immediately or wholly, to be his own. He seems always careful to let no structure of thought arise which might stand by itself without his intervention, to let no method intrude between him and his fancies. He prefers, rather, looking on ironically, to let his mind build little houses of cards which he blows down again before they grow too large.

And yet these "mental exercises" reach a greatness, a truth and a profundity, when he follows himself into the twilight borderlands of his consciousness, on the edge of sleep, dreams, distraction, torpor, and death—in those corners where consciousness, Montaigne's consciousness, first becomes fully realised, that is, detached from every connection with the extraneous. These are the places in which he reaches furthest, and we can learn from them not to content ourselves too lightly with Montaigne's seeming superficiality; for much of the dawdling and dallying of the *Essays* amid the banal and the trivial is, in the same way, a kind of half-sleep of the unconsciousness, in which it permits itself, unknowingly, to be observed. To be sure, many thoughts are brought to light in this way whose interest and even greatness is in themselves; but they are by-products of a thought directed to other ends. For Montaigne, it is not a question of taking the measure of his eyes. The way in which he sees things, now so, now otherwise, leads to no conclusions about the things, only about himself.

"Montaigne against miracles; Montaigne for miracles," Pascal noted. Montaigne is both at once. He brought together tirelessly and indiscriminately a whole chamber of curiosities, full of all the possible conclusions of his own and all other philosophies, not to play them off against each other, but to display the range and possibility of human thought, and with a little prompting he would accept them all—and the most unusual with the most alacrity. They contradict each other?—yes, but all together they mark out the borders of human awareness, with all its manifold possibilities. "Truth is the whole." To the *Essays,* too, Hegel's dictum applies, but altered: Michel de Montaigne's truth is the sum of his contradictions. And this truth of his he demonstrates in his book as Dionysius the Cynic demonstrated motion by walking; there he stands, a whole man, in whom all these contradictions come to harmony.

Truth of another, general, superpersonal kind he does not possess and is not looking for. "I do not see the whole of anything," he says, and adds, smiling: "Nor do those who promise to show it to us." This renunciation troubles him so little that almost every general opinion passes as equally valid with him; rather than worry his head over it, he prefers to hold fast to those opinions customary in his land and his family, certainly as good as any other. He is at pains to set them outside the reach of all human possibility of knowing—this is the whole content of the "Apology for Raymond Sebond"—the better to put them at a distance. They are unattainable, and they do not trouble him. His essays, those little strolls of thought, never set out in search of such truths, but always and only, in search of Montaigne. The whole, which he calls God or Nature, Fate or Order, almost without distinction, gets along very well without him, and he without it: or rather, he is embedded and hidden in it, like the mole or the plant louse, who also knows nothing of how things stand with the universe.

It is this placid, unquestioning taking of things for granted which roused Pascal to indignation. "There are only three types of men: those who serve God, having found Him; those who exert themselves to seek Him, not having found Him; and those who live without seeking Him and without having found Him." It is plain to which of these categories of Pascal's Michel de Montaigne belongs. Whatever he was, a god-seeker he was not. He fulfilled his religious obligations as he fulfilled those of this rank, his marriage, and his public office, and there is no reason to doubt that he fulfilled them honourably and earnestly. But it was not as something of his own, not out of personal conviction, or as an expression of his own essence; it was rather as something expected of him, in the station allotted him by birth and heredity. The separation is astonishingly clear through the *Essays,* and it requires gross bias not to see it: where Montaigne is speaking in general and about generalities he seldom neglects to weave into his discourse the rhetoric of orthodoxy which was especially advisable in his age of religious persecution; when he speaks of his external behaviour, his morals and habits, he takes pains to note his crossing of himself, his saying of grace, and his attendance at Mass; but when he really turns to himself, when he is no longer speaking of mankind, life and death in general, but of himself, his life and his death, then faith is left behind, as habit and philosophy are left behind, and he is alone with himself.

This then is Montaignean scepticism. But the philosophic label does not really suit him. Certainly, the description of sceptical thought given by Hegel in the *Phenomenology of the Spirit* sounds word for word as if it were meant for Montaigne; it is perfectly true that he "only deals with the particular and wallows in the accidental," that his style of thought is "this senseless drivel alternating from one extreme of undifferentiated self-awareness to the other of chance awareness, confused and confusing," and "it perceives its freedom sometimes as a revolt against all the confusion and accidentalness of being and at other times as a falling back into the unessential and a frolicking about in it." It is, too, "only . . . a musical thinking which never arrives at . . . the objective concept" and "so we see only a personality restricted to, and brooding on, itself and its own little activities, as unfortunate as it is unhappy." How well-aimed this description of the sceptical mind is—and how widely it misses Montaigne! The man who steps before us in the *Essays* is as little a representative of Hegel's "unhappy consciousness" as he is the damned and despairing figure of Pascal. And just this is perhaps the scandal of Montaigne: to be so aware of that limitation which does not allow him to grasp "the whole," to content himself with the imperfect and the fragmentary, and yet to be so wholly untragic. His scepticism, philosophic as well as religious, is no sorrowful renunciation, because it is not a philosophy, but a form of spiritual hygiene; a device to help hold off the extraneous and give room for what is his own. His truthfulness applies other, but no less stringent, criteria to truth: is it mine? does it fit me? does it remain mine even in sickness, in pain, and in death?

One can only speak of Montaigne in contradictions, and as he himself rambled on from one thing to another, so one can ramble on in speaking of him, for his subject is himself, in which all other subjects are mirrored. He imposed no method on himself, not even a method for self-knowledge, and there is no such method except unconditional honesty with oneself. Those astonishing journeys of exploration he made on the frontiers of the unconscious were only possible because through long acquaintance with himself he had found the right distance to keep, in order—as he says once—to consider himself impartially "like a neighbour, or a tree." One can follow precisely this process through the development of the *Essays*, the process by which Montaigne wins that distance from himself, that lack of a *parti pris*, which is the hardest part of truthfulness.

The first two books of the *Essays,* in their earlier form, are full of the general truths of Stoic wisdom; these are the essays of which Montaigne later said that they "smelt a little of the property of others." But then that spiritual hygiene begins to operate, the sceptical questioning of his own wisdom—how do I come to it, I, Michel de Montaigne, landed nobleman of Perigord, fifty years old, a little below average height, afflicted with incipient kidney stones? What does it mean to *me?* This is the beginning of Montaigne's marvellous truthfulness, this return to self, this limitation of truth to his personal measure; and the *Essays* have remained unique in the consistency with which they follow the path of honesty—the most personal book in world literature. Unique, perhaps, because they took this path not a priori but artlessly and unintentionally at first, then with a growing joy of discovery. For the personal belongs also to things one does not achieve by a purposeful striving after them; the self that, without long detours, at once reaches itself, has in reality gone no distance at all and remains empty. To take the measure of one's eyes it is necessary to seek first the measure of things.

Montaigne reflected very earnestly on things outside himself, on the nature and destiny of man, on the state, on law, virtue, marriage and education, on belief in miracles, on the passions, and, over and over, on the possibility of objective knowledge, always with reference to himself but never with reference only to himself. So this book of self-knowledge is no confession, no autobiography, no self-justification or self-accusation, no *Ecce Homo.* Montaigne does not start from himself, he comes to himself quite simply, as one comes to the point.

In Montaigne all the usual motives for self-description are lacking. He did not write out of a sense of his own uncommonness, his "otherness" or his exemplary quality, either for good or evil; on the contrary, his experiment was all the more valid because of his ordinariness, and one often senses that he is emphasising this ordinariness, that he is making himself more ordinary than he is. In this way he escaped all the dangers of conscious self-description, the danger of self-enchantment and the perhaps even greater danger of self-abasement, that "sly humility" of confessionals, whose authors tread themselves into the dust in order to demonstrate how high they have raised themselves above themselves. There is no *Weltschmerz,* remorse, rebellion, accusation, inner strife, grief against others or against himself, nothing of all of that which since Rousseau has driven so many failures to spit in the world's face, so many beaten people to write

their *De Profundis,* so many sinners to summon the world to a last judgement on themselves. This is the unusual thing: here a rich, healthy, and
fairly happy man makes himself known, one who has thoroughly mastered
his life and played his part with honour in the public affairs of his city and
his countryside. He does not write in order to create a role for himself, but
to lay one aside, and come to himself.

"*Mundus universus exercet histrioniam*";—the word "person" itself,
is etymologically, "mask." In this comedy where all must act a role chosen
or imposed, in character-masks which everyone finally accepts as his real
visage, with commitments, articles of faith, and dogmas which we "believe
we believe" and to which we must adhere out of loyalty to ourselves, without much knowing how we really came to them: in this comedy Montaigne's role was thoroughly in order. To set himself at a distance from the
mere "making of books," he underlines, rather emphatically on occasion,
the man-of-the-world element in himself. He surrounded his ancestry with
an aura of old warrior nobility it was not at all entitled to; he notes with
pride that as the mayor of his city he had a marshal to precede him and
another to follow him; and, with a vanity full of imperceptible self-irony,
he quotes the entire Latin text of his Roman patent of nobility. These
traits, too, noted by his Jansenist critics with bitter derision, are essential
to him, and they are mirrored in the *Essays* without dissimulation. He did
not renounce the world in order to find himself: he sought to find himself
in the world.

But what is left now of the personality he is seeking? Everything that
holds it together, ancestry, education, milieu, habit, convention, principles,
relations, beliefs, rank, name, and position comes to it from outside, they
are allotted, accidental roles, and yet they make up almost the whole conscious "I." The more closely he considers himself the more his contours
blur, the more individuality is dissolved into that many-coloured, unstable,
iridescent, and fleeting chaos he never, in his contradictoriness, grows tired
of describing. Yes, one should play one's role fitly, he says—but always as
a role, without identifying oneself with it or losing oneself in it. And this
attitude can be followed on the title pages of the early editions of the *Essays;* if the first two editions, conforming to the custom of the period, still
display the full splendour of the titles possessed by the royal knight, coun-
cillor, and mayor, Michel de Montaigne, there is left on the title page of
the last edition, supervised by Montaigne himself, only his name.

For the stepping out of his role in which the actor betrays himself, a
special ear for the undertones of consciousness is needed. All the splendid
life of the *Essays* springs from this keen listening of Montaigne's to his re-

laxed and outward-turned self. It is true that this kind of thinking goes in circles. But the circle grows smaller and smaller until at last it circles only around the one point at which Montaigne finds himself alone—death. Here all acting ends; "that is a business for one man alone." The thought of death engaged him early, and we can follow the process of his self-discovery in nothing so clearly as in his relation to death. In death he found the ultimate test of truthfulness. To come to terms with it was what Montaigne sought, in the beginning, from philosophy. *Hic Rhodus, hic salta!* "To philosophise is to learn to die," he titled the long chapter on death in his first book, written when he was still full of the wisdom of the ancients about life and death; and all the consolations of Stoicism are here summoned up. Montaigne always understood as philosophy this spiritual elevation of man in the face of his sad, confused, and ephemeral humanity, and that was what he still meant by it when he said later, of himself, "I am no philosopher." He has reached the end of the way when, considering the calm and natural death of the simplest men in the plague year 1585, he rejects Cicero's phrase about the philosophic preparation for death as idle boasting: What is it, to be able to do what every fool and every beast can and must do? to strike a pose in order to endure what everyone must endure anyway? If philosophising is to learn to die, "well then, let us go to school with stupidity." To learn to live, not die, is wisdom. The essays of his first and last period can be endlessly contrasted, for with the change in his attitude towards death all the perspectives and measuring-rods of life change too.

Yet the last judgements do not cancel the first; nothing is taken back, only added to and deepened. In the beginning it is man, life, and death that occupy him, in the end it is only "my life" and "my death," and he is no longer dealing with a philosophic allegory of death, but experiencing and enduring his own slow dissolution. He, Michel de Montaigne, can no longer push death out of his consciousness, and no speculation can prevail against this. Here he no longer grants himself the doubt that makes everything else, even miracles, possible; death is the end, and whatever may be on the other side, he, Michel de Montaigne, remains on this side. The consolations of philosophy, like those of religion, he never denies, he leaves them undecided; he accepts extreme unction and the sympathy of friends, but they do not concern him; these are the last actions of a life lived according to custom and usage, since it was not granted him to die unmolested—"quite alone"—journeying and far from home. A man must act his role in life to the last instant.

The Stoic, like the Christian, contempt for death is grounded in the contempt for physical life, but the more Montaigne feels himself disappearing the more deeply he feels that this life is all he has, and that it is much and precious. Now he finds in all contempt for life the overweening pride of the human spirit, the will to lift itself over and beyond itself towards the absolute, a revolt against the unbearable thought of existing today and ceasing to exist tomorrow—against the natural order that embraces both life and death. His last essay, already full of the presence of death and the readiness for it, closes with a hymn to this existence. *"C'est une absolue perfection, et comme divine."* In the presence of death Montaigne learned to love life, to "hold it fast with tooth and claw," to savour it to the last drop. Life is earthly, but not therefore void; transitory but not therefore despicable; losable, but not absurd; precious beyond words in its very fragility and unsureness.

In these last dialogues with old age, sickness, and death, there is no more art and no more cleverness, only obedience and assent to the riddling laws of life and death—*amor fati*. But if this is wisdom, then it is wisdom of the humblest and most unassuming kind, the wisdom of all creation, which goes hence unquestioning, without puzzling over the universe in which it lives and dies; the wisdom of the obedient. And if such thankful obedience to the unknowable is piety, then this is piety—but a piety that is wholly of this world. How much of the beauty of the *Essays* is due to the fact that their movement so truly describes the curve of life through ripeness and to death—the whole of life!

Why did Montaigne write them? He himself posed the question over and over, without finding an answer. Yet we must believe his foreword: he did not write them for us. He wrote them for himself, for his own sake, out of inner necessity; and yet he needed the unknown reader in order to reveal himself to himself. Self-description was the instrument of his self-discovery. For, and this is the last contradiction, there is no self-knowledge which does not make itself known, and no truthfulness without communication. "Whoever does not live a little for others hardly lives for himself." The consciousness of self that remains mute and unexpressed cannot attain self-knowledge. Perhaps there lay, at the source of Montaigne's decision to write down his thoughts, the death of his friend, Etienne de la Boétie, who shared with him common ideas and ideals. The *Essays* are the continuation of a broken-off conversation. The whole first period of the *Essays* is an echo of this intimate association of two humanistic minds, both in love with antique greatness and the wisdom of Stoicism. Now Montaigne was alone, bereft of that "other I" who "alone possessed my true image, and took it with him," and it was "as if I had been cut in half." But this lost image of himself which he tried to reconstruct was hardly the one that emerges in the *Essays;* the undertaking led him further than he had intended.

We can infer Montaigne's image from the portrait he sketches of La Boétie; how impersonal, how declamatory in spite of all its real emotion, this essay is! We sense the humanistic enthusiasm for antique greatness "as our century no longer knows it" in which these two come together, the spirit of emulation of the Scipios and Catos which one finds also in La Boétie's posthumous *Contr'un.* It was only slowly that Montaigne freed himself from the spell of that image of ideal manhood proposed by the Stoa, which was embodied for him in Etienne de la Boétie. He cannot maintain himself on such heights—in such a role—alone, and the great generalities of virtue, truth, and freedom remain empty, for they find no echo. Hesitantly, in a few tentative thrusts, whose keenness for a late-Renaissance mind still filled with the spirit of antiquity we are hardly able to measure any more, he begins to question not mankind itself but these standards for mankind, and to seek the criteria of judgement within himself. And in shaping this new and quite personal image of man he attained his full reality. His book was the triumphant bursting loose of the free man from late-humanistic epigonism. And through it, Montaigne himself became what he was. Montaigne noted finely the reciprocal process in which he and his book were engaged: "And even if no one were to read me, should I have wasted my time? I no more made my book than it has made *me.*" His book has become a true collaborator, and through it the reader becomes one too—"my book," Montaigne says, as he would say "my friend," and, reading his book, we are drawn into this intimacy too. Whence the inexhaustible freshness which speaks to us from this book across more than three and a half centuries, as from no other book of his time, and few of all time.

In the end the richness of this book is the richness of the personality which shared itself with it, wholly and without holding back. It is not the monologue of a crank in his library, brooding over himself. The man who wrote this lived open-eyed among men caught up in the most merciless of civil and religious wars; he stood in his time with both feet, at the end of that colossal century in which the new world was discovered and the world of antiquity rediscovered, which saw the Christian church tottering on its foundations, and the anthropocentric model of the universe overturned, the century of the conquistadors and the great rebels: Cortez and Copernicus, Luther and Machiavelli, Calvin, Loyola, and Giordano Bruno.

The book, too, is of this time—and what a time! Montaigne began to write his essays in the year of the St. Bartholomew massacre, which gave the signal for slaughter throughout France, and entered history as the ineradicable symbol of betrayal, baseness, and murder in the name of the highest certainties of faith; the night of butchery in Paris, and of the thanksgiving mass with which it was greeted in Rome. All his life Montaigne saw religious war smouldering or blazing all around him, in his city, in his own family, and among his brothers and sisters, three of whom adhered to Calvinism. The twenty years during which he wrote the *Essays* were twenty years of civil war, hardly interrupted by the worthless peace treaties and edicts of toleration, broken before they came into force. Montaigne's retreat in 1571 "to the lap of the learned Muses, where he will pass in calm and security the days left him to live," was of short duration; the next year he was with the royal army in Poitou sent against rebellious La Rochelle, then bearer of the king's commands to the Parliament of Bordeaux, and in the following year we meet him again and again as agent and mediator between the warring camps. The news of his election as mayor of Bordeaux reached him on his "extended journey" in Italy, and King Henry III wrote to him in Rome to summon him to the immediate and pressing assumption of his office—a difficult one in a city torn by outer and inner quarrels, and become a storm-centre of the Huguenot wars.

But the Michel de Montaigne faithful to church and king was also the confidant and adviser of Henry of Navarre, the chief of the Protestant party, who visited him in his castle and appointed him, already chamberlain to Henry III, to be his own ex officio chamberlain too. An unelevating role, and one hard to understand, like the role of all those who issue no calls to battle and wage no wars, but seek to make peace instead; suspect, like all moderation; dangerous, like all will to balance in times of fanaticism. So Montaigne also passed, as he once complains, "for Guelf among the Ghibellines and Ghibelline among the Guelfs"—for a Papist among the Calvinists, and a heretic, or, what was almost the same thing, a lukewarm believer, among the Catholic zealots.

He has been called with justice, if also with some exaggeration, the philosopher of Henry IV, who brought peace and order to the French state, and to whom Montaigne, in one of his last essays, dedicated the verses Virgil wrote for Augustus. But if he was the philosopher of Henry IV, it was before the latter's victory, which he did not live to see. Montaigne had party loyalty, but it was not to the party of a dogma. His loyalty was to the old order, embodied in the monarchy which fell to pieces under the blows of both religious parties, the Calvinists as well as the

Catholic League. If one wishes to range him with a party then it must be with the *"parti des politiques,"* as his contemporaries called that "third force" made up of moderate and tolerant spirits which—hence its designation as "political"—drew a distinction between religious conviction and political practice.

When hereditary succession made the Protestant Bourbon, Henry of Navarre, heir to the throne of the weak and degenerate Valois, the split became open; while the Catholic League sought to deliver the crown of France into the hands of the Spanish Hapsburg, Philip II, or the Lothringian Duke of Guise, the legitimist party of "the politicals" became simply the patriotic party. But it was only by going over to the religious faith of the majority of his people that Henry IV could finally become the "prince of peace," the "good king" who has entered legend. For those sick alike of the oligarchic city-republics of the Calvinists and the caricature of democracy created in Paris by the League through the long reign of terror enforced by a fanaticised mob, the monarchy appeared as salvation. That the paternal and tolerant régime of Henry IV prepared the way for the absolute monarchy which less than a century later began to destroy his work, is part of the history of another epoch, which had gone on to new problems; for history knows no "solutions" by which everything works out as smoothly as in the arithmetic books and ideological primers, only the triumph of new formulations of a problem over the old ones, the replacement of the religious formulation by the political, and the political by the social—all of them, however, only new forms of the old. What Montaigne says of the political problems of his time is spoken out of that time and his personal experience: it is uncontemporary to us. And yet, in a far deeper sense, it *is* contemporary.

Nowhere is politics the subject of this book. Nowhere does Montaigne draft an ideology or a programme of even the most modest kind; here too it is a question solely of *his* relation to politics and ideology. He was involved in these disorders as a citizen and an official, not as Michel de Montaigne, and the self-contemplation of the *Essays* is once again the means, in a time of ideological murder and carnage, to gain distance from the struggle, to come to himself, in the full sense of the phrase, to win the inner freedom that the party follower loses. In politics, too, it is a book of spiritual hygiene.

Here again scepticism above all fulfills its cleansing function. In the blackest impasse of the civil war, sharpened to ultimate bitterness by the betrayal of St. Bartholomew's Night, while the unity of the kingdom itself was for the first time put in jeopardy, and the "natural right" to rebellion and to execute kings was seized on in turn by Calvinist theoreticians and the zealots of the Catholic League, Montaigne read Sextus Empiricus's "Outline of Pyrrhonism," struck off his philosophical coat-of-arms, showing the arms of a scale poised in wavering equilibrium and the motto "*Que sais-je?*"; and began to set down his "Apology for Raymond Sebond," the only really polemic essay in his work. All certainties are overturned here, with a true lust for destruction and an undiscriminating insatiability, all dogmas reduced to mere opinion, illusion, and conjecture, one as good as the next and each a mere curiosity in the cabinet of human fantasy. Everything is reduced to one level, man and beast, wise man and fool, intellect and instinct, belief and delusion, science, speculation and old wives' tales, and every supposed certainty cancelled by mere confrontation with a dozen contradictory and just as evident certainties. Montaigne notes sarcastically that two hundred and eighty-eight sects arose in antiquity out of the dispute over the highest good alone, and Pascal later copied this remark into his *Pensées.* Religion too is brought into this sphere of mere human supposition, for "it is clear and distinct that we accept our beliefs only in our own fashion and from our own hands, just as other religions have been accepted," according to the accidents of place, birth, and education: "A different latitude, different parents, similar promises and threats, could have produced in the same way a quite contrary belief. We are Christian in the same sense that we are German or Perigordian." Curious defence of the good Sebond, who wished "to demonstrate the truth of our religion by the conclusions of reason!"

No one, probably, will ever succeed entirely in clarifying the strange labyrinth of this polemical piece, for Montaigne himself has taken pains to make sure that no one will be able to pin him down to anything—not even doubt. Perhaps such a mock battle, with reversed weapons, in which Montaigne undertakes to defend Sebond's proof of religion by reason while pushing reason (and all human certainties with it) into the void, was the only way in which a free spirit of that age could create room for itself to breathe between inexorably hostile dogmas—one thinks of the quite otherwise motivated, but very similarly constructed, *Defense of Herodotus* by Henri Estienne, which undertook to prove the credibility of the wildest fables of the ancient Greeks by assembling a selection of the even more grotesque miracle stories and fairy tales which the priests of his time had imposed on a credulous people. . . . Yet one need not therefore impute to Montaigne a case of plain fraud. Here, as everywhere in the *Essays,* the occasion and point of departure for the essay, Sebond's "natural theology," turns quickly into a mere pretext for following Montaigne's own thoughts down every sideway and bypath. Nor is it a question of simple enlightened denial or doubt of an article of faith. The possibility of divine revelation remains open to rare and chosen spirits; but it is clear that it is not these spirits who are drowning France in fire, murder, and warfare, while they battle for the mastery of the country. By themselves the genuinely religious would hardly be numerous enough to form a troop of militia. The others—and are these others not, in reality, all?—are possessed, not by the truth, but by blood-frenzy, greed, and hunger for power. If they weighed truly the fragility of their convictions, the uncertainty of their murderous certainties, if they were in possession of, instead of beside, themselves, would they not sheath their swords?

He too, Michel de Montaigne, belongs not at all to the graced who have received the light of holy truth; he too is a Christian like the multitude, as he is a Perigordian, by heredity and habit. It is for just this reason that he stands fast; precisely because he cannot decide by himself what the truth is, he holds to that truth which is his by birth—"and since I am in no position to choose, I follow the choice of others, and remain in the rut in which God has set me. For otherwise I would roll and roll without end." With this he contents himself, to this he clings, but modestly; it is a personal, historically limited faith, which makes no claim to be binding on those whom God has set in another track. "What sort of truth is it that ends on this side of the mountains and is a lie for the world beyond?" It is a rule of behaviour, a "local ordinance," to which Montaigne submits himself in his ignorance; blind, but conscious of his blindness.

So he rejects the Reformation, not as sin and error, but as disorder and a sectarian arrogance of spirit which presumes to pass personal judgement on what is ultimate truth; not because his certainty is better but because he knows the questionableness of all certainties. It would take passionate conviction to change his faith, but it requires only mild conviction to hold to the old one. All the more because Calvin's Genevan papacy was both more demanding and less tolerant than pre-Tridentine Catholicism— and the introduction of the Tridentine creed into France had long been successfully resisted by the Gallican *politiques*—which contented itself with external submission to churchly usage, and gave its approval to the *Essays* as a tract written in defence of the old faith, until a new wave of fanaticism, two generations later, repudiated as anti-Christian both the *Essays* and, characteristically, the religious tolerance of the Edict of Nantes. Of course, the zealots were not wrong. Montaigne was indeed, in Sainte-Beuve's pointed phrase, a good Catholic in the exact measure that he was a lukewarm Christian. He, personally, was prepared to let pass every belief and every superstition, "to light one candle to St. Michael and another to the dragon," and with Socrates he held that "the truest opinion of the supernatural is to have no opinion."

Montaigne's loyalty to the old faith does not therefore contradict his scepticism, it is grounded in it. He defended the hereditary church as a conservative, not as a fighter for the true faith; as a politique, not as a crusader against heresy. He did not put the light on one side and the darkness on the other, he reserved the freedom to look around him, and to see what became of his convictions in the fists and mouths of their defenders, "who believe they believe because they do not know what belief is," and to recognise the human qualities and virtues of their opponents. He speaks often, in the *Essays,* with curiosity and astonishment, of the strange phenomenon of party passion, that human loss of self in a "role" thanks to which men work themselves up over things which do not in the least concern them. *"Je m'engage difficilement"* is a key sentence of the *Essays;* he is "not easily inclined to belief nor to disbelief"; and the essay in which he reports how he exercised his mayoral office bears the magnificent title, "On the Management of the Will." His political ethos is the rejection of passion.

He refuses to be passionate even about the tradition he upholds. Every traditional form of order is an inheritance, and nothing else. Church, crown, state, law, family, and marriage are institutions which earn the esteem of a citizen in his role as citizen, but only in that role; they can claim no compulsion over his way of thinking or his conscience. What exists is neither holy, nor good, nor even reasonable; it has no other virtue but that it exists. Order, the state, law and justice are nothing else but disorder, lawlessness and violence, established and grown venerable by age, and often enough laughable, inhuman, and absurd. "The laws are not law, because they are just, but because they are laws." All human order is nonrational, neither derivable from, nor justifiable by, reason; every schoolboy is able to demonstrate its senselessness, but he had better let it stand: he knows nothing better.

For there is no rational order. Society has grown not out of the test tubes of reason but the disorder of history, not as an abstract logical construction for abstract logical men, but as an empirically discovered form of the living-together of human beings. For the state too, what is truth this side of the Pyrenees is a lie on the other. Like all historical reality it cannot withstand the scrutiny of reason, for it is grounded not on truth but on custom; and yet it is infinitely superior to reason, for it is actual. And the older and more customary it is, the better, for it has survived its violent birth pangs and found its inner equilibrium, it has shown its usefulness and vitality by its survival, and grown to be the normal state of affairs with which everyone is familiar, because he is born to them, and which therefore allow the highest measure of freedom. Whoever assails it risks a relapse into the rule of the fist. Montaigne's whole polemic against the "innovators" is an indictment of the power-pretensions of abstract reason in its attempt to create an order outside historical contingency, and he has only scorn for the ideal states of philosophy, which have no place and no time. Every idea which presents itself as an ideology and claims power over men as a universally valid principle of order, is hubris and folly, arrogant transgression.

But even to the existing order he did not concede the right to impair his private freedom: "If the laws I serve threatened me even with their little finger I would go immediately in search of others, wherever they might be. . . . I am so greedy for freedom that I would feel hemmed-in if I were denied access to no matter what corner of the Indies." He acquiesced in the external order precisely for the sake of this freedom: freedom, too, he drew to himself as *his* freedom, not as a public postulate; and practical conformity seemed to him a small price to pay in order to defend it. He played the part that was allotted him, in a bad time, as Frenchman, Catholic, Perigordian, citizen, and mayor of Bordeaux, dutifully and without passion, with calm acceptance of his historic "contingency," and thereby preserved the inner freedom to remain Michel de Montaigne, sceptic and citizen of the world. Thus this political attitude flows back into the self-knowledge from which it issued, into the open-eyed acceptance of that contradiction of freedom and obligation, individuality and conformity, in which Montaigne found his own nature—"So I am."

The best fruit of this self-possession is its absolute openness to other things and other men. This deeply liberal spirit was tolerant without that tinge of sufferance, of the magnanimous concession granted by Truth to Error, that so often clings to the word—a word Montaigne does not even know. This enemy of all ideology had an insatiable, unprejudiced curiosity about all ideas, this scorner of all pretensions to special knowledge had an unbounded readiness for learning, this sceptic in regard to every dogma was open to the whole endless variety of spiritual possibilities, the life-forms and life-truths of other men and other peoples, and he treated with respect even those possibilities which were closed to him. Willingly, playfully, he tests his capacity to assume another opinion and seek its justification, and it often happens that the game turns to earnest in the process, and he abandons his own to adopt the opinion he began by combatting.

To be sure, a great deal also escaped this mind, which grasped so much in the attempt to grasp itself. The soaring lights of inspiration, the mystic vision of the world, the passion for knowledge and perhaps passion itself he sensed only by imaginative intuition, without really experiencing them: the border forms of human existence, the seer, the hero, and the saint, like the radically evil, were foreign to him. The psychic phenomena of transport and ecstasy he traced in himself and others again and again, with a mixture of curiosity and aversion; but his whole effort is in the opposite direction: to come to himself, not to allow himself to be transported, to possess himself, not to be possessed. He found this way to himself not by negating, but by affirming what was outside his nature, by the affirmation even of what was to him foreign, mysterious, and incomprehensible.

This rare and precious faculty for setting himself in the place of another being and respecting its inner laws as equal to his own he pushed to its utmost reach: "When I play with my cat who knows if she does not amuse herself more with me than I with her?" All of Montaigne lies in that casual sentence.

Truthfulness is not only a great, it is a difficult virtue. It demands not merely an open character but a clear head, and that, for a man of Montaigne's time, as for our own, was difficult indeed to achieve. Every time of disorder is also a time of dishonored minds who know all about God and the world, the cause of things and their background, the meaning of history and the destiny of man—all about everything except themselves. And in such times nothing is more necessary than to come, in the spiritual and even in the clinical sense, to oneself. That is the spiritual hygiene Montaigne practised as his joyful wisdom, and his only teaching. "With him I would live," Nietzsche wrote, "if the task were set me to make myself at home on earth." It is just this task, perhaps, that we have all been set again.

DONALD  M.  FRAME

# The Whole Man, 1586–1592

### THE NATURE OF MAN

In the early essays Montaigne often seems to question whether there is
such a thing as human nature. He sees little but chaos and inconsistency
in the individual, little but diversity in the race. His sense of differences in
man and men is one of his vitalizing contributions to human psychology;
but it makes any generalization virtually impossible.

At the end of his life, however, he finds unity both within each man
and in mankind. Having already shown all that education can do for the
individual, he now stresses the fact that it cannot do everything:

> Natural inclinations gain assistance and strength from educa-
> tion; but they are scarcely to be changed and overcome. . . . We
> do not root out these original qualities, we cover them up, we
> conceal them. . . .
>
> Just consider the evidence of this in our own experience.
> There is no one who, if he listens to himself, does not discover
> in himself a pattern all his own, a ruling pattern *(une forme
> sienne, une forme maistresse)* which struggles against education
> and against the tempest of the passions that oppose it.

Montaigne still sees more difference than resemblance in mankind,
but now he sees both: though our faces, he says, are different enough to
tell us apart, they are enough alike to tell us from the animals. He finds
that his long self-study has made him a good judge of others, often better

From *Montaigne's Discovery of Man: The Humanization of a Humanist.* © 1955
by Columbia University Press.

able than they to explain their conduct to them. Evidently, his observations have general validity. "I set forth a humble and inglorious life," he writes; "that does not matter. You can tie up all moral philosophy with a common and private life just as well as with a life of richer stuff: each man bears the entire form of man's estate."

Montaigne's sense of kinship and solidarity now extends, more seriously and less paradoxically than in the early essays, to many large groups: the people of the New World, foreigners in general, the populace of Bordeaux, freaks, and women. Now he senses, and fully shares, a broad strain of common humanity.

For Montaigne, the basic fact of man's nature is that he is made up of body and soul. And his basic deduction is that these two are equal parts.

Most moral philosophy since Plato, and much before, considers the soul a likelier candidate for immortality than the body, and therefore the better of the two. Often it carries this preference further and regards the soul as good, the body as bad; or further still, and calls the body the prison of the soul. Christian doctrine is generally more balanced, believing as it does in the ultimate resurrection of the body, which is the gift and the temple of God. When Montaigne mentions the Christian attitude, it is in this vein.

Montaigne's emphasis on the body is not new in the late essays. "It is not a soul," he had written earlier, "it is not a body that is being trained; it is a man; these parts must not be separated." He had rejected Plato's doctrine of the immortality of the soul on the grounds that to separate our two main parts thus is the death and ruin of our being. Now he writes that there is nothing in us purely either corporeal or spiritual, and that wrongly we tear apart a living man. "To what purpose," he asks, "do we dismember by divorce a structure made up of such close and brotherly correspondence?" Again and again he reminds us of the importance of the body, which we tend to forget or ignore. Man's condition, he writes, is wonderfully corporeal; likewise life is "a material and corporeal movement, an action imperfect by its very essence, and irregular." For the same reason he warns that since our life is part folly, part wisdom, whoever writes about it only reverently and regularly leaves out more than half of it.

The body as Montaigne sees it is simple, earthy, solid, sane, slow to change. It appears to be entirely subject to nature, in which it is fortunate; for nature makes even pain contribute by contrast to its pleasure and places its greatest pleasures in the satisfaction of its needs. The body can sometimes even help the soul by giving its stability.

The soul is very complex and infinitely powerful for our good or ill.

Centrifugal, erratic, never at rest, it is always trying to improve on nature and succeeds only in making us miserable. Properly directed, however, it can do wonders.

Its parts or functions are not always clear. The mind (*esprit*) sometimes represents the entire soul, sometimes its knowing and reasoning function. The imagination is the most flighty part of the soul, undiscerning between truth and falsehood, often needing consolation from the mind. Reason *(raison)* has at least two distinct meanings or aspects for Montaigne—that of *reasoning,* which is rash, plausible, and dangerously irresponsible, and that of *reasonableness,* which is excellent. Understanding *(entendement)* and judgment, which are virtually synonymous, test new appearances by comparing them with present and past evidence and then assign them the appropriate degree of truth or falsehood, good or evil. Judgment is the master quality, of which conscience appears to be one function. Where judgment rules the soul harmoniously, all will be well; where it does not, mind and soul are dangerous even to their possessor.

Located within us, the soul, or mind, has no direct contact with externals. It receives the reports of the senses on the impacts that objects make on them and tries to find the truth from these reports. In this it has no assurance of success, since it accepts things always in its own fashion. But this same arbitrariness gives it infinite power for our happiness.

> Things in themselves may have their own weights and measures and qualities; but once inside, it [the soul] allots them their qualities as it sees fit. . . . Health, conscience, authority, knowledge, riches, beauty, and their opposites, are stripped on entry and receive from the soul new clothing, and the coloring that it chooses . . . and which each individual soul chooses. . . . Each one is queen in its realm. Wherefore let us no longer make the external qualities of things our excuse; it is up to us to reckon them as we will. Our good and our ill depend on ourselves alone.

Since the soul is so powerful, it should help the body, as Montaigne had seen earlier. In particular it should protect man against the tyranny of age. Montaigne's body was hard for his soul to control in his youth because it was lusty; now the reverse is true: "This body flees irregularity and fears it. . . . It dominates in its turn, and more roughly and imperiously. . . . I defend myself from temperance as I formerly did from sensuality. . . . Wisdom has its excesses, and needs no less moderation than folly." For our apparent reform in old age is really a decline, a "cowardly and rheumatic virtue" produced by sourness and weakness; we do not really abandon our vices but only change them, usually for the worse. If Montaigne is to be master of himself as he wants, his mind must combat this deformation: "Let it grow green, let it flower meanwhile, if it can, like the mistletoe on a dead tree." His body, he tells us, is often depressed; his soul, when it is not actually blithe, is at the very least tranquil and cheerful. If his body were as governable as his soul, he would be well off indeed.

Since the soul deceives the senses even as it is deceived by them, it may exercise its power through pleasant delusion. No matter; the point is that it has the power:

> The body has, except for a little more or less, only one gait and one bent. It [the soul] is diversifiable into all sorts of forms and adapts to itself, and to its condition, whatever this may be, the feelings of the body and all other accidents. Therefore we must study and investigate it, and awaken in it its all-powerful forces. There is neither reason, nor prescription, nor force which has power against its inclination and its choice. Of so many thousands of biases that the soul has at its disposal, let us give it one suitable for our repose and preservation, and we are not only safe from all injury but even gratified and tickled, if it seems good to it, by injuries and evils.
>
> It makes its profit from everything indiscriminately. Error, dreams serve it usefully as a lawful means to place us in security and contentment.

All this, of course, is vanity: the senses gullible, the soul deceptive and irresponsible, the body decadent from youth, disobedient to the soul and rivaling it in importance. This is a far cry from the usual bright Renaissance picture of man as the little universe, the microcosm.

Moreover, vice comes as naturally to us as vanity. Ambition, jealousy, envy, vengefulness, superstition, despair, cruelty—the seeds of these are inborn, and to destroy them would be to destroy the fundamental conditions of our life. However, we also have it in us to recognize vice and control it. To know it is to hate it; repentance follows it as the night the day. Thus although vice is important, vanity remains the keynote: "I do not think there is as much unhappiness in us as vanity. . . . We are not so much full of evil as of inanity."

Vanity is not a new idea to the author of the "Apology for Raymond Sebond." He merely argues it now better and oftener, making it a theme of most of the essays of book 3.

It is man's wisdom, not man's follies, he writes in "Three Kinds of Association," that makes him laugh. Is there anything except us in nature, he asks in "Diversion," that feeds on inanity and is controlled by it? "Some Verses of Virgil" treats the vanity of our physical makeup. The whole world revolves about the urge for copulation, which we call love; yet no other action so comically reveals us as the plaything of the gods. "Husbanding Your Will" shows mostly vanity in public affairs and the motives that drive us into them; "Cripples," our love of the vanity of speculation and dispute; "Physiognomy," the vanity of artificial reason and knowledge, which do us more harm than good as defenses against the fear of pain and death. Finally, "Experience" finds vanity in our very essence: "I who boast of embracing the pleasures of life so assiduously and so particularly, find in them, when I look at them thus minutely, virtually nothing but wind. But what then? We are all wind. And even the wind, more wisely than we, loves itself for making a noise and moving about, and contents itself with its own functions, without wishing for stability and solidity, qualities that do not belong to it."

Vanity is the heart as well as the title of chapter 9. Montaigne admits that there is vanity in his love of travel. "But where," he asks, "is there not? And these fine precepts are vanity, and all wisdom is vanity. 'The Lord knoweth the thoughts of the wise, that they are vain.' " Vanity is a part of our condition, and a large part at that. There may be little that we can do about it, but at least we should know it. Montaigne's conclusion is particularly eloquent:

> If others examined themselves attentively, as I do, they would find themselves, as I do, full of inanity and nonsense. Get rid of it I cannot without getting rid of myself. We are all steeped in it, one as much as another; but those who are aware of it are a little better off—though I don't know. . . .
>
> It was a paradoxical command that was given us of old by that god at Delphi: "Look into yourself, know yourself, keep to yourself. . . . It is always vanity for you, within and without; but it is less vanity when it is less extensive. Except for you, O man," said that god, "each thing studies itself first and, according to its needs, has limits to its labors and desires. There is not a single thing as empty and needy as you, who embrace the universe: you are the investigator without knowledge, the magistrate without jurisdiction, and all in all, the fool of the farce."

Our essence, then, is vanity. But the equation works both ways. Van-

ity is our essence; and we are fools if we despise our essence. Montaigne
had attacked this malady of self-disdain earlier, and now, in the chapter
on vanity itself, he returns even harder to the attack.

To be sure, we must recognize our vanity, our great limitations. We
are very physical, very variable, often comical, something less than omni-
scient. To ignore this is to invite arrogance, presumption, and self-disdain,
dangerous faults but easily curable. But at the same time we must recognize our possibilities, which are richly adequate for living. The little learning that we need to live at ease is in us; and if we cannot find it by ourselves, Socrates will teach us how. His greatest service was precisely that
of showing all that human nature can do by itself. We may not even need
his help if we look within us as Montaigne does, and try to become authorities not on Cicero but on ourselves. "In the experience I have of myself," Montaigne writes, "I find enough to make me wise, if I were a good
scholar." The best cure for our vanity, indeed for all our errors—anger,
inconstancy, ignorance, bad judgment, and all the rest—is not to read
about them in books but to see them, truly and steadily, in ourselves. It is
not really at our own expense, as he had written earlier, that we become
wise in this way; it is only at the expense of our self-conceit. "Let us only
listen: we tell ourselves all we most need."

These are the main facts of human nature for Montaigne. Our limitations are great, but our resources for living well are greater. If we look into
ourselves, we shall find them.


## THE JOY OF LIVING

In all man's limitations and all his resources Montaigne finds tremendous possibilities for happiness or unhappiness, for good or evil, for wisdom or folly. These pairs of opposites are closely related. Happiness produces neither goodness nor wisdom, though it is favorable to them;
goodness produces happiness but not wisdom; wisdom produces both
goodness and happiness and depends on neither. Thus wisdom is basic.
The surest way to seek goodness and happiness is through wisdom.

Perhaps, indeed, it is the only way. Only a miraculous intervention of
God, Montaigne believes, can make radical changes in our intellect or
morals. By ourselves we cannot force our "ruling pattern" or extirpate our
vices. However, we can control these by a wise use of our virtues. The essence of a good education is not to impose on us "right" ways of thinking
and acting but to train our judgment to make us wise, and therefore good,
with a wisdom and a goodness that is our own. We should "know how to

do all things and like to do only the good." Only such free choice has moral meaning.

Wisdom, for Montaigne, consists entirely in knowing how to live. This involves four things: knowing ourselves, accepting ourselves and our life, learning what to expect of ourselves, and learning our duty to ourselves and others. Here the basic element, on which all the others depend, is self-knowledge. Ethics must be firmly rooted in psychology: what we should be, in what we are. Acceptance is equally necessary. For unless we accept as well as know ourselves, with our strengths and our weaknesses, we will expect too much or too little of ourselves, and in either case fall short of our best possible moral effectiveness. And unless we accept life with its joy and its pain, we will fall into the vice of sourness and ingratitude.

The last two parts of wisdom guide us in our main responsibility here on earth, namely our conduct. To do what is fitting and best we must first know what is fitting and best. To know this for ourselves alone is not easy; to know it for others as well is still harder. But the challenge is as rewarding as it is difficult.

For Montaigne this is the only way to seek real goodness. As long as there is inner strife, we cannot be entirely good, and we fall short of the ideal. Judgment, the voice of wisdom in us, must rule within; but it rules by persuasion, so that our whole selves join in our action. Only a soul in harmony with itself can be wholly good. Integration is a condition of integrity.

The most difficult thing is to know what we owe to ourselves and to others. Montaigne's final conviction of this is a measure of his growth. In the early years of his retirement, as we have seen, he had called it the greatest thing in the world to know how to belong to oneself. Now his sense of solidarity makes him reject this ideal as one-sided and incomplete. The problem is to belong to oneself and to the human race as well. Its most obvious aspect is the question to what extent public service is a duty.

"I am of this opinion," Montaigne now writes, "that the most honorable occupation is to serve the public and be useful to many." However, in the next breath he adds that he himself abstains from this partly from laziness, partly from conscience. At first glance his paradox seems perplexing. But actually laziness is not an important motive. What Montaigne probably means is simply that he loathes the lack of freedom of public life and knows that his loathing could be called laziness. His real reason for turning his back on a way of life that he admires is the difference between the norm and the rarely attained ideal. He finds that vices are necessary to hold the state together; that the general welfare may demand at any time that a public person do evil, sacrificing the honorable to the useful. Rare are the men who, like Epaminondas or Montaigne's father, can keep their integrity in public office.

> Public life must have relation to other lives. The virtue of Cato was vigorous beyond the measure of his time; and for a man who undertook to govern others, a man dedicated to the public service, it might be said that it was a justice, if not unjust, at least vain and out of season. . . .
>
> The virtue assigned to the affairs of the world is a virtue with many bends, angles, and elbows, so as to join and adapt itself to human weakness; mixed and artificial, not straight, clean, constant, or purely innocent. . . . He who walks in the crowd must step aside, keep his elbows in, step back or advance, even leave the straight way, according to what he encounters. He must live not so much according to himself as according to others, not according to what he proposes to himself but according to what others propose to him, according to the time, according to the men, according to the business.
>
> Plato says that anyone who escapes with clean breeches from handling the affairs of the world escapes by a miracle.

In other words, in public we can live neither as we like nor even as good a life as we like. This is where conscience motivates Montaigne's abstention. If he had to, he feels, he could adapt himself to public life; but he would rather not. The more he has experienced it, the more he is disgusted with it. He is better at private life, he thinks, as well as happier. Let those who are happier—and presumably no worse—in public life do their own dirty work.

"Husbanding Your Will" (bk. 3, chap. 10), whose subject is Montaigne's mayoralty, goes to the heart of the larger question of duty to self and to others. In a way that Pascal was to remember when he wrote on diversion, Montaigne analyzes the motives that drive most people out of themselves, whether into public office or elsewhere, and finds mainly ambition and a sort of centrifugal force bred of emptiness, laziness, and bad conscience. As importunate to themselves as they are serviceable to others, most men seek business simply for the sake of being busy. They do so with a good conscience, since everyone accepts uncritically the notion that public life is intrinsically altruistic, private life intrinsically selfish. But this notion is false. Self-abdication need not be self-abnegation, nor self-possession selfishness. We must remember our principal duty. "The principal responsibility that we have," Montaigne insists, "is to every man his conduct; and that is why we are here.... You have plenty to do at home within you; don't go away."

No longer will complete withdrawal do for Montaigne: "He who lives not at all with respect to others *(à autruy),*" he now writes, "hardly lives with respect to himself *(à soy).*" But the opposite is equally foolish and unnatural: "Just as anyone who should forget to live a good and saintly life, and think he was quit of his duty by guiding and training others to do so, would be a fool; even so he who abandons healthy and gay living of his own to serve others therewith, takes, to my taste, a bad and unnatural course."

The ideal balance lies in proper self-possession, which means lending but not giving ourselves to others. Its opposite, self-abdication, Montaigne finds ineffective and often bad: ineffective when we let our work possess and control us instead of controlling it; bad when we abdicate our judgment, reason, and conscience in favor of our passions or those of others. Then we become mere partisans, obliged upon command to distort the features of truth and goodness. Our judgment must see the good with the bad in the enemy, the bad with the good in our own side; it must distinguish the mask from the face, the mayor from Montaigne. Constructive moderation, so badly needed in violent times, comes not from passion but only from self-possessed loyalty.

Proper self-possession in general lies in a delicate balance of conflicting duties. It would be fairer and better for man, Montaigne believes, if he consciously included himself in applying the golden rule. His argument rests not on hedonism but on justice. Excessive self-devotion defeats itself; but excessive self-abnegation, however admirable (like that of Montaigne's father as mayor), is also unjust. The true point of justice, Montaigne believes, is to contribute all fitting duties and services to society, but with the aim of applying our experience to our own lives. We owe friendship not only to others but also to ourselves: not a false friendship that drives us to frantic pursuit of false goods such as glory, learning, riches; nor an overindulgent one that breaks down our character as the ivy does the wall it clings to; but "a salutary and well-regulated friendship, useful and pleasant alike." The true point of this friendship is difficult to find but all-important, a secret mystery of the temple of Pallas. "He who knows its duties and practices them . . . has attained the summit of human wisdom and of our happiness."

Montaigne sometimes calls goodness easy, because it follows nature instead of resisting it; sometimes he seems to call it hard, to combat the common illusion that public life is harder than private. In public, he says, we play a part, wear a mask, display our "art"; in private we reveal ourselves, our own face, our "nature." In private we need the reality of goodness, which is character; in public we need only its semblance, which is personality. It is easier to simulate goodness than to practice it.

Moreover, the incentive of glory makes public life easier. It is a brilliant thing to win a battle, to conduct an embassy, to govern a people. It is a rarer matter, more difficult, and less noticeable, to be pleasant and just with ourselves and our household, not to let ourselves go, not to be false to ourselves. Thus, despite popular opinion, private lives accomplish duties as harsh and strenuous as other lives, or more so. Moreover, private goodness is more appropriate and important than public: "Alexander's virtue seems to me to represent a good deal less vigor in his theater than does that of Socrates in his humble and obscure activity. I can easily imagine Socrates in Alexander's place; Alexander in that of Socrates, I cannot. If you ask the former what he knows how to do, he will answer: 'Subdue the world'; if you ask the latter, he will say: 'Lead the life of man in conformity with its natural condition'; a knowledge much more general, more weighty, and more legitimate."

Since our raison d'être is our conduct, private life is our proper function and domain. To live it well is the greatest masterpiece of all.

> We are great fools. "He has spent his life in idleness," we say; "I have done nothing today." What, have you not lived? That is not only the fundamental but the most illustrious of your occupations. "If I had been placed in a position to manage great affairs, I would have shown what I could do." Have you been able to think out and manage your life? You have done the greatest task of all. . . . To compose our character is our duty, not to compose books, and to win, not battles and provinces, but order and tranquillity in our conduct. Our great and glorious masterpiece is to live appropriately.

In order to perform this masterpiece, we must recognize and accept ourselves as children of nature. From the "Apology" and "Cannibals" to "Physiognomy," Montaigne continues to insist on this point. We belong in nature, but we will not admit it. In our reckless attempts to improve on her by art, we have lost her track; we have changed her into all sorts of forms, as perfumers do with oil, so that we no longer recognize her in ourselves and must seek her in simple people or animals. We have been fools to abandon a guide who led us so happily and so surely.

Nature helps us in every way. She uses our inconstancy to divert our grief; gives us better laws than our own, since she knows her business better than we do; makes pain serve pleasure, and our needs pleasant to satisfy; teaches us how to die, and in fact all we need to know to be content. She is a sweet guide, but no more sweet than prudent and just; we cannot fail if we follow her, and the more simply we follow her the better.

Artificiality is our undoing. Foolishly we take its glister for gold. Sometimes—and here Montaigne speaks from personal experience—we let it spoil our lives. We beset ourselves with all sorts of fears, like that of death, which may not even be natural; we give ourselves more trouble in preparing for death than we would in dying; we make death the goal of life instead of merely the end. For all her grateful children nature takes care of these things better than ever we can and on a moment's notice.

From the refusal to accept ourselves as children of nature comes presumption and its offspring, the wildest of our maladies, self-disdain. Because we think of ourselves as above and apart from the order of creation, we cut our obligations to fit a higher being than ourselves, and so order ourselves to be necessarily at fault. We like to think that the higher our aim, the higher will be our attainment. But Montaigne disagrees, like Socrates, whose motto, "According as one can," he often borrows. Our nature, he finds, simply does not work that way: constant failure, however inevitable, makes us give up trying, either through discouragement or through too easy acceptance of the inevitable. There is the danger also that it will make us actually worse; for our normal impulse to cover up perhaps a minor vice will add to it the ugly vice of hypocrisy. "Between ourselves," Montaigne writes, "these are two things that I have always observed to be in singular accord: supercelestial thoughts and subterranean conduct. . . . They want to get out of themselves and escape from the man *(eschapper à l'homme)*. That is madness: instead of changing into angels, they change into beasts; instead of raising themselves, they lower themselves."

In Montaigne's eyes this is perhaps our greatest folly: to want to escape from man's condition. It is not natural but purely man-made, a product of our erratic mind. We would be wiser, happier, and better, he insists, to accept ourselves as we are, to let our conscience be content with itself not as the conscience of an angel or of a horse but as the conscience of a man. Self-knowledge is the road to this acceptance: "We seek other conditions because we do not understand the use of our own, and go outside of ourselves because we do not know what it is like inside."

For self-study reveals our resources to us as well as our limitations. Socrates, whose principal rule was "Know thyself," can help us to see them. Whereas the peasants are a good corrective, he is a perfect model and guide. He has shown human nature how much it can do by itself; he can teach us the little learning that we need for happy living. Beyond these resources, which are natural, all others are practically vain and superfluous. By our usual standard of values, which sets art above nature, the simplicity of Socrates is low and backward. With relish Montaigne points up the paradox by portraying him in these terms:

> He was always one and the same, and raised himself, not by sallies but by disposition, to the utmost point of vigor. Or rather, he raised nothing but rather brought it down and back to its original natural point. . . .
>
> By these vulgar and natural motives, by these ordinary and common ideas . . . he constructed not only the most regulated, but the loftiest and most vigorous beliefs, actions, and conduct that ever were. . . . See him plead before his judges. . . . There is nothing borrowed from art and the sciences; the simplest recognize their means and their strength; it is not possible to go back further and lower.

Thus in Montaigne's opinion the paradox works both ways. By trying to escape man's condition and be angels, men become beasts. By accepting his lot, humbly and simply, as a child of nature, Socrates became the best man that ever lived. Acceptance such as his is a condition of goodness.

Even the preceding remarks, however, show that for Montaigne self-acceptance alone is not enough; a measure of self-improvement is also needed. The peasants are good, or at least innocent; but Socrates is perfect. He has improved himself, as they presumably have not, by applying his reason to his natural resources. Their goodness is primarily natural; his is fully human.

Montaigne is often at odds with himself—verbally at least—on the question of self-improvement. It is no wonder that his moral countenance has appeared to different readers as anything from earnest reformer to complacent hedonist. Often it is his love of sally and paradox, humor and irony, that leads him into inconsistency of statement; but there are other reasons, too. In respect to himself, frankness makes him say that he has sought to be better, and perhaps in some measure succeeded; but frankness and modesty make him regard this measure as small. Moreover, he considers self-acceptance bad in excess but good in moderation: in excess the enemy of self-improvement, in moderation the conditon of it. Since most people put all the emphasis on self-improvement, Montaigne usually stresses his lack of it. "I have not corrected, like Socrates," he writes, "my natural dispositions by force of reason. . . . I let myself go as I have come,

I combat nothing." What virtue he has, he calls a sort of accidental innocence.

Yet even in this same context, while saying that he has restricted his vices too little, he admits that since they aid and abet one another, he has kept them apart and confined, as isolated and simple as he could. Such statements seem more candid than the others and closer to the center of his thought. Without boorish conceit he could not claim much more than he does when he says that he has put all his efforts into forming his life. And still more revealing is a later comparison of himself with the stoics: "What they did by virtue, I train myself to do by disposition *(complexion)*."

The somewhat surprising use of the term *complexion* (as something trained and acquired) is a result of Montaigne's conception of the mechanics of self-improvement. It is through habit, he finds, that wisdom works to produce goodness. Habit is all-important, all-powerful; a second nature, as Aristotle says, and no less strong than the first. Virtue can work by fits and starts, and in that way we can do almost anything. But what we really are we are constantly, by habit. One of the reasons why Montaigne sets Socrates so high is that by habit he had made his goodness a second nature. When Montaigne trains himself to do well by disposition, he is following what he considers the best way to be good and the only way to be really and wholly good.

For we can improve on nature, good and strong as she is. Our native state seems to be a sort of balance of conflicting elements: the vices on the one hand, and on the other hand conscience and repentance. As we grow, either side may prevail, or neither. Education can do much but not everything; we may control, but we cannot extirpate, our natural propensities. Reason will normally tell us to follow nature, but not always; when it does not, it is reason we must follow.

Montaigne's main hope of human betterment lies in an inborn seed of universal reason. Although he is sincerely religious, the Protestant experience and the religious wars apparently make him feel that religion has failed as a moral stimulus, presumably because it has not allowed enough for human limitations. With his intense practicality, he cares hardly at all for belief, almost exclusively for individual and civic morality. The one passage where he speaks his mind clearly on this matter is worth quoting at length:

> Shall I say this in passing: that I see held in greater price than it is worth what is almost alone practiced among us, a certain idea of scholastic probity, slave to precepts, held down beneath

fear and hope? What I love is the kind that laws and religions do not make but perfect and authorize, feeling in itself enough to sustain itself without help, born in us of its own roots from the seed of universal reason imprinted in every man who is not denatured. This reason, which straightens Socrates from his inclination to vice, makes him obedient to the men and gods who command in his city, courageous in death not because his soul is immortal but because he is mortal. It is a ruinous teaching for any society, and much more harmful than ingenious and subtle, which persuades the people that religious belief is enough, by itself and without morals, to satisfy divine justice. Practice makes us see an enormous distinction between devoutness and conscience.

Just as Montaigne rejects nature as the arbiter of our morals, so he rejects religion as their base. He dislikes its constraint, its self-seeking motivation by fear and hope. He not only accepts us as neither horses nor angels, he does not want us to be anything but men. He seems to feel that in giving us reason to help us rise above mere nature, God has put us quite on our own to be fully ourselves.

In the early essays, doubtful of our ability to become good, Montaigne had mainly urged us to be natural. Now he still urges that, but most of all he wants us to be human.

Our vices, for example, he regards as natural but not human. Most of those that he hates worst—disdainful treatment of social inferiors; contempt for the body and its rights; eagerness to make others sad by our misery; lying, disloyalty, mob violence, torture, cruelty—he clearly connects, by statement or suggestion, with inhumanity.

Meanwhile his highest praise for ideas, actions, or men is to call them human. The philosophical opinions he likes best are, he says, "the most solid, that is to say the most human and the most our own." An honorable man will not lie, for he wants to be seen just as he is inside, where "either all is good, or at least all is human." Epaminondas deserves a place among the best of men because even in the sternest of actions he exercised goodness and humanity. Even for a god the term is high praise: Vulcan's generosity to his unfaithful wife Venus is "of a humanity truly more than human." And the concept is central in Montaigne's statements of his ideal: "The most beautiful lives, in my opinion, are those that conform to the common human pattern. . . . There is nothing so beautiful and legitimate as to play the man well and duly."

To be natural and yet naturally to surpass the rest of nature; to accept ourselves and yet by the means God has given us to improve ourselves: this for Montaigne is to be truly human.

For all his stress on the need of accepting the limitations imposed on us by nature, Montaigne wants no others. Truly representative of his age, his ideal is to live not only simply but also as richly and fully as possible. Already before 1580 he had recommended versatility in his essay on education when he advised that a young man should be able to do all things and do good only from free choice. In the late essays he stresses this value even more and also treats a new aspect of it—the problem of encroaching age.

He fears aging, as we have seen, as a diminution. "I hate that accidental repentance that old age brings," he writes. "I shall never be grateful to impotence for any good it may do me. . . . Miserable sort of remedy, to owe our health to disease!" He held these views in youth as in age. Now that his sluggish body drags him down, his mind must fight to stay green. Man, he feels, must strive to be limited by neither youth nor age. The ideal is to be whole.

Montaigne's main praise of versatility in general is in "Three Kinds of Association" and "Experience." Versatility is close to his ideal of simplicity in that it usually means the ability to relax as well as be tense, to move and act happily and gracefully on lower social and intellectual levels than one's own. "The fairest souls," he writes, "are those that have the most variety and adaptability."

Here again, habit is the great power that makes us what we are. The great danger is that it will enslave us to our usual ways and spoil us for varied living. It can also be used, however, to make us and keep us adaptable: "I would admire a soul with different levels, which could be both tense and relaxed, which could chat with a neighbor about his building, his hunting, and his lawsuit, and keep up an enjoyable conversation with a carpenter and a gardener."

Praise of this ability to relax graciously fills much of the conclusion of Montaigne's last chapter. In the midst of great wars, he tells us, Caesar and Alexander found time to enjoy natural pleasures, and Brutus to make notes on Polybius. For all their severity, both Catos accepted and enjoyed our human bondage to Venus and Bacchus. Epaminondas and Scipio the Elder spent pleasant hours singing and playing with youngsters. Socrates again is our best model. Courageous, noble, patient and self-restrained in every sort of hardship including death, he could lose himself in some beautiful thought for hours at a time yet could also drink the rest of the army quietly under the table when that was in order, or play gracefully and happily with children at their games. Such rich versatility is wholly admirable. "We should never tire of presenting the picture of this man as a pattern and ideal of all sorts of perfection."

Thus the main components of Montaigne's ethical ideal meet in Socrates—the natural simplicity of self-acceptance, the human virtue of self-improvement, the rich versatility of a life lived fully on all levels. His was life at its best, fully and purely human.

"It is an absolute perfection and virtually divine to know how to enjoy our being lawfully *(loyallement)*." Thus Montaigne, almost in conclusion, attempts, not for the first time, to compress into a formula the heart of his message. It is a reminder that we should accept ourselves and life and live appropriately; it is also a statement that the proper enjoyment of our being is a form of perfection.

Montaigne had not always felt and talked in this way. On the contrary, until his illness he had even mistrusted life. Paradoxical, but only in its Epicurean extremeness, is his bleak statement from the "Apology": "Our well-being is only freedom from being badly off. . . . To have no pain is to have the most good that man can hope for." But now his confidence makes him contradict this view when he adds: "I am glad not to be sick; but if I am sick, I want to know that I am; and if I am cauterized or incised, I want to feel it. Truly, if anyone rooted out the awareness of pain, he would extirpate at the same time the awareness of pleasure, and in the end would annihilate man. . . . Evil is a good to man in its turn. Neither is pain something for him always to flee, nor pleasure for him always to follow."

This is the second of the two important concepts that give Montaigne confidence in life. To the arbitrariness of the soul he has added, apparently since his illness, the interdependence of pleasure and pain. Now he finds life full of contrasts which our soul must learn to accept and to harmonize: "Our life is composed, like the harmony of the world, of contrary things, also of different tones, sweet and harsh, sharp and flat, soft and loud. If a musician liked only one kind, what would he have to say? He must know how to use them together and blend them. And so must we do with good and evil, which are consubstantial with our life. Our existence is impossible without this mixture, and one group is no less necessary for it than the other." Naturally, we will prefer pleasure to pain and encourage it, but we will regard both sanely and accept them as necessary elements of our life. They are not completely pure; there is pain in pleasure and pleasure in pain. To live well and happily we must use them wisely, like the musician in the passage above: "They are two fountains: whoever draws from them the right amount, from the right source, at the right time, whether city, man, or beast, he is very happy."

It takes attention to exercise this artistry in living, but it is a pleasant and rewarding occupation. Montaigne enjoys life twice as much as others, he believes, for enjoyment depends on application. As the life that remains to him grows shorter, he works to make it deeper and fuller. We must study, savor, and ruminate our joys, he finds, in order to be properly grateful to him who grants them to us.

The basic condition is acceptance: of ourselves, our condition, and our life, with all the limitations and possibilities that nature has placed in them. We are not to reject, like some, the natural pleasures of the body, for to do so is to reject our condition; we are to accept them not avidly but simply and gratefully. Nor are we in effect to cast life aside by always seeking to "pass the time"; it is too precious to be allowed to slip through our fingers. It is Montaigne's grateful and gracious acceptance of all that human life means that gives such happy and steady serenity to his comments on the pains and drawbacks of his declining years: "If I had to live over again, I would live as I have lived. I neither regret the past nor fear the future. . . . I have seen the grass, and the flower, and the fruit, now I see the dryness—happily, since it is naturally."

Montaigne's earlier friends the Stoics had also believed in the goodness of life; but the difference in the underlying reasoning is complete. They started, in effect, by accepting the belief in a supreme and good intelligence that governs the universe for the best. Thus what seems a particular evil must be in reality a good; and if we are to be wisely in tune with nature, we must learn to accept it as good and call it that. Montaigne's conviction carries weight because it is not at all a preconception. Though his Christian God is all-good and all-powerful, he is too remote to play a part here. Montaigne's optimism is the fruit of his meditations on a life rich in experience, painful as well as pleasant.

> As for me, then, I love life and cultivate it just as God has been pleased to grant it to us. I do not go about wishing that it should lack the need to eat or drink . . . nor that we should beget children insensibly with our fingers or our heels, but rather, with due respect, that we could also beget them voluptuously with our fingers and heels. . . . Those are ungrateful and unfair complaints. I accept with all my heart and with gratitude what nature has done for me, and I am pleased with myself and

proud of myself that I do. We wrong that great and all-powerful giver by refusing his gift, nullifying it, and disfiguring it.
Himself all good, he has made all things good.

It is the long meditative journey Montaigne has traveled that gives
power and persuasion to his final triumphant hymn of gratitude. The critical apprehensive early stages, summed up in the famous "Que sçay-je?"
had led to deep self-examination. Self-examination, trial by illness, and experience have led at last to confidence in self, in man, and in life. For the
final stages and the journey as a whole, Montaigne's final motto is the true
one: "*Viresque acquirit eundo*—He acquires strength as he goes."

MAURICE MERLEAU-PONTY

# Reading Montaigne

*I commit myself with difficulty.*
—(*Essays,* bk. 3, chap. 10)

*We must live among the living.*
—(*Essays,* bk. 3, chap. 9)

We think we have said all there is to say about him when we say he is
a skeptic, that is, that he questions himself and does not answer, refusing
even to admit that he knows nothing, and holding himself to the famous
"What do I know?" None of this takes us very far. Skepticism has two
sides. It means that nothing is true, but also that nothing is false. It rejects
*all* opinions and *all* behavior as absurd, but it thereby deprives us of the
means of rejecting any one as false. Destroying dogmatic, partial, or abstract truth, it insinuates the idea of a total truth with all the necessary
facets and mediations. If it multiplies contrasts and contradictions, it is because truth demands it. Montaigne begins by teaching that truth contradicts itself; perhaps he ends up recognizing that contradiction is truth. "I
do indeed contradict myself at random; but truth, as Demades said, I do
not contradict at all." (All quotations of Montaigne are taken from book
3 of the *Essays.*) The first and most fundamental of contradictions is that
by which the refusal of each truth uncovers a new kind of truth. Thus we
shall find in Montaigne a doubt which rests upon itself and is endless, we
shall find religion, and we shall find Stoicism. It would be useless to pre-

---

From *Signs.* © 1964 by Northwestern University Press.

tend that he excludes any of these "positions," or that he ever makes any one of them *his own*. But perhaps in the end he finds in this ambiguous self—which is offered to everything, and which he never finished exploring—the place of all obscurities, the mystery of all mysteries, and something like an ultimate truth.

Self-consciousness is his constant, the measure of all doctrines for him. It could be said that he never got over a certain wonder at himself which constitutes the whole substance of his works and wisdom. He never tired of experiencing the paradox of a *conscious being*. At each instant, in love, in political life, in perception's silent life, we adhere to something, make it our own, and yet withdraw from it and hold it at a distance, without which we would know nothing about it. Descartes will overcome the paradox and make consciousness mind: "It is never the eye which sees itself . . . , but clearly the mind, which alone knows . . . the eye and itself" (Leon Brunschvicg, *Descartes et Pascal lectures de Montaigne*). Montaigne's consciousness is not mind from the outset; it is tied down at the same time it is free, and in one sole ambiguous act it opens to external objects and experiences itself as alien to them. Montaigne does not know that resting place, that self-possession, which Cartesian understanding is to be. The world is not for him a system of objects the idea of which he has in his possession; the self is not for him the purity of an intellectual consciousness. For Montaigne—as for Pascal later on—we are interested in a world we do not have the key to. We are equally incapable of dwelling in ourselves and in things, and are referred from them to ourselves and from ourselves to them.

The Delphic oracle must be corrected. It is well to make us return to ourselves. But we do not escape ourselves any more than we escape things. "It is always vanity for you, within and without, but it is less vanity when it is less extensive. Except for you, O man, said that God [at Delphi], each thing studies itself first, and according to its need, has limits to its labors and desires. There is not a single one as empty and necessitous as you, who embrace the universe; you are the scrutinizer without knowledge, the judge without jurisdiction, and, after all, the fool in the farce." Confronted with the world of objects, or even the world of animals resting in their nature, consciousness is hollow and avid. It is consciousness of all things because it is nothing; it grasps at all things and holds to none. Involved in spite of everything in this flux they wish to be unaware of, our clear ideas risk being masks we hide our being beneath rather than the truth about ourselves.

Self-understanding for Montaigne is dialogue with self. It is a questioning addressed to the opaque being he is and awaits a response from. It is like "essaying" or "experimenting on" himself. He has in view a questioning without which reason's purity would be illusory and in the end impure. Some are amazed that he should want to speak about even the details of his mood and temperament. It is because for him every doctrine, when it is separated from what we do, threatens to be mendacious; and he imagined a book in which for once there would be expressed not only ideas but also the very life which they appear in and which modifies their meaning.

So beneath clear ideas and thoughts he finds a spontaneity abounding in opinions, feelings, and unjustifiable acts. "Myson, one of the seven wise men . . . , questioned as to why he was laughing to himself, replied: 'For the very reason that I am laughing to myself.' How many stupid things I say and answer every day in my own eyes, and thus how much more frequently I am apt to do so in the eyes of others." Consciousness has an essential foolishness, which is its power to become no matter what, to become itself. In order to laugh to ourselves we need no external cause; we need only think that we can laugh to ourselves and be company for ourselves. We need only be dual and consciousness.

> What is taken to be rare about Perseus King of Macedonia—that his mind attached itself to no rank but went wandering through all kinds of life and representing customs to itself which were so vagabond and flighty that it was not known to himself or others what man this was—seems to me more or less to apply to everyone. We are always thinking somewhere else,

and it could not possibly be otherwise. To be conscious is, among other things, to be somewhere else.

The very powers found in animals and related to the body are in man transformed and distorted because they are caught up in the movement of a consciousness. We see dogs who bark while they dream; so they have images. But man does not have just a few images painted into his brain. He can live in the realm of the imaginary. The sight of actors "so deeply involved in a mourning role that they still weep about it in the dressing room" is a wondrous one, as is the sight of a man by himself who fashions a crowd around him, grimaces, is astonished, laughs, fights and is triumphant in this invisible world. Or this prince who has his well-beloved brother killed as a result of a bad dream, or that other one who kills himself because his dogs howled. If the body alone is considered, the penis ought to give only a precise pleasure, comparable to that of other bodily functions. But

> throughout most of the world, this part of our body was dei-
> fied. In the same province some skinned theirs in order to offer
> up and consecrate a chunk of it, while others offered up and
> consecrated their semen. In another province, young men
> pierced theirs publicly, opening them in various places between
> flesh and skin, and through these openings they passed skewers,
> the longest and biggest they could bear; and afterwards made a
> fire from these skewers as an offering to their gods, who were
> held to have little vigor and chastity if they happened to be as-
> tonished at the force of this cruel suffering.

Thus life is borne away outside itself; the extreme of pleasures resembles pain. "Nature itself, I fear, attaches some instinct for inhumanity to man." It is because our body and its peaceful functions are traversed by the power that we have to devote ourselves to something else and give our-selves absolutes. Besides, there is no desire which goes to the body alone and does not seek another desire or an assent beyond the body. "Thus these men say it is the will that they contract for, and they are right. . . . I am horrified at imagining that a body deprived of affection is mine." Love is not just love of the body, since it intends someone; and it is not just love of the mind, since it intends him in his body. The word "strange" is the one that most often recurs when Montaigne speaks of man. Or "absurd." Or "monster." Or "miracle." "What a monstrous animal he is who horri-fies himself, whose pleasures weigh upon him, who clings to misfortune!"

Descartes will briefly confirm the soul and body's union, and prefer to think them separate; for then they are clear to understanding. Montaigne's realm, on the contrary, is the "mixture" of the soul and body; he is inter-ested only in our factual condition, and his book endlessly describes this paradoxical fact that we are. That is to say that he thinks of death, the counterproof of our incarnation. When traveling he never stopped in a house without wondering if he might be sick there and die comfortably. "I feel death continually gripping at my throat or loins." He spoke very well against meditation upon death. It deforms and misses its object; for it con-cerns distant death, and distant death, being everywhere in our future, is harder than present death, which advances before our eyes in the form of an event. It is not a question of corrupting life by thinking about death. What interests Montaigne is not death's pathos—its ugliness, the last sighs, the funereal trappings which form the customary motif of discourses on death and are images of death used by the living. "These men do not consider death itself at all; they make no judgment about it whatsoever: they do not bring their thought to rest on death but run toward, intend a new being." Those who listen to the consolations of the priest, lift up their eyes and hands to heaven, and pray aloud, "these flee the struggle, turning their consideration away from death, as we amuse children while we intend to prick them with a lancet." Montaigne wants us to measure nonbeing with an incisive glance and, knowing death in all is nakedness, know life laid wholly bare. Death is "the act of one person alone." In the confused mass of being, death cuts out that particular zone which is ourselves. It puts in matchless evidence that inexhaustible source of opinions, dreams, and passions which secretly gave life to the spectacle of the world. And thus it teaches us better than any episode of life the fundamental accident which made us appear and will make us disappear.

When he writes: "I study myself more than other subjects. It is my metaphysics and my physics," these words must be taken literally. He rejects in advance the explanations of man a physics or a metaphysics can give us, because it is still man who "proves" philosophies and sciences, and because they are explained by him rather than he by them. If for example we wanted to isolate mind and body by relating them to different principles, we would hide what is to be understood—"the monster," the "miracle," man. So there cannot in all good conscience be any question of solving the human problem; there can only be a question of describing man as problematic. Hence this idea of an inquiry without discovery, a hunt without a kill, which is not the vice of a dilettante but the only appropriate method for describing man. "The world is only a school for inquisitioners." Hence too the attention he gives to thoughts' streaming and the spontaneity of dreams, which makes him anticipate at times Proust's tone, as if for him already the only victory over time lay in expressing time.


Having set out in this way, attentive to all that is fortuitous and unfinished in man, he is at the opposite pole from religion, if religion is an explanation of and key to the world. Although he often puts it outside the range of his inquiries and beyond his reach, nothing he says is a preparation for belief. "We are in the midst of the world's peat and dung," tied to "the deadest, most stagnant part of the universe." Animal instinct is more perfect than our reason. Our religion is a matter of custom: "we are Christians in the same way we are Perigordians or Germans." Circumcision, fasting, Lent, the Cross, confession, the celibacy of priests, the use of a sacred language in worship, the Incarnation of God, Purgatory—all these elements of Christianity are found in pagan religions. In each village miracles are fabricated beneath our eyes through ignorance and hearsay. A Platonic legend has Socrates born of a virgin visited by Apollo. Men have looked for and found in Homer all the oracles and predictions that they needed. In short, revealed religion is not very different from the folly men cause to appear on earth. It remains to be seen whether we must conclude from this, as Montaigne does at times, that barbarian religions are already inspired—or that our own is still barbarous. How can there be any doubt as to his answer when he even reproaches Socrates for his *demonries* and *ecstasies*? In morals as in knowledge, Montaigne contrasts our terrestrial inherence to every supernatural relationship. We can repent an action, he says; we cannot repent being ourselves; and yet according to religion this is what we would have to do. There is no new birth. We cannot annul anything we have done: "I customarily do what I do completely, and proceed all of a piece." He makes an exception in the case of a few men who already dwell in eternity, but casts suspicion upon them by adding: "just between us, supercelestial opinions and subterranean customs are things I have always judged to be in singular accord with one another."

What he retains of Christianity is the vow of ignorance. Why assume hypocrisy in the places where he puts religion above criticism? Religion is valuable in that it saves a place for what is strange and knows our lot is enigmatic. All the solutions it gives to the enigma are incompatible with our monstrous condition. As a questioning, it is justified on the condition that it remain answerless. It is one of the modes of our folly, and our folly is essential to us. When we put not self-satisfied understanding but a consciousness astonished at itself at the core of human existence, we can neither obliterate the dream of an other side of things nor repress the wordless invocation of this beyond. What is certain is that if there is some universal Reason we are not in on its secrets, and are in any case required to guide our lives according to our own lights. "In ignorance and negligence I let myself be guided to the general way of the world. I will know it well enough when I perceive it." Who would dare to reproach us for making use of this life and world which constitute our horizon?

But if we reject religious passion, must we not reject all other passions as well? Montaigne often speaks of the Stoics, and favorably. This man who wrote so well against reason, and showed that we can in no case get beyond opinion to see an idea face to face, has recourse to the "seed of universal reason embedded in every man who is not perverted." As there is the invocation of an unknown god in Montaigne, there is the invocation of an impossible reason. Even though nothing is wholly "within our power," even though we are not capable of autonomy, must we not at least withdraw and carve a corner of indifference for ourselves from which we look upon our actions and our life as unimportant "roles"?

This view is found in Montaigne, among other things. "We must lend ourselves to others and give ourselves only to ourselves." Marriage, for example, is an institution which has its laws and its conditions of equilibrium. It would be madness to mix passion with it. Love which "enslaves us to another" is acceptable only as a free and voluntary practice. At times Montaigne even speaks of it as of a bodily function which is a matter of hygiene, and treats the body as a mechanism we need not make common cause with. So much the more will he place the State among those external devices we find ourselves joined to by chance and ought to use according to their law without putting anything of ourselves into them. Imagination and prestige always reign in our relationships to others. And much more so still in public life, which associates us with those we have not chosen, and with many blockheads. Now "it is impossible to deal in good faith with a blockhead. At the hands of such an impetuous master, not only my judgment but my conscience as well is corrupted." In public life I become mad with the madmen. Montaigne strongly feels that there is a witchcraft in social life: here everyone puts in the place of his thoughts their reflection in the eyes and idle chatter of others. There is no longer any truth; there is (Pascal will say) no longer any self-consent to oneself. Each is literally alienated. Let us withdraw from public life. "The common weal requires us to betray and lie and massacre; let us resign this commission to those more pliant and obedient." It is true that we are not always able to abstain, that furthermore to do so is to let things slide and that after all there is certainly a need for men of state or a prince. How can they help it? The prince will have to lie, kill, and deceive. Let him do it, but let him know what he is doing and not disguise crime as virtue. "What remedy is there? There is no remedy. If he was really bothered between the two extremes, he had to do it; but if he did it with no regrets, if it did not weigh upon him to do it, this is a sign that his conscience is in a bad state." And we who look on? All there is left for us to do is (as it will be said later) to obey despising what we obey. We must despise, since the State is against everything that matters in the world: against freedom, against conscience. But we must obey, since this folly is the law of life with others, and since it would be another folly not to deal with the State according to its laws. Yet Plato puts the philosopher in the government. He imagines a just city and sets out to construct it.

> But is there any evil in a polis which is worth being fought
> against with such a mortal drug? . . . Plato . . . does not con-
> sent to violence being done to his country's peace in order to
> heal his country; he does not accept an improvement which
> costs the blood and ruin of its citizens, but establishes it as the
> office of a virtuous man to leave everything as it is in such a
> case.

It is absurd to want to rule a history made of accidents by reason.

> In my time I have seen the wisest heads of this Kingdom assem-
> bled, with great ceremony and public expense, for treaties and
> agreements about which the true decision nevertheless de-
> pended in all sovereignty upon the desires of milady's chamber
> and the inclination of some silly little woman.

Foresight and laws will never be equal to the variety of cases; reason will
never be able to judge public life. In a time when public life is split into a
thousand particular conflicts, Montaigne does not even suspect that a
meaning can be found for it. It is impossible to be reconciled with this
chaos. To live in public affairs is "to live according to others." Montaigne
is clearly inclined to live according to himself.

And yet is this his final word? He sometimes spoke differently of love,
friendship, and even politics. Not that he simply contradicted himself in
doing so. It is because the Stoic separation of external and internal, necessity and freedom, is abstract, or destroys itself; and because we are indivisi-
bly within and without. We cannot always obey if we despise, or despise
always if we obey. There are occasions when to obey is to accept and to
despise is to refuse, when a life which is in part a double life ceases to be
possible, and there is no longer any distinction between exterior and interior. Then we must enter the world's folly, and we need a rule for such a
moment. Montaigne knew it; he did not swerve from it. And how could
he have? He had described consciousness, even in its solitude, as already
mixed according to its very principle with the absurd and foolish. How
could he have prescribed that consciousness dwell in itself, since he thinks
it is wholly outside itself? Stoicism can only be a way-point. It teaches us
to be and judge in opposition to the external world; it could not possibly
rid us of it. What is most peculiar to Montaigne may be the little bit he
has told us about the conditions and motives for this return to the world.

It is not a question of reaching a reassuring conclusion at no matter
what cost, nor of forgetting at the end what has been found on the way.

It is from doubt that certainty will come. So we must measure the extent of it. Let us repeat that all belief is passion and makes us beside ourselves, that we can believe only by ceasing to think, that wisdom is a "resolution to be irresolute," that it condemns friendship, love, and public life. And so here we are back to ourselves again. And we find chaos still, with death, the emblem of all disorders, on the horizon. Cut off from others, cut off from the world, incapable of finding in himself (like the Stoic wise man) and in an inner relationship to God the means of justifying the world's comedy, Montaigne's wise man, it would seem, no longer has any conversation except with that life he perceives welling madly within him for a little while longer, any resource except the most general derision, any motive except despising himself and all things. In this disorder, why not give up? Why not take animals for a model—these neighing horses, these swans who sing as they die—why not join them in unconsciousness? The best thing would be to go back to the "puerile security, the ignorance" of beasts. Or to invent, against the feeling of death, some natural religion: "the extinction of a life is the way to a thousand other lives."

This movement is to be found in Montaigne. But there is another one too, which appears just as often. For after all the doubts, there remains to be explained—precisely because we know that every attempt to know multiplies questions and obscures what it wants to clarify, and that for each head severed, the Hydra of ignorance grows three new ones—why there are opinions, why we believed to begin with that we held truths, and why doubt needs to be learned. "I know what it is to be human better than I know what it it to be animal, mortal, or rational." Descartes will remember this saying. It means that the mind's movement and irresolution are only half of the truth. The other half is the marvel that our volubility has stopped, and at each moment stops again, in appearances which we may indeed show cannot withstand examination, but which at least had the air of truth and gave us the idea of it. Thought, when it questions itself, never stops prolonging and contradicting itself; but there is a thought in act which is no little thing, and which we have to take into account. The critique of human understanding destroys it only if we cling to the idea of a complete or absolute understanding. If on the contrary we rid ourselves of this idea, then thought in act, as the only possible thought, becomes the measure of all things and the equivalent of an absolute. The critique of passions does not deprive them of their value if it is carried to the point of showing that we are never in possession of ourselves and that passion is ourselves. At this moment, reasons for doubting become reasons for believing. The only effect of our whole critique is to make our passions and opinions more precious by making us see that they are our only recourse, and that we do not understand our own selves by dreaming of something different. Then we find the fixed point we need (if we want to bring our versatility to a stop) not in the bitter religion of nature (that somber divinity who multiplies his works for nothing), but in the fact that there is opinion, the appearance of the good and true. Then regaining nature, naivete, and ignorance means regaining the grace of our first certainties in the doubt which rings them round and makes them visible.

In fact, Montaigne did not simply doubt. Doubting is an action; thus doubt cannot demolish our action, our doing, which is in the right against it. The same author who wanted "to live according to himself" felt passionately that we are among other things what we are for others, and that their opinion reaches us at the core of our being. "I would gladly come back from the other world," he says in sudden anger, "to give the lie to the man who would shape me differently than I was, even though it were to honor me." His friendship with La Boétie was exactly the kind of tie which "enslaves us to another." He did not think he knew himself better than La Boétie knew him. He lived beneath his eyes, and after his death he continued to do so. It is in order to know himself as La Boétie knew him that Montaigne questions and studies himself; "he alone possessed my true image and took it away with him. That is why I decipher myself so curiously." We rarely see such a complete gift. Far from La Boétie's friendship having been accidental to his life, we would have to say that Montaigne and the author of the *Essays* were born of this friendship, and that for him, in sum, existing meant existing beneath his friend's gaze. The fact of the matter is that true skepticism is movement toward the truth, that the critique of passions is hatred of false passions, and finally, that in *some* circumstances Montaigne recognized outside himself men and things he never dreamed of refusing himself to, because they were like the emblem of his outward freedom, and because in loving them he was himself and regained himself in them as he regained them in himself.

Even in pleasure, which he sometimes speaks about as a doctor, Montaigne is not after all cynical.

> It is madness to devote all one's thoughts to it and commit oneself to it with a furious and indiscreet affection. But on the other hand, to get mixed up in it without love and willing obligation, in the manner of actors—in order to play a common role of the age and its customs and put nothing of one's own into it except words—is in truth to provide for one's safety, but in a very cowardly way, like the man who would abandon his

honor or advantage or his pleasure out of fear of danger. For it is certain that those who set up such a practice cannot hope to gain from it any fruit which would touch or satisfy a noble soul.

As an old man, Montaigne says that success in seduction depends upon choosing the right moment. But what does this late wisdom prove? When he was young and amorous, he never carried on his love affairs like battles and according to tactics.

I often had a lack of luck, but sometimes of enterprise as well; God save the man who can still joke about it! In this century it requires more temerity, which our young people excuse under pretext of ardor; but if they looked more closely, they would find that it comes more from scorn than ardor. I feared superstitiously to offend, and I gladly respect what I love. Not to mention that whoever takes away reverence for this commodity rubs away its luster. I like a man to be a bit of the child and fearful servitor in his love. If this is not enough, I have besides some aspects of the stupid shame Plutarch speaks about, and have been in the course of my life wounded and spotted by it in different ways. . . . I have as tender an eye for sustaining a refusal as I do for refusing; and it weighs upon me so much to weigh upon others that on those occasions when duty forces me to test someone's will in something which is doubtful and costs him dear, I do it sparingly and in spite of myself.

There is a very tender cynic. Fate did not have him love from love as he did from friendship, but he himself had nothing to do with it.

He entered the bewitched realm of public life; he did not withhold himself. "I do not want a man to shrink from attention, steps, speeches, and if need be sweat and blood in the responsibilities he assumes." The people named him mayor several times. "I wish them all possible good; and certainly, if the occasion had arisen, I would have spared nothing to serve them. I was as disturbed for their sake as I am for my own." How was he able to live a public life if he was "disgusted with mastery, both active and passive?" He obeys without liking obedience and commands without liking command. He would not even like to be a prince. The prince is alone. He is not a man, since he cannot be challenged. He does not live, he sleeps, since everything gives way before him. But the passion to obey is ugly too, and useless. How could a man who delivers himself up body and soul be esteemed? Capable of giving himself unconditionally to a master, he is also capable of changing masters. Yes, we must take sides, and follow the consequences to the very end; but "just opportunities" are less frequent than is believed, and we must not choose too readily, for then it is no longer the cause but the sect we love.

> I am not subject to these penetrating, intimate mortgages and commitments. Wrath and hatred are beyond the call to be just, and are passions serving only those who do not hold strictly enough to their duty simply through reason. . . . We must not (as we do every day) give the name "duty" to an intestine bitterness and acerbity which is born of private interest and passions; nor "courage" to a treacherous, malicious behavior. They call their propensity to spitefulness and violence "zeal." They fan the flames of war, not because it is just but because it is war. When my will is given to a party, it is not with such a violent obligation that my understanding is infected by it.

A man can serve a party and be a harsh judge of what is going on there, find intelligence and honor in his enemy, in short, continue to exist in the social world. "I have been able to get mixed up in public responsibilities without swerving from myself by a hair's breadth, and to give myself to others without abandoning myself."

Perhaps it will be said that these rules make snipers, not soldiers. That is true, and Montaigne knows it. He is able at times, and lucidly, to force himself to lie; he does not make a habit or a way of life of it. "Whoever wants to make use of me as I am, let him give me things to do requiring rigor and freedom, and conduct which is short and to the point yet still risky, and I shall be able to do something for him. If long, subtle, laborious, artificial, crooked conduct is required, he would do better to ask someone else." Maybe there is some scorn here. But it is also possible that Montaigne means more than that. We always ask questions as if they were universal, as if in an instant we chose the good of all men in choosing our own. But what if this were a presumption? Being what he is, Montaigne will never be partisan. We do well only what we do willingly. He must not affect a lofty manner. He can serve better and more outside the ranks. Is it unimportant, this weight attached to his words because men knew he neither lied nor flattered? And did he not act all the more effectively because he did not care too much for action?

Passions seemed to be the death of the self, since they swept it away outside itself, and Montaigne felt threatened by them as by death. Now he tries to describe to us what have since been called "free passions." Having experienced that what he loves is at stake, out there, he resolutely confirms the natural movement which was bearing him outward. He joins the human game. Upon contact with this freedom and courage, passions and death which overcomes death. The good arguments are "those which make a peasant and whole peoples die just as steadfastly as a philosopher," and they all come back to a single one—we are living beings, it is here we have our tasks, and as long as we draw breath they are the same. Meditation upon death is hypocritical, since it is a morose way of living. In the movement which throws him at things, and precisely because he has shown what is arbitrary and perilous in it, Montaigne discovers the remedy for death.

> It is my impression that it is indeed the end, yet not the aim of life; it is its end, its extremity, yet not its object. Life should have itself as its aim and design; its proper study is to govern, conduct, and undergo itself. Among the several other offices that this general and principal chapter comprehends is this article of knowing how to die; and if our fear did not give it weight, it would be among the lightest.

The remedy for death and passions is not to turn away from them, but on the contrary to go beyond them as everything bears us beyond them. Others threaten our freedom? But "we must live among the living." We risk slavery there? But there is no true freedom without risk. Action and attachments disturb us? But "life is a material and corporeal movement, an action that by its own essence is imperfect and disordered; I occupy myself with serving it as it is." There is no sense cursing our fate; both good and evil are found only in our life.

Montaigne tells that the doctors had advised him to lace himself tight with a napkin when he traveled on shipboard, in order to fight seasickness. "Which I did not even try," he adds, "having accustomed myself to contend with my defects and master them by myself." His whole morality rests upon a movement of pride through which he decides to take his risky life in hand, since nothing has meaning if it is not in his life. After this detour toward himself, all seems good to him again. He said he would rather die "on horseback than in his bed." Not that he counted on the warrior's anger to help him, but because he found in things, along with a threat, a viaticum. He saw the ambiguous link that bound him to them. He saw that he was not required to choose between himself and things. The self is not "serious"; it does not like to be tied down. But "is there anything as certain, resolute, disdainful, contemplative, solemn, and serious as an ass?" It is unconditional freedom which makes us capable of absolute attachment. Montaigne says of himself: "I have been so sparing in promises that I think I have kept more than I have promised or owed." He sought and maybe found the secret of being simultaneously ironic and solemn, faithful and free.

LOUIS MARIN

# Montaigne's Tomb,
## or Autobiographical Discourse

$F$our propositions:

Proposition I: If autobiography means the writing of one's *own* life and of its outstanding events, this writing can only begin and end with two statements which are, strictly speaking, unutterable: "I was born," and "I died," and can only be constituted by a *single* infinitely reflexive statement: "I write that I write that . . . *ad infinitum* my own life."

Proposition II: Autobiographical narrative can only be carried out with the help of a trick of writing, manipulating the past time/tense of the story with the present of narration, and producing the subject of the narrative utterance as the simulacrum of the situation of the enunciation.

Proposition III: The operator of this trick will be a figure occupying in the text the unoccupiable place of the subject of enunciation, a figure representing the mortal situation in which the gaze grasps itself in its eye (death and reflexivity).

Proposition IV: The autobiographical text will, in the place of its subject, be worked on by an originary, inaudible voice, and will constitute itself as the echo of this in its signifiers.

And by way of introduction, this enigmatic definition of "syncope" from Littré's Dictionary:

From *The Oxford Literary Review* 4, no. 3 (1981). © 1981 by *The Oxford Literary Review*.

1. "Sudden and momentary interruption of breathing, conscious sensations and voluntary movements," in other words, the *body interrupted* and self-consciousness with it.

2. "The dropping of a letter or syllable in the middle of a word," in other words, *writing interrupted,* and the voice taking up and effacing this interruption.

3. "The linking of the last note of a bar with the first of the following bar, so as to produce the effect of a single note," or the *syncope* of voice or song or music, in which *an end* can be heard *at the same time as a beginning,* but, equally, the opposite of this: "when two notes are heard successively, and of these the second has a value twice that of the first," this succession—and no longer simultaneity—produces to the ear an effect of *rhythm,* a repetition which is no other than the intensification of an absence and a presence.

We shall here be concerned to read the narrative of a *syncope:* the essay on "Exercise or Practice," chapter 6 of book 2 of the *Essais.* It will be a presupposition of this reading, despite the digressive nature of Montaigne's writing, that we take the text as a whole, and our objective will be to retrace (to write or rewrite) the itinerary of its writing, which has as its point of departure the observation that there is no communicable experience of death, and as its point of arrival the questioning of the undertaking of *writing oneself,* of writing Me, and of the communication of that Me.

Again, it will be noted that this journey is a journey in the very time of the undertaking of the *Essais,* since this curious essay takes as its starting point a development of the first edition of 1580, and has as its point of arrival an addition in the so-called Bordeaux copy, which can only be assigned the date 1592, the year of Montaigne's death. This arrival is written, if I can put it like this, in the margin of the original text and at the approach of its author's death. The question on the question of the writing of self is at the frontier of life and text, of a text which makes the point that it is not possible to write—to communicate—one's own death as death. Would not the writing of self (*s'écrire soi-même*), as supplement, come to fill the lack of this ultimate experience? What then is the strange relationship which, once again, links these two motifs together? Between, that is, the impossible and necessary *cogito* of *death,* and the writing of one's own *life,* autobiography?

What is it to write onself, if it is not possible to write one's own death? This is the paradoxical relationship inscribed in the text of the Bordeaux copy: the writing of self and the question this involves are marginalia of the writing of one's own death or of its impossibility—the supplement of a lack.

But this first positioning of the essay is too hasty, for it would make the relationship between the two motifs dependent on the register of the *discours* and not that of the *récit*, a discourse on an impossibility and on a question. In this beginning and this end—positioned as reciprocal supplement of the margin and the body of the text—it is a question of writing the conditions of possibility (or impossibility) of one or the other of the attempts to, (1) write one's own death, and (2) write Me (the Self), but also of writing their conditions of legitimacy: *de facto* conditions and *de jure* conditions, forming the discourse of what is transcendental to autobiothanatographical writing. And yet, as we also know, this transcendental discourse forms an integral part of that very writing, from Augustine to Rousseau, from Descartes to Stendhal, or from Lévi-Strauss to Leiris. Autobiothanatography is thus indissolubly both auto- and metagraphy; thus it poses the question of the margin and the text; thus it raises the problem of the grounding of writing.

However, between the starting point and arrival point of the essay, there is a narrative, the narrative of a story *(histoire)* dated in historical time: "During our third or our second troubles," the conclusions of which, "this relation of such a minor event would be vain enough were it not for the instruction I drew from it for myself," will induce the great marginal, final addition. The conclusion of the narrative is already the matrix of the end of the essay, the margin is already potentially in the body of the text: the narrative is the body whose thinking head is the reflection that it is not possible to write one's own death, and whose matrix is the question, "Ought one to write oneself?" Let us note here in passing the *transition* from observation to question, from the constative modality of an impossibility to the prescriptive and interrogative modality of a duty: one cannot write one's own death—ought one to write one's own life? A transition, then, from the *de facto* question of the conditions of possibility of the ultimate experience (that of death) by a subject—*or the communication or objectification of a subjective experience*—to the *de jure* question of the *conditions of legitimacy of the writing of self*—a transition, then, from the *cognitive* plane of the possibility of giving an *objective value* to a subjective experience, to the plane of *ethical,* moral, practical value: no longer an objective theoretical validation of an *extreme* experience, but a practical valorization of the experience of the *entre-deux* (as Pascal would put it), between origin and end: the experience of Self.

In other words, the narrative which is the body of the text operates the conjunction between the two questions—the theoretical and the practical—between knowledge and value. And yet these two questions function in a chiasmus within the text since the possibility of writing one's own death *(if that possibility existed)* is from the outset endowed with its legitimacy in Montaigne, and since it is in describing its conditions of possibility that he will defend the *value* of the writing of self. It is just as difficult— not to say impossible—to write one's own death (even though one ought to) as it is to write one's own life (even though one ought not to, "so they say"). Theory and practice, objective validity and ethical value cross over and change places, just as do the writing of death and the writing of self. Such would be Narcissus's formula: wanting to know oneself to the point of writing oneself is to be seduced by one's own death. And conversely, to try to write one's own death would be to seduce oneself.

At the point at which these two questions changes places, we find a narrative (the body of the text), the narrative of a real event—an accident—which happened to Montaigne, and which he describes as the simulation of death. A real subjective experience is narrated (written—Montaigne writes himself in this experience) as a simulation of the impossible extreme experience. At this point of its narrative, the writing of self by oneself *simulates* the real extreme experience of death, and by this writing of self as simulation of the real, the subject is constituted as subject. Between the theoretical and the practical, at the point of their crossing, where it is a question of the subject itself, of the self of the subject *(du sujet même, du même du sujet)*, we read a narrative of the real which is a simulacrum of the real experience itself, that of death. Perhaps the real only ever comes about in simulation. In (the) place of the subject, we find a figure: "I" is never in adequation with *(au point de)* the real; the real is what is always lacking *for the subject.* "I" is never in the place of the real, where *it thinks itself* and *is thought.* It is perhaps only ever *the fiction of this point.*

Broadly speaking, such would be the schema, the frame and the problematic of my reading of this essay, chosen as a figure and paradigm of Montaigne's autobiographical writing. A chosen figure in which my own writing or rewriting of the essay is thus only a critical fiction, or else the autobiographical narrative of my own reading, and nothing more.

## ON THE POSSIBILITY OF WRITING ONE'S OWN DEATH

In the very opening sentence, Montaigne raises the question of what has appeared to constitute the two poles of the essay, the theoretical and the practical, the cognitive and the ethical: what is the relationship between discourse and action? Between saying (writing) and doing? Even if we believe in what we say (or in what is said to us) and although discourse has a power of its own, discourse does not lead us on into doing, into action: the practical is not deduced from the theoretical by the operation of the power proper to theory. There is need of a mediation, experience/ experiment, taken here as indissolubly theoretical and practical, cognitive and active, as at once experience and exercise: in short, an essay (to essay, to experiment). Between saying and doing, experience is an axiom of theoretical reason and a maxim of practical reason. However, axiom and maxim both suffer a single exception on a single point in a single case, which is, in Montaigne, the *essential* case: death as my death. Theoretical validity and practical value in general are theoretically and practically invalidated by a single and universal event, by the universal singular: death/universal: "all men are mortal"/as my death/singular: "my ultimate experience." There can be no experience of death since death is my death and it is unique.

Montaigne's considerations on this subject converge towards a double motif: first of all, a certain temporal structure is *essential* to the consideration of death/my death. Wisdom, virtue, philosophy are defined by an *economy* of time (in all senses of the word "economy": thrift, care, a distribution *[un ménage, un ménagement, un aménagement]* of duration structured by an intention, a project and a conservation, a memory, by the balance between an expense and a reserve). Now death/my death is a passage, and as such it excludes all retrospection through memory, and therefore through discourse and writing. It is an *absolute expense,* admitting of no reserve, in which all duration and the economy of duration which is wisdom are instantaneously consumed. Death, my death, is the instant of a passage, the point of a movement. Whence the second motif as yet scarcely sketched out: that of visibility, of the theoretical. Is it possible to *see* the instant of a passage? Can one *see* the dynamic infinitesimal which is the point of a movement?

However, in defining (but is it a definition?) death/my death as a point of passage, Montaigne discovers a duality in the moment: death as a point *and* as a passage. The instant is a point, but it is also this point's dynamic divergence *(écart)* with respect to itself, a limit but also the "apostasis" of that limit: and it is by *playing* on the apostasis, the gap *(écart)* (the gapping) of the limit that the "I" will be able to elaborate its *strategy.* I use the word "strategy" because we are still dealing with a general discourse and not an experience/experiment.

It is now that the "I" makes its appearance in the text itself: "it seems to me that there is a way of taming death, of trying it out *(essayer)* to some extent." There is a "means of mediating" *(moyen de moyenner)*. This means, playing on the structure of the instant, consists in reflecting (at the level of the discourse of generalities) on experiences/experiments (in the plural), on real, concrete situations in which death is simulated, simulation being characterised by a certain form of repetition of the "simulation," and at the same time, by a certain form of memory, and therefore of inscription in signs, and therefore of writing.

"Playing on" and also "putting into play" the structure of the instant, at once a point without duration *and* a gapping at the limit, at once infinitesimal and differential: the technique of "play" will consist in enlarging (in the photographic sense of the term) the gap at the point which hides the instant as passage. Simulation will consist in making the instant last, and perhaps this is only possible through writing, which is thus simultaneously the effect of a real simulation and the instance producing the simulation. Reading the text, we see that Montaigne distinguishes "joining" death and "approaching" or "recognising" it, distinguishes too its centre—its "fort"—and its "avenues" (approaches) which can be used and seen. (Discrete images, then, of cynegetics [hunting] and poliorcetics [military tactics]). The fort is death's fortress, but also the dense thicket where the wild beast hides; the avenue is the road but also the path leading to a bird trap *(pipée:* the type of trap where birds are caught in lime after being attracted by the simulated cry of an owl); recognising is not here identifying by memory what is already known, but rather exploring an unknown land, clarifying the enemy's position (Fr. "reconnaître", cf. Eng. "reconnoitre"—trans.); taming is making the wild animal less fearful and less savage, and more precisely, in an interesting ambivalence of active and passive, making oneself familiar with death and death with oneself, making it approach our private domain and also approaching "its lair" *(son privé):* in short the simulation of writing, the production of the simulacrum simultaneously consists on the one hand of putting into *spatial* terms the *temporal* limit (and the gap at the limit) of the instant by defining the point (unreachable and impregnable in itself) by its surroundings, its neighbourhood, its circumstances; in a word, of constructing a topological model of the temporal instant, and, on the other hand, of substituting for science or for a general, total consciousness of what is in and by itself unknowable—for what is a-poretical—an art of means, of approaches, of neighbourhoods, of singular proximities, of specific and unique circumstances, an art of ruses (of hunting or of war): strategy has become a tactic.

This topological model of the instant leads to the production of three figurative analogies which I shall classify rapidly as that of resemblance, that of imagination, and that of the simulacrum. Resemblance or the analogy of sleep and of death; imagination or that of illness and death, the simulacrum or that of the *syncope*. Each indeed aims to recognise (reconnoitre) the *edges* of the ultimate, incommunicable experience of death as my death, but the resemblance of sleep and death, despite getting at the universal and the singular which characterise the event of death, lets its *unique* character escape, since the experience of sleep is repetitive. As for imagination, anticipating illness as death, it indeed operates in the approaches, on the edges, the proximities, but it is an operator of *metrical* modifications which operates in order to subvert the "Euclidian" geometry of reason in its relationship to things, by reintroducing the agitations of body and soul into the abstract space of order and measures: by "passionalising" the proximities and neighbourhoods. The whole problem of the essay—both theoretical and practical—will, then, consist in disentangling the imagination from the affair by simulation, which is a totally practical reason of effects, as Pascal was to say: an art, a technique for the topological distribution of effects. Our sufferings, our actions and our operations, Montaigne tells us, need time: there is no feeling without leisure. All passional, pathological consciousness is duration. But the instant, the point, has a zero effect: it is imperceptible. Only the effects of circumstances and surroundings are to be feared, but we have a hold over them in that we can practice them. Hence the value of the violent accident and of the *syncope* which brings together proximity to the point of death and its imperceptible effect, and which, through "real" simulation and simulation through writing, will allow some practical knowledge of death: namely the dynamic differential of the gap at this point.

## THE SIMULATIONS OF DEATH

We must then move on to the central narrative, the body of the text of the essay. Now this narrative is of a formidable complexity and, when one thinks about it, of a strange complexity, since on the one hand it is interrupted, cut by a long discourse into two narrative sequences, and on the other hand because the second of these sequences is *at once* the sequel of the narration, what comes after the first part ("As I approached home"), and also a displaced repetition of it, a structural repeat: it is in short very precisely the textual *syncope* of the narrative of a *syncope*.

The first sequence of the narrative, that of the accident itself, is an enigmatic story. I shall "centre" my reading of it on the status of the narrating "I," taking into account the story of the event, and on the question of time, at once the time of the story *(histoire)* and that of the narrative *(récit),* in order to approach in my turn the present of the writing's enunciation. Montaigne begins the narrative of his simulated death by articulating it onto the time of history in general ("during our second or third troubles. I can't remember exactly": the memory thus instituted is uncertain, but that is not what is in question). The point of reference, the centre of perspective, is "me," but a me defined less in itself than by its situation in geographical space and historical time, a "chez moi" in which, instantaneously, the name of a place and that of the person who says "I" cross over, a "chez moi" defined as a "setting" *(assiette),* a stable, fixed place ("chez moi qui suis assis"). This stable centre of gravity is "the hub of all the civil-war troubles in France": the hub of a wheel is the part which is *closest* to the axle, the fixed axis around which the wheel turns. The hub, stable and yet mobile, centre and yet edge of the centre, is Me insofar as "chez moi," a centre insofar as it is the local surrounding of a fixed point, a stability insofar as it is the smallest movement among historical movements. The narrative begins with a small divergence *(écart)* from this centre. "I" diverges dynamically with respect to "chez moi": a little horse-ride, a gap of the gap in the neighbourhood of the centre. And here, all at once, is the event in its sudden instant, "a powerful charger with a desperate mouth, ridden by a big strong horseman" bolts and bears down like thunder in its toughness and heaviness, on the "little man and little horse," Montaigne: an instantaneous instant of impact at the point of intersection of two trajectories, the dynamic point of instance of two contrary forces, the throw *(coup:* also "blow"—trans.) of chance and necessity: in short, an accident, a blank, the white blinding flash of death.

Yet the narrative continues: "And there is the horse knocked down and lying in a daze, myself dead ten or twelve paces beyond, prostrate on my back, my sword more than ten paces beyond: I had no more movement or feeling than a log." Very oddly in this first-person narrative, a Euclidian geometer or a forensic pathologist leans over the victim to measure his position, a policeman draws up his statement: geometer, pathologist, policeman who are none other than the dead man today recounting his death. "There . . . me . . . dead": this is how "I died"; the unutterable *cogito* of death is declined in the subject through the simulation of a consciousness transcending the body fallen backwards. The syntax of the scene and of the narrative of the scene is here essential: first indicator, the prostrate horse, and "Me" is positioned by it (ten or twelve paces beyond): second indicator, "Me," and the sword is positioned by it (ten paces beyond). Me beyond the horse which is here but here with respect to the sword which is beyond. Beyond in the other world and yet in this world, both topo-graphically (syntax of the scene) and semantically (syntax of the narrative). "Me" is placed and elided in a place which it both occupies and does not occupy, at once beyond and this side of, neither there nor here. But now let us see how, by *metaphorical* simulation, *writing* brings him back from death to sleep, "There . . . me . . . dead," "with no more movement or feeling than a log." But one sleeps like a log: one does not die like a log. Thus death—my death—is little by little displaced towards loss of move-ment and consciousness and then, by explicit comparison, towards sleep. Montaigne is alive. But he is alive already anyway, since he is recounting his death. The writer interrupts the narrative: "that is the only time I have fainted to this day" (at which time I am writing the narrative of my syn-cope). A simulation, as I said, but an "objective" one. What does this mean? Montaigne does not calculate how he is going to simulate his death in the story of his faint. The simulation is objective in that it is carried out and operated by the very structures of language, of the quite specific mo-dality of enunciation of this strange narrative. Who is speaking?

If we attempt to reestablish the deep narrative structure, we obtain the following statement: "My companions told me that they thought I was dead ten or twelve paces beyond my horse." The text is thus struck by three *syncopes:* the first is that of the narrative enunciating instance: "My companions told me." The second, that of their erroneous knowledge: "that they thought that." The third: "I was dead," that of the verb in a personal form, in a past tense, and also that of the subject of the utterance. On the other hand, and following the very structure of the *syncope,* all of these elisions in the text of the narrative are *substituted* for by "Me dead"; that is, by the proper name of the "I" ("Me" as autonym of "I") and by the *qualifier* "dead" (in place of "I was dead") *plus* a supplement, *"voilà,"* a deictic. *Vois/là* (see there), beyond, this side of: "me-dead" can only be understood in relation to the place of the subject uttering it, in relation to his position in space, the position of a subject who *presents* to another (the reader, himself?), by a sort of verbal gesture, the scene at some distance from him, *making* that other see it from his own viewpoint, and, finally, recalling by anaphora and cataphora the narrative of the scene just written and which will continue to be written, positioning at once a past reference and a statement to come. In short, we have here a strange narrative in the form of a nominal sentence. I shall take up the analysis of it again only in order to point up two essential characteristics: on the one hand, since the assertive element of the sentence is nominal, the term reduced to its seman-tic content alone is not susceptible of the determinations carried by the ver-

bal form: it is thus intemporal, nonmodal, and above all cannot place the
time of the event in relation with the time of the discourse on the event: it
is disconnected from the speaker. And on the other hand, in that it poses
an absolute, a truth proffered outside time, person or circumstance, it no
longer depends on the *récit*, but on the *discours*. "Me dead": "Me," the
proper name of the "I," subject of the utterance but *in its proper name;*
"dead": both past participle referring to the past event recounted today,
but also a quality asserted as pertaining to the subject of the utterance outside of all relationship with the speaker. And yet: *"voilà,"* just as much as
"me," reconnects (if I can put it like this) utterance and enunciation, narrative and narration. Deconnection and reconnection: no, yes; yes, no: what
is recounted here is recounted by nobody, neither by Montaigne nor by his
companions: what is recounted recounts *itself* all by itself, starting from
the split I have just pointed out, from the interruption; this is how the interruption speaks: this is the *narrative of the syncope.* In this way a double
gap is written; at the point/instant in *space,* and at *the place of enunciation.* A topological gap is thus inscribed in the gap between two modalities
of enunciation. The topological structure of space in the scene would, then,
be the metaphor or rather the *analogon* of a semantic structure: a matrix
of writing which is none other than that of autobiography.

From this *place* (in the semantic and topological senses) *of the "syncope,"* this place which is unoccupiable and yet necessary, there begins a
return, a transfer, a metaphor. "I began to stir and breathe . . . I began to
come back to life a little, but it was slowly . . . I began to see, but my sight
was so feeble and dead that I could only make out light." Breath returns
with the "I" in position of subject and with the vomiting of his own swallowed blood; then sensation—without its being able to find a stable seat—
and finally sight. Not yet looking *(regard)* however, but a simple seizure of
the eye through the medium of visibility, that is, light, the necessary condition of perceptual synthesis and of object recognition. From orality to visibility, from breath to light, this movement of return comes to an end in
the self-constitution of the subject in the seeing of self: *I saw myself.*
"Me": this is the first object constituted by the gaze, to the rhythm of
darkness and light: "Now opening, now shutting my eyes, like a man half
asleep and half awake," writes Montaigne quoting Tasso.

Two remarks before concluding on this point, two remarks in which
life and death are linked, and where they are to be read in the very writing
of the text. First of all, between first sensations and visibility, an interruption of the narrative instance breaks the narrative for a moment, "this
memory which is deeply imprinted in my soul, representing the face and

idea of death so naturally, reconciles me with it somewhat." A memory, then, which is at once an imprint and a representation, an inscription; a mark in the soul and an image. This would seem, then, to be a memory anterior to the first thought, to "seeing," to the first functions of the soul, an archaic and as if originary memory of death, *not* as an event—since in "truth and reality" Montaigne is not dead—but as a mark or indelible trace, which is forever past without ever having taken place, without ever having been a present. It would be this trace or mark which is retraced by a representation as a very life(death)like figure of a "face and idea," which is so close to nature, to an irrecuperable original, only thanks to a chance event, an accident, a syncope: a representation, a *figure* after the event, a fiction drawn today by the writing of a narrative without a subject in the text. Could it be that this imprint engraved into the soul without bearing the seal of the *event* of death—could it be that this is death itself? Perhaps death is only ever a pure proximity, the place of constitution of the subject as its simple effect? Perhaps the subject can only identify itself, in this writing which is death, by retracing the trace, and diverging from it?

Second remark: the sudden accident of the *syncope* is the occasion of an instantaneous regression of life: the sudden projection to the edge of death (which *is* death) is a projection to the edge of the origin. In the accident, the approach which is death allows the simulation of a birth in a sort of conversion of the Christian theological theme marked by Augustine in chapter 6 of the *Confessions:* "To die is to be born, to be born is to die." Here there is a convergence at—or near—the same point, of birth and death, in this beginning three times repeated and three times in progress from breath to vision; and this *beginning* is a slow *regression* to the origin or rather beyond it—we need only read the text: "It seemed to me that my life was hanging on only to the edges of my lips: I closed my eyes to help—or so it seemed—to push it out of me. This was an imagination which did no more than swim superficially in my soul, tender and feeble as all the rest, but in truth not only free of unpleasure but inmixed with the sweetness felt by those drifting into sleep." Closing one's eyes, breathing out the breath of life, letting oneself go and sink and slip—this is not pleasure but happiness *(bonheur)*. Here all limit between I and Me is annulled in the floating imagination, the free flux of a "this side" of death and a "beyond" of birth, in the happiness of letting oneself slide, letting oneself drift with the current and with expiring breath. At this point of the text, a double proximity of death and birth is marked: this side of death, "I was born, I died," at once unutterable and necessary; the structure of the *real itself* wherein Me finds origin and end and wherein autobiographical writing is founded in its necessary and unutterable initial and final statements. What then is this structure of the real itself in the accident of its contingency and the occasion of its necessity? It is that of a proximity, of a place which exists only through its edges. I am always a little before or a little after; "I" is never in adequation with the real, the real is always that which it lacks, that which the story of its life will do nothing but fill tirelessly.

## COMING ROUND

At this point there is a lengthy interruption of the narrative: after the impossible narrative of the "I," now comes the discourse of the other; after the topology of death as my death, of its recognition by its approaches, there develops a semiology of the death of the other, of the recognition of the other as "I," by the interpretation of the signs of this approach—bodily movements, gestures, features and voices. What Montaigne implicitly explains is that the narrative he has just given is impossible. It is not possible for the soul to recognise *(reconnaître)* while in a state of *syncope*, nor for the "I" to recount his death as that of another simply by reading its signs. How can the circumstance of death be "de-passioned"? How can the imaginary and the pathetic be disimplicated from its approach? Montaigne's tactic, his ruse which is indissolubly cognitive and ethical, speculative and practical, has consisted—by the simulation of his own death as death—in recognising the circumstance of the point-as-passage, that is, in signifying it, telling its story, giving its signs and a text, in order to show its *unassignable* character, unassignable except by imaginary and therefore false inferences.

After the interruption comes the resumption: the continuation of the foregoing narrative in chronological and narrative time, and its displaced structural repetition. To the birth or rebirth of motor and respiratory, sensory and visual functions there follows and corresponds that of perceptive syntheses, but not yet of object-recognition: speech is echolalia, emotions automatic mechanisms, vision not yet recognition and identification. But above all the conclusion of this return "home" *(chez moi)* which is both, undecidably, the space of dwelling and the as yet empty site of self, is the same as that in the preceding narrative: that of a fictive death, simulated in and by the "this side" of the point of death, ("It would have been—I do not lie—a truly happy death") which plays and mimes the beyond of birth, the movement of an infinitely slow regression to the happiness of the maternal breast: "Je sentis une douceur infinie à ce repos . . . je me laissais couler si doucement et d'une façon si douce et si aisée que je me sens guère autre action moins pesante que celle là était"—written phrases which

sound with internal echoes and whispers, with the repetitions and allitera-
tions of liquids and sibilants. In order to describe, writing becomes a voice
again, a murmur, a muted slipping, a whispering which, in the *hearing,*
plays out the euphoria of an archaic voice present anew.

In commenting on the two following narrative sequences in which,
twice more, the event of death is repeated fictively according to a double
difference, I shall point up only two passages in which this event is inscribed in the tactics of writing in order, *finally,* to circumscribe and constitute the site of the subject. "When I came back to life again . . . I felt myself suddenly in touch with pain again and thought I should die again, but
more sharply, and I can still feel the shock of that brush with death." To
live is to *come back to life,* to feel reflexively, to feel *again,* to suffer and
to die *again.* The second death repeats the first, but in the unhappiness of
suffering: it is life, the pain of life in the body, which is thus given a self-
consciousness to the extent that "I can still feel the shock of that brush
with death." Death has left a trace, it *is* that trace left in the body up to
this moment at which I write the story of my memory. What I write now is
thus this old present of my death—that event in the past—but this present
inscription of the past, of death as past (whose only function is to give me
being as a subject in and through writing) is already inscribed as a mark
in my body, a mark present while I write as a pain, a mark imprinted into
my body: writing in order to identify oneself as subject comes down to
transcribing the ever-present mark of death, the mark as permanent death
in my body, *transcribing this mark as a sign,* giving the mark being as a
sign, transcribing my body, always already marked by death, into a textual
body, a signifying corpus. By this very fact, I give myself being, I am born
to myself. Second death, second birth: no longer, then, the simulation of
the neighbourhood of the point of death and regression to the undifferentiated happiness of maternal, primordial water, but pain, the unhappiness
of life, and the transcription of the mark into signs.

The second passage I shall comment on is the final sequence of the
narrative: "I do not wish to forget that the last thing in which I could resit-
uate myself was the memory of the accident . . . it seemed to me it was a
lightning-flash striking my soul with shock and that I had come back from
the other world." A remarkable strategy of writing is here elaborated
which is at once a circumscription of the subject's place in terms of its
edges and a ruse played with time. A negative desire of forgetting is here
substituted for the will or positive desire for memory; not, "I want to remember this," but, "I don't want to forget this, now that I am writing."
Writing now is a negation of a negation; wanting to write oneself is to
open the enigmatic space of a neuter, of a position which is none other

than the gap between a negative will and a loss of memory. The present of the subject's position with respect to itself, the present identification of self to self, is, in the first instance, this syntactic gap: "I don't want to forget now that I had previously forgotten my death." A double split, then, of the *subject* in the present, and of *time* in the past. Thus is posited and inscribed in the narrative autobiographical text, the relationship of the subject (of the I) to the present moment, in the double apostasis referred to by Aristotle in the text of the *Physics*.

But this operation carried out by negations of negations is also a manipulation of time. For what happened first, the accident in its sudden punctuality, is what comes back last in representation: the last memory to appear as an event in the story is that of the event which happened first, in the same story. In other words, the story (as sequence of events) doubles back on itself, reflects itself, represents itself by inverting its order. On the other hand, the narrative of this story began with the narrative representation of the first event, and ended on its last event: the appearance of the final memory. The time of the narrative *(récit)* maps onto the time of the story *(histoire)*, but the narrative representation is temporally disconnected from a self-representation of the story. Between this story which represents itself (since its last event is the representation of the first), and the narrative of this story which has told itself (since the narrator was not there to recount its first events), in this gap between two sequences of representation, the enunciating instance is at once caught up at the end of the irreversible movement of time and placed at its beginning. This instance accompanies (if I can put it like this) the inexorable flux of time (which is nothing but a permanent death), but, equally, inverts it, and recuperates it in the process. And it is thus, by the manipulation of time by writing, that the present presence of the subject to himself is circumscribed.

That this circumscription has something to do with the sudden instant of death, with its proximity and its imminence, is shown by the last sentence of the narrative, since the final representation of the first event has the temporal characteristic of that event (the sudden flash); but its dynamic is the reverse, since instead of sending Montaigne into the beyond it brings him back. "When my memory came round to the representation of the state I had been in when I saw them bearing down on me . . . it seemed to me it was a lightning-flash striking my soul with shock, and that I had come back from the other world."

## THE SKELETOS-TOMB

In conclusion, I should now like to move on to the last part of the essay, the final addition, in the margin of the narrative of death. Let me recall the general problematic: it is not possible to write, to transmit, to communicate death as one's death. It is impossible and yet it is essential, for it is the ultimate experience in which each man singularly identifies himself in his particular truth, in his propriety *(dans son propre)*. And yet, through the narrative of the singular accident simulating death, there has been something *like* a writing of death as my death, in the proximity of the edge of death. What then is it to write oneself? And has one the right to communicate to others what one knows about oneself? This is the next stage of Montaigne's reflection. The problem is this: what is the relationship between writing one's own death and writing oneself, between the fact of writing death and the right to write oneself? Why *write* the narrative of my own death (in simulated form) since the experience is absolutely personal and incommunicable? And, more generally, why write oneself, since what is transcribed in any writing of self is a purely private, individual, personal and incommunicable experience? "If I play the fool it is at my own expense and of interest to no one, for it is a madness which dies in me, and has no consequence." What then is autobiographical writing if not the very writing of madness, since it is a writing of death with every sign traced? It is the *very* writing of madness in that it is the writing of singularity and uniqueness, a private narrative in which the "I" is its own object, a writing of absolute difference and to that extent absolutely indifferent to others: and to this same extent it is mortal madness, since what I attempt to seize and register by it is no other than the "I" in the unique and puctual instant of its presence. I write, not to conserve, appropriate and publish *myself,* but in a sort of absolute expenditure. This is a madness which dies in me, a writing which consumes and consummates me entirely at every moment: autobiographical writing is the madness of private writing, of writing as my death, of writing as instantaneous and absolute expense since it is at once its beginning and its end. Why then write oneself? Montaigne's first reply is that such writing does no one any harm—this is the reply of humour.

The substance of the second reply is this: I do not write in order to communicate, but in order to know who I am—and the only way I have of knowing who I am is to write myself. For writing is the only instrument I have with which to retrace the trace of a flux which beats no track, and to fix it in the drift *(errance)* of this flux, which is not bound by any structure or preexistent form: this wandering flux which is my mind. Writing, the only instrument for tracing this movement and this force is also the only instrument which allows me to see, to penetrate with my gaze the opaque depths of my mind, the dark locus of the Self. How can writing be

gaze and illumination? Only in that the opaque depths of the mind are
born of another, more fundamental configuration. The mind (the self) is
only an infinity of *folds:* its reality is nothing but a multiple folding, the
infinite abyssal movement of self-reflection. To write is to *see,* insofar as
writing will consist in a tireless unfolding of the folds, an "explication" of
the folds. And to write is, finally, at once to choose and to arrest the tiny
airs of the agitations of being, airs which have to be understood in three
senses: (1) movements of air which are scarcely noticeable, ungraspable, in
constant transition; (2) ephemeral expressive manners, the changing turns
and fashions of the soul; (3) little pieces of music, little scarcely audible
songs in between sounds and words, hummed by the Self in many parts,
discreet and insane cacophony. The written signs cut up the continuous
transitions, select and constitute states of manners, inscribe the inaudible
scores of the Self, constituting something like a science, but a science which
is instantaneous, noncumulative, repeating itself without end in its own
obstacles—an endless task appropriating nothing, infinitely descriptive. "I
am myself the only aim of my thoughts; I examine and study only myself."
A private science, this, a mad consciousness in and through the writing of
self which, excluding all other objects, has no object beyond that of retracing indefinitely the infinite self-reflexive movement of the "I." On the other
hand, "if I study anything else it is immediately to apply it *(le coucher)*
onto—or, better, into—myself." The gesture of writing is a gesture of appropriation of the other: to apply something to myself is to apply it to the
paper; to put something in writing is to reduce the other to the state of
signs: but at the same time "Me" is none other than the paper on which
"I" writes, and is, more than a surface, a bodily depth in which the other
is imprinted, inscribed, marked as a sign. To apply the other by writing
onto myself, into myself, is to let myself be penetrated by the other—the
writing of the self is this activity of reception, both seductive and auto-
erotic. Montaigne does not write (himself) in order to *seduce himself by
seducing the other as the self, in the self,* not to make himself known and
seen, but rather, in the strange dual process of seduction, to recognise himself as other and as self.

Has one the right to write oneself? Through a continuous slippage,
the motif of the questions, "What is it to write oneself?," "How to write
oneself?" has become transformed into that of right and legitimacy. Here
the paradox of *autography* is resolved: it is indeed reprehensible to talk to
the public of oneself, but it is right and good to talk to them of the vanity
involved in so doing. By publishing the quasi-impossibility of communicat-
ing oneself in one's singularity, the "I" communicates itself to the other in

its incomparable difference. But once again, it is not a question of transmitting to the other a piece of information about oneself, but of offering oneself up for seduction, of giving rise to the double difference of self and other—their personal differences—in the very process of seduction. "My trade, my art, is that of living." To write is to write oneself, and *that* is living: the *art of writing is the art of living.* Living is not the result of science, knowledge, study, but a practical business, the cunning technique of the origin and the end, the art of the machinations and means of writing through which I cause myself to be born and to die, through which I am my own author, or at least never stop trying to be.

Montaigne now returns to this art of writing or of living, to autobiographical writing, in the last page of the essay, from which—given the lack of space to rewrite the rest—I shall extract only the following passage in which, it seems to me, all the motifs I have laid out come together.

Like Stendhal evoking "Félix Faure making himself a peer of France," along the straight road of consideration and prestige, Montaigne replies to an objection: "all right, you'll say, but to live is to bear witness to oneself, to signify oneself to others through one's acts, through effects, and not only through words." The reply is this: acts and action are effects of chance; they are fragmentary, particular and uncertain *personae,* the dispersed marks of the contingency of the world, and not proofs or signs of self. Who then am I if not this site of dispersion where the particularities of influences and social roles meet and are exchanged in chaos? In order to answer the question, "Who am I?," one must decidedly choose *the effects of the writing of self,* preferring these to the effects of external contingency, turning away from "reality" and its effects (our works and acts) in favour of the effects of writing: in other words, in favour of the identification of self. Here is the passage: "I paint my cogitations, a formless subject which cannot fall into workaday production. Only with the greatest difficulty can I lay myself *(coucher)* on this aerial body of voice . . . I lay myself out: it is a *skeletos* where, in a glance, veins, muscles and tendons can be seen, each in its place. I do not write of my deeds; I write myself, my essence." An extraordinary text, this, where in the space of a few lines, Montaigne slips from thoughts to writing, from the *formless* subject of the interior of the soul or the mind (less a void than the multiple chaos of cogitation), *to the Self in essence and in truth,* i.e., *in the written text,* a monument of signs which is less a tomb (memorial to glory and history) than a cenotaph in which the essence and truth of the Self are not enclosed, but in which they are none other than the signifying architecture, holding itself up by the internal force of words and phrases strategically disposed, endlessly written and rewritten. In this way the form of the essence "Self" can inform the formlessness of cogitations, the multiple "I"s of thought. Speech is a body insufficient to take on voice, its aerial body, articulated breath, because it is ephemeral like them. And yet this tomb of writing, the Self, the essence, is not exactly the same as the tomb found *empty* by the holy women on the morning of the resurrection and where, instead of the body to be anointed, they heard the voice, the message of the *aggelos:* "he is not here, he is elsewhere," the message of history. Montaigne's tomb contains a dried-up body, a mummy, a *skeletos;* not the aerial body of the angel, nor the body as ritual object of infinite mourning, but the anatomical model *(écorché)* of a dead body; less a double than the figure of the fiction of the "I" writing itself and whose only object is to write itself: a figure occupying the place of the I-Me in the text, the unoccupiable place of the subject of the enunciation, a figure showing *everything in a single look.* The *skeletos* is indeed the singular truth and essence, ("Me," in a word), but it is a figure, the deep architecture of the autobiographical text, and, in the final discourse, the double of the body laid out on its back, bloody from the intermediary narrative of the *syncope.* It is the effect of the internal edge of the monument of signs, built in the evening of life, and in which the subject identifies himself in his fiction because he has, decidedly, put himself at stake in his writing.

TERENCE CAVE

# *Problems of Reading in the* Essais

All literature, it can be argued, depends for its existence on the literary texts which preceded it, whether or not it draws directly on them as its sources, and the proposition is nowhere more palpably true than in the *Essais*. Montaigne quotes, alludes to and borrows from other writers at every turn. In "Sur des vers de Virgile," having discussed explicitly the question of literary imitation, he claims that he is going to leave books on one side and speak "plus materiellement et simplement"; but in the very next sentence, he refers to Zeno and Cratippus and quotes Claudian; shortly after, there is a quotation from Horace, a reference to Plato, and paraphrases of sayings of Alexander and Aristotle (bk. 3, chap. 5). The Montaigne of the *Essais,* as opposed, for example, to the Montaigne who was mayor of Bordeaux, is above all a reader: a highly intelligent one whose dialogue with the books he reads is instructive more—as he himself would say—for its method than its matter. Indeed, reading is one of the themes to which Montaigne recurs most often in the *Essais,* taking its place next to such major concerns as virtue, happiness and death. He discusses his preferences and deficiencies as a reader, the difficulty of discovering the correct meaning of a text, the dangers of overinterpretation, the question of authorial intention, and many other aspects of the topic which are still debated in our own day. In consequence, the practice of reading, and reflections on that practice, form an integral part of Montaigne's self-portrait.

From *Montaigne: Essays in Memory of Richard Sayce,* edited by Ian D. McFarlane and Ian Maclean. © 1982 Oxford University Press.

The example cited above already suggests that reading is not always the innocent and straightforward activity it may at first sight appear to be: it presents problems. In particular, it refuses to be tied down or relegated to a subordinate domain. Even when Montaigne thinks (or we think) it has been set aside, it infiltrates everything he writes; and, likewise, precisely because the question of reading is inherent in the fabric of the *Essais* as a whole, our own reading of the text is fraught with problems which are the more acute because they are often hidden. These problems cannot be finally solved, for reasons which will become apparent in due course. They can be explored and elucidated; the rest is up to the reader.

This essay will consider three principal aspects of the question of reading as it appears in the *Essais*. The first section will present a sketch of Montaigne's practice of reading: the kinds of books he avowedly read and preferred, the uses to which he puts his reading, and the evaluative or descriptive comment he makes. The second section explores some of the ways in which Montaigne's readings are assimilated into the *Essais* by means of quotation, a process which affects the whole of Montaigne's text and raises all the key questions. The third section considers how the *Essais* themselves are offered to the reader. As the very notion of a self-portrait implies, Montaigne is no less conscious of his own readers than he is of himself as a reader: he approaches them with disarming gestures, he uses devices like irony and paradox to outwit their conventional responses, he at once ignores and embraces them. In this third section, Montaigne's explicit reflections on reading—both his own and his reader's—will play an important part; but the other two sections will not exclude reference to them where relevant. It is, I believe, a mistake to attempt to make too sharp a distinction between the explicit and the implicit, or between theory and practice, in Montaigne. The two categories are in a constant relationship with one another; or, to put it another way, Montaigne's "theory" is so intermittent, so deliberately unsystematic, that to attempt to make of it a coherent structure of thought which could be used to explain his practice would be to ignore and falsify the character of his discourse.

The chronological development of the *Essais* will be taken into account as far as clear evidence exists and where it is relevant to the question. It can be shown, for example, that Montaigne had different reading habits and incorporated his reading into the *Essais* in a somewhat different way in his later years. But the three principal strata of the text as indicated in modern editions only provide a rough guide to chronology. In many respects, the decisive period of development occurred in the period 1572–80. What came later is undeniably rich and, for modern readers at least, intellectually and aesthetically satisfying; but the essentials of Montaigne's method, his range of themes, and the notion of self-portraiture, are established by 1580, as is the crucial invention of the title. What the later versions provide above all, for present purposes, is an endless series of examples of the way in which Montaigne read his own text and incorporated it, as it were, into a new and expanded text.

## MONTAIGNE'S PRACTICE OF READING: "JE FEUILLETTE LES LIVRES, JE NE LES ESTUDIE PAS"

As a reader, Montaigne belonged to, and helped to shape, the late Renaissance. Earlier generations of scholars had laboriously acquired expertise in the ancient languages, edited virtually the whole corpus of classical writings, elucidated them in prefaces and commentaries, and begun to codify their insights in their own (mainly Latin) writings. Greek texts were made more accessible by translation into Latin, and the most popular Greek and Latin texts were rendered in the vernacular. This process was still continuing at the time when Montaigne was beginning to write the *Essais:* two Latin editions of Sextus Empiricus's *Hypotyposes* were published in France (1562 and 1569), and Jacques Amyot translated Plutarch's *Lives* into French (1559), adding the *Moralia* in 1572. Had these publications occurred twenty years later, Montaigne's *Essais* would have been inconceivable in the form in which we know them.

Although Montaigne's Greek was apparently only elementary, he had acquired in early childhood a fluent reading knowledge of Latin, and was thus in a position to exploit most of the vast store of materials opened up by earlier humanists. He himself affected no great erudition, edited no texts, wrote no commentaries and used the vernacular as his medium. It was no longer necessary, in 1570, to be a professional scholar in order to read and reflect on the writings of the ancient world.

The reading materials which find their way in one form or another into the *Essais* are drawn from the whole range of these writings, which should be taken to include the Bible and St. Augustine's *City of God.* Modern vernacular authors—Boccaccio, Ariosto, Castiglione, Marguerite de Navarre, Rabelais, Marot, Du Bellay, Ronsard—are referred to, together with neo-Latin poets such as Buchanan, Bèze and Muret. But Montaigne has some marked preferences. The three genres which formed the core of the humanist educational programme, history, poetry and moral philosophy, are his favourite quarry, since they all provide insights which are germane to human experience and can be assimilated without lengthy

training. By contrast, the logic and metaphysics of Aristotle and his medieval heirs are treated with caution, irony or even, at times, withering scorn.
Unlike many of the humanists, Montaigne has little time for rhetoric as a
formal discipline leading to a discourse in which elegance is given priority
over truthfulness. In this, he concurs with Erasmus and other sixteenth-
century "anti-Ciceronians," for whom Cicero is a prime example of aesthetic perfection allied with dubious morals.

It would be wrong, however, to think of Montaigne's tastes as being
rigorous and exclusive. He is as unsystematic in this respect as in all others.
He can take advantage of any material which he happens to recall or to
come across in the course of reading, and will view it in a positive or negative (or neutral) light according to his momentary purpose. Ciceronian *exempla* and aphorisms are often cited in support of his argument; "De l'experience" begins with a tag (unacknowledged) from Aristotle. The practice
of reading to which the *Essais* bear witness is one in which the original
text is treated less as a whole than as a repository of potentially instructive
materials or insights. Montaigne often speaks of himself as skimming
through books, reading them superficially or hastily, while his notorious
lack of memory, whether genuine or not, provides another motive for the
fragmentation of his reading. Once again, this approach has important humanist antecedents. From the beginning of the sixteenth century, Erasmus
and others had popularized methods of extracting pithy sayings, images
and examples from the classics and storing them under convenient head-
ings, to be redeployed later by the writer as occasion arose. The compen-
dium or miscellany is no less important a channel of transmission of antique culture than the original literary works themselves. Erasmus's
*Adagia, Apophthegmata* and *Parabolae* were among the most popular
books of the age, as were other miscellanies such as those of Ravisius Tex-
tor, Petrus Crinitus and Maurice de la Porte. It should be added that certain classical works—the *Natural History* of the elder Pliny or the *Attic
Nights* of Aulus Gellius—were themselves collections of heterogeneous materials awaiting reassembly, as it were, in some future continuous work.
Furthermore, some of the leading moralists of classical antiquity adopted
an eclectic method which deeply appealed to sixteenth-century humanists.
The most famous of these was Plutarch, who was admired and exploited
by Erasmus and Rabelais long before he became Montaigne's favourite
author.

What humanist readers from Erasmus to Montaigne valued above all
in their readings was adaptability. It was considered important to attempt
to understand the original or intended meaning of a text, but still more

important to be able to utilize that text, or fragments of it, in a new context: in other words, to regenerate its meaning. Erasmus in particular—and in this he is followed by vernacular theorists like Du Bellay—elaborated a theory of imitation of the ancients according to which the modern writer assimilates and digests his reading materials and reproduces them as a reflection of his own personality, his own moral vision. Merely copied passages are lifeless and inert, however great their value in the work they came from. Classical antiquity must be first disassembled, then reassembled in a new form, according to the needs of a modern sensibility. In humanist exegesis of classical texts, it is true, the original context is paramount in determining the authentic sense; but in humanist theories of education, the reading of the classics is chiefly of value insofar as it may respond to fresh contexts and give rise to fresh meanings.

Montaigne is the direct heir of this latter principle. It determines the evolution of the *Essais* from their earliest form as *leçons* (more or less fragmented "readings" of classical and other works) to the exuberantly expansive chapters of the later years, where the flow of writing which surrounds the borrowed materials is both deeper and more powerful. It informs many of his remarks on reading as a heuristic exercise. And it corresponds closely to his practice of reading insofar as that practice demands that each instance of reading be also an exercise of the judgement. The judgement can and should, according to Montaigne, try itself out on every sort of material; books have no priority, in principle, over the direct experience of the world. But the wealth of experience which can be discovered in or recovered from books is nevertheless formidable, and for a written text like the *Essais,* other written texts necessarily provide the best adapted notations of experience.

If many of Montaigne's remarks give the impression that he adopted a nonchalant and even facile method of reading (e.g., 2.17; 3.12), others make it clear that he was well aware of the rarity of discriminating literary judgement. The most extended of these occurs in "De l'art de conférer" (3.8[c]), but a similar observation is made in relation to poetry in "Du jeune Caton" (1.37[c]) and the idea is already present in embryo in the 1580 edition, where Montaigne speaks of Aesop as an "autheur de très-rare excellence et duquel peu de gens descouvrent toutes les graces [author of very rare excellence, although very few people have discovered his whole charm] (2.37[a]). It is precisely because Aesop would not normally be classed as a difficult author that the remark has the widest of implications.

In his own reading of texts, Montaigne's frame of reference is predominantly ethical. The vast collection of anecdotes, examples and sayings which he culls from other texts in order to weave them into the *contexture* of the *Essais* has the function above all of illustrating the infinite variety of forms of human behaviour. It is the training ground of the judgement, seen here as, a faculty of moral discrimination. Since the potential discrepancy between language and moral substance (or language and action) is one of the most insistent of Montaigne's topics, it is not surprising to find that he frequently explores the relationship between an author's writings and his life. Thus in "Un traict de quelques ambassadeurs," he claims that he pays particular attention, in a writer's works, to those matters in which the writer was expert: in this instance, an anecdote recounted by the diplomat Guillaume Du Bellay, Sieur de Langey, about the way François Ier's ambassadors reported a defiant speech by the Emperor Charles V (1.17[a]). The principle established here is exemplified also in ["Observations sur les moyens de faire la guerre de Jules César"], (2.34), which analyses the superiority of Caesar's writings on war among books suitable for "chefs de guerre." Such instances concur with Montaigne's concern to find reliable and authoritative witnesses rather than ones who may distort their report by adding their own interpretations (see 1.31).

The most characteristic examples, however, are the ones in which Montaigne infers the moral character of an author from his works, or uses external evidence to reconstruct that character and then bring it to bear on the writings. The chapter on Caesar itself contains an example of this procedure: "il me semble lire en plusieurs de ses exploits une certaine resolution de se perdre, pour fuyr la honte d'estre vaincu [it seems to me I read in many of his exploits a determined resolve to lose his life, to avoid the shame of being vanquished]" (2.34[a]); another occurs in "De l'art de conférer," on Tacitus: "Si ses ecris rapportent aucune chose de ses conditions, c'estoit un grand personnage, droicturier et courageux, non d'une vertu superstitieuse, mais philosophique et genereuse [If his writings tell us anything about his qualities, Tacitus was a great man, upright and courageous, not of a superstitious but of a philosophical and high-minded virtue]" (3.8[a]); and more fleetingly, in "De la moderation," a poet is presumed to be suffering from sexual frustration because he tells a story of Jupiter succumbing to an unusually vigorous access of passion for his spouse Juno (1.30[c]). In "De la gloire," external evidence is used to corroborate Montaigne's impression that a letter dictated by Epicurus just before his death betrays the concern for reputation which Epicurus had decried in his writings (2.16[a]). The principle is, of course, most acutely relevant where writers on ethics are concerned, and in "De la colere,"

Montaigne not only judges the relative sincerity of Cicero, Seneca, Plutarch and others, but also describes his method explicitly: "Je ne voy jamais autheur, mesmement de ceux qui traictent de la vertu et des offices, que je ne recherche curieusement quel il a esté [I never read an author, especially of those who treat of virtue and duties, that I do not inquire curiously what kind of a man he was]" (2.31[a]).

A similar procedure is apparent in Montaigne's assessment of Amyot's translation of Plutarch at the beginning of "A demain les affaires":

> Je n'entens rien au Grec; mais je voy un sens si beau, si bien joint et entretenu par tout en sa traduction, que, ou il a certainement entendu l'imagination vraye de l'autheur, ou, ayant par longue conversation planté vivement dans son ame une generale Idée de celle de Plutarque, il ne luy a aumoins rien presté qui le desmente ou qui le desdie.

> [I understand nothing of Greek; but I see throughout his translation a sense so beautiful, coherent and sustained, that either he has clearly understood the real thought of the author, or at least, having by long acquaintance implanted vividly in his own soul a general idea of Plutarch's soul, he has attributed to him nothing that belies or contradicts him.]
>
> (2.4[a])

The remark implies an acceptance of the central principle of sixteenth-century translation theory, namely, that the translator should strive to capture the thought *(imagination)* of his author rather than to produce a word-for-word version. But it also suggests that, in reading the works of a given author, he applied a criterion of internal coherence in order to determine the sense. This does not, it must be stressed, necessarily mean that Montaigne believed that literary works are only meaningful if they are wholly consistent. It will become apparent later that Montaigne was perfectly able to conceive of inconsistent or even fragmentary works (the *Essais,* for example) as having their own authenticity. But it does suggest that he believed a work to be imprinted by its author with characteristic features which, when discovered, provide the key to the reconstruction by the reader or translator of its true meaning.

As an instance of reading, the case of Amyot's Plutarch (and, it should be noted, of Montaigne's Amyot) transcends the moral domain. It does, however, fit exactly into the moralist's constant desire to discern the underlying mechanisms or patterns of human behaviour. The literary text is viewed here as the discourse of a man whose independent existence confers meaning on it; its quality is judged on the one hand by its consonance with its author's life, on the other by the extent to which it is functional in suggesting norms of moral behaviour to the reader. The reading of a text is, in this respect, parallel to the interpretation of the comportment of other people still living, except that in the latter case visible action, facial expressions and so on provide a part of the evidence. The parallel emerges with especial clarity in a passage in "De l'experience" where Montaigne claims that his long experience in judging himself has given him a happy capacity to judge others:

> À mes amys je descouvre, par leurs productions, leurs inclin-ations internes; non pour renger cette infinie variété d'actions, si diverses et si descoupées, à certains genres et chapitres . . . (c) Les sçavans partent et denotent leurs fantasies plus specifique-ment, et par le menu. Moy, qui n'y voy qu'autant que l'usage m'en informe, sans regle, presente generalement les miennes, et à tastons. Comme en cecy: (b) je prononce ma sentence par arti-cles descousus, ainsi que de chose qui ne se peut dire à la fois et en bloc. La relation et la conformité ne se trouvent poinct en telles ames que les nostres, basses et communes.

> [I reveal to my friends, by their outward manifestations, their inward inclinations. I do not attempt to arrange this infinite va-riety of actions, so diverse and so disconnected, into certain types and categories . . . The scholars distinguish and mark off their ideas more specifically and in detail. I, who cannot see be-yond what I have learned from experience, without any system, present my ideas in a general way, and tentatively. As in this: I speak my meaning in disjointed parts, as something that cannot be said all at once and in a lump. Relatedness and conformity are not found in low and common minds such as ours.]

> (3.13)

By representing his interpretation metaphorically as a book explaining the "inclinations internes" of his friends, Montaigne nicely discloses his ten-dency to seek a correlation between living human behaviour and written texts.

All this will, no doubt, not seem very surprising to a modern reader, who can hardly have avoided at some point using the "life and works" approach to literature. But it is important to stress that methods of reading are not timeless and universal: they have their own history, and Montaigne is a major contributor to the success of the view of literature indicated above. If humanist readers did not themselves invent these procedures, they certainly revived them and gave them an enormous and lasting impetus at a time when quite other methods were well established. The same might be said of Montaigne's exercises in "practical criticism," the most celebrated of which are the comparison of Latin poets in "Du jeune Caton" and the analysis of a passage from Lucretius in "Sur des vers de Virgile." Using a metaphorical and emotive vocabulary based, initially at least, on classical Latin accounts of literary effect, Montaigne colourfully conveys his response to both subject matter and style. He is able to point with great precision to the word or phrase which determines a given effect, as well as to command the reader's assent by his strategy of carefully graded comparison. Once again, Montaigne is helping to forge a discourse of literary appraisal based on a presumption of shared good taste and fine discrimination, rather than on methodical application of rhetorical categories.

But, to return to the biographical principle, it may also be argued that the equivalence between reading texts and reading people is not as straightforward as at first appears. The passage from "De l'experience" quoted above asserts the difficulty of making judgements which are other than piecemeal, such is the diversity and discontinuity of human behaviour. In a subsequent development, the point is made still more clearly:

> Je laisse aux artistes, et ne scay s'ils en viennent à bout en chose si meslée, si menue et fortuite, de renger en bandes cette infinie diversité de visages, et arrester nostre inconstance et la mettre par ordre. Non seulement je trouve mal-aisé d'attacher nos actions les unes aux autres, mais chacune à part soy je trouve mal-aysé de la designer proprement par quelque qualité principalle, tant elles sont doubles et bigarrées à divers lustres.

> [I leave it to artists, and I do not know if they will achieve it in a matter so complex, minute, and accidental, to arrange into bands this infinite diversity of aspects, to check our inconsistency and set it down in order. Not only do I find it hard to link our actions with one another, but each one separately I find hard to designate properly by some principal characteristic, so two-sided and motley do they seem in different lights.]

> (3.13[b] )

Montaigne's image of man as a creature of chance and circumstance, the image which dominates the celebrated opening passage of "Du repentir," renders at least problematic the model of a text made coherent by the char-

acter of its author. Two potential exceptions are allowed: superior souls—
Cato and Socrates, perhaps—unlike our "low and common" ones, may aspire to consistency; and scholastic philosophers ("artistes") may succeed in
imposing order on the wealth of human experience. But even these exceptions are suspect. The word "artistes" strongly recalls the opposition between art and nature which is one of Montaigne's fundamental themes.
"Art" is artifice; it deals in surfaces, appearances; it is the realm of the
specious. Nature may have its own profound pattern; but if so, it is mostly
hidden from us, and can be perceived only in glimpses, after long and cautious probing. Even the harmony of superior souls may be only an effect
of art. For the most part, the phenomena of human behaviour present
themselves to us discontinuously. Furthermore, whereas the circumstantial
analysis of one's friends' behaviour is subject to a criterion of sorts (we can
ask them if they agree), this is not the case in the reading of texts by dead
authors. All we can do is examine in turn their shifting "visages" and "lustres," and make provisional, unresolved judgements. There can be no unequivocal guarantee for our readings.

One might juxtapose with this late passage a brief chapter in book 1
where Montaigne considers some of the ways in which chance can create
effects of rationality or of aesthetic purpose. The theme is already elaborated with several examples in the 1580 text, but it is most pithily expressed in a late insertion: "Semble il pas que ce soit un sort artiste? Constantin, fils d'Helene, fonda l'empire de Constantinope; et, tant de siècles
après, Constantin, fils d'Helene, le finit [Doesn't this seem to be an artistic
fate? Constantine, son of Helen, founded the Empire of Constantinople;
and so many centuries later, Constantine, son of Helen, ended it]"
(1.34[c]). Once again, the effects described here are specious; they are governed by no unifying intention. But if the history of Constantinople has
only a fortuitously aesthetic symmetry, might not the same be true of much
historical narrative? Chance, as an artist, can rival the "artistes" of "De
l'experience" who make neat patterns out of the confusion of actions and
events. One of the most striking features of Montaigne's view of history is
precisely the absence of cause-and-effect narrative, or of speculations
about the necessary order of things. His reading of history is always fragmentary; episodes taken from quite different periods and national contexts
are juxtaposed according to the temporary (and random) perspective of the
reader. The factual status of his examples is not paramount: probability
provides an adequate basis for the operation of the moralist's judgement
(see the conclusion of 1.21). On the other hand, not surprisingly, Montaigne tends to be suspicious of fiction. In "De trois bonnes femmes," he
condemns fiction explicitly, and suggests that it would be valuable to com-

pose an amalgam of "true" (i.e., plausible) stories, loosely linked like Ovid's (implausible) *Metamorphoses*. This is, in effect, what he himself is doing in "De trois bonnes femmes"; indeed, it is not too far removed from the character of the *Essais* as a whole. The writer, like the reader, recreates the workings of "fortune" without too many of its miraculous coincidences.

It is clear, then, that Montaigne's practice of reading is subject to the same oscillations and apparent contradictions as his thought in general. In some contexts, the intuitive conviction of right judgement, or the sense of an underlying continuity, will predominate. In others, certainty crumbles, and the world dissolves into a heterogeneous collection of ambiguous "visages" and "lustres"; chance infiltrates all of our attempts to make sense of things (see the(c)-text which concludes 1.47). The presence of an original, authentic intention which stabilizes the meaning of any text is always presupposed, and may in some cases be uncovered with confidence; on the other hand, the reader—and above all perhaps the discerning reader—will often find a text to be elusive and equivocal, hiding its true intention and thus giving rise to many possible reconstructions.

A group of passages may be taken to illustrate briefly the consequences of this uncertainty. The earliest is a 1580 passage in "Des livres," where Montaigne blames the weakness of his judgement when he is unable to discern the value of one of Plato's dialogues:

> Il s'en prend à soy, et se condamne, ou de s'arrester à l'escorce, ne pouvant penetrer jusques au fons, ou de regarder la chose par quelque faux lustre . . . Il pense donner juste interpretation aux apparences que sa conception luy presente; mais elles sont imbecilles et imparfaictes.

> [It blames and condemns itself either for stopping at the outer bark, not being able to penetrate to the heart, or for looking at the thing by some false light . . . It thinks it gives a correct interpretation to the appearances that its conception presents to it; but these are weak and imperfect.]

> (2.10[a])

In this instance, the hidden value is guaranteed by the reputation of the author, and the reader's interpretation is considered defective. Also in the (a)-text, but greatly elaborated after 1588, is an application to reading of the sceptical arguments of the "Apologie de Raimond Sebond": "il n'est aucun sens ny visage, ou droict, ou amer, ou doux, ou courbe, que l'esprit humain ne trouve aux escrits qu'il entreprend de fouiller [there is no sense

or aspect, either straight, or bitter, or sweet, or crooked, that the human
mind does not find in the writing it undertakes to search]" (2.12[a]). The
difficulty of grasping the true sense of Scripture is presented as a first example, followed by the ambiguity of oracles and "fables divinatrices" (prophetic myths); subsequently, a (c)-text, embroidering on a reference to Homer in the 1580 version, asks whether Homer could possibly have
intended all the meanings attributed to him by different readers. The argument as a whole is designed to show that we perceive everything in our
own terms, that we read into texts meanings which suit our own preoccupations and meet our own needs.

A slightly different account of the problem of overinterpretation is
given in the opening pages of "De l'experience." Here the target is the ma-
nia for writing interpretative commentaries, setting in train an infinite regression from the original sense of the text: "Nous ne faisons que nous
entregloser [We do nothing but write glosses about each other]" (3.13[b]).
It is a celebrated passage, requiring no further analysis here. Together with
the examples from "Des livres" and the "Apologie," it demonstrates that
Montaigne was sharply conscious of the apparently infinite capacity of a
text for generating meanings. The tone is pejorative in every case: these
supplementary meanings are said to be spurious and even pernicious (in
the case of Scripture). But it should be remembered that Montaigne's negative arguments are seldom a blind alley: they have a habit of opening up
avenues in unexpectedly positive directions.

In "Divers evenemens de mesme conseil" (and already in the (a)-text),
the argument that works of art owe much to fortune is sketched out. A
mild irony towards artists is apparent here, as in "La fortune se rencontre
souvent au train de la raison" (1.34; 3.8[b]), but the conclusion of the passage turns the irony to the advantage of the reader:

> La fortune montre bien encores plus evidemment la part qu'elle
> a en tous ces ouvrages, par les graces et beautez qui s'y treu-
> vent, non seulement sans l'intention, mais sans la cognoissance
> mesme de l'ouvrier. Un suffisant lecteur descouvre souvant ès
> escrits d'autruy des perfections autres que celles que l'autheur y
> a mises et apperceües, et y preste des sens et des visages plus
> riches.

> [Fortune shows still more evidently the part she has in all these
> works by the graces and beauties that are found in them, not
> only without the workman's intention, but even without his
> knowledge. An able reader often discovers in other men's writ-

ings perfections beyond those that the author put in or perceived, and lends them richer meanings and aspects.]

Here it is the capable reader, not the inadequate one, who discovers in a
text meanings other than those the author put there (or ones which, if he
did put them there, he was not himself conscious of). The vocabulary is
markedly positive ("suffisant," "perfections," "plus riches"): the imaginative reader can make capital out of chance. Likewise, in "De l'institution
des enfans," a post-1588 addition develops Montaigne's earlier assertion
that history should not be learnt but judged by suggesting that this is the
subject "à laquelle nos esprits s'appliquent de plus diverse mesure. J'ay leu
en Tite-Live cent choses que tel n'y a pas leu, Plutarque en y a leu cent,
outre ce que j'y ay sceu lire, et, à l'adventure, outre ce que l'autheur y avoit
mis [to which we apply our minds in the most varying degree. I have read
in Livy a hundred things that another man has not read in him, Plutarch
read a hundred things in him, plus what I read in him and, by chance,
added to what the author himself had put in]" (1.26[c]). Montaigne is here
claiming to be a "suffisant lecteur," while acknowledging that Plutarch can
do even better.

Thus the plurality of readings to which texts can be subjected may
appear as a rich and fertile phenomenon. It is worth recalling here that
earlier humanists had taken the view that privileged texts such as the Bible
or Homer's epics are infinitely pregnant with meaning. Erasmus asserts
(following Augustine) that, even if a meaning was not certainly intended
by God, it is valid, provided always that it is consonant with evangelical
doctrine and the rule of faith. Montaigne, too, has his criterion of validity,
although it is secular rather than sacred: it is clear from his practice of interpretation, if not from his overt statements, that any reading is acceptable if it is profitable to the reader, that is to say if it prompts self-awareness or helps to train the judgement. In other words—and here we return
to Montaigne's extension of the humanist doctrine of imitation—the coherence of an individual's reading materials lies ultimately in their application to his own character and circumstances, rather than to those of the
defunct author. No doubt he will attempt to judge his contemporaries
through their speech and actions; but the appropriation and digestion of
all these materials for his own benefit remains his primary aim. Speaking
of the way a teacher should ideally instruct his pupil, Montaigne says:

> Qu'il ne luy demande pas seulement compte des mots de sa
> leçon, mais du sens et de la substance, et qu'il juge du profit
> qu'il aura fait, non par le tesmoignage de sa memoire, mais de

sa vie. Que ce qu'il viendra d'apprendre, il le lui face mettre en cent visages et accommoder à autant de divers subjets, pour voir s'il l'a encore bien pris et bien faict sien.

[Let him be asked for an account not merely of the words of his lesson, but of its sense and substance, and let him judge the profit he has made by the testimony not of his memory, but of his life. Let him be made to show what he has just learned in a hundred aspects, and apply it to as many different subjects, to see if he has yet properly grasped it and made it his own.]

(1.26[a])

This principle governs the whole field of reading as envisaged by Montaigne.

### QUOTATION: "UN AMAS DE FLEURS ESTRANGERES"

The problem of the appropriation of borrowed texts may be approached with greater precision through a study of the rôle of quotation in the *Essais*. Many of the early readers of Montaigne's writings considered them above all as a florilegium of *sententiae, exempla* and other topoi. As Mlle de Gournay remarked in 1601:

Ce que ses écrits ont gagné de réputation publique jusqu'à ce jour, ce n'est pas par la meilleure de leurs parties, qui reste plusqu'à demi couverte, c'est par la moindre: comme exemples, histoires, et riches allégations: ces choses seulement les font rechercher du commun.

[What his writings have gained in public reputation up till today, it is not through their best part, which remains more than half-hidden, it is through the slightest part of it: as examples, stories, and rich allegations. These things only make them sought after by common minds.]

Or as Montaigne himself puts it: "Comme quelqu'un pourroit dire de moy que j'ay seulement faict icy un amas de fleurs estrangeres, n'y ayant fourny du mien que le filet à les lier [Even so someone might say of me that I have here only made a bunch of other people's flowers, having furnished nothing of my own but the thread to tie them]" (3.12[b]). Of these borrowings, a small but significant proportion are specifically quotations. Even a modern reader will be struck by the number of passages in verse and in prose, mainly in Latin, but some in Greek, French or Italian, which are scattered seemingly at random throughout the *Essais:* there are in fact some 1,300 quotations proper (excluding translated or paraphrased passages). Marked off typographically by italics and, in the case of verse, by indentation, these are the most self-evidently foreign bodies in Montaigne's text, the least digested elements of his discourse. They thus provide a test case for the way in which his readings are integrated into a new context.

A question of definition arises here. It is not too difficult to distinguish by the criteria indicated above between quotation proper and the various other forms of borrowing which pervade Montaigne's writing, but the borderline is nevertheless in many respects an arbitrary one. The translation of a letter by Epicurus, or of a passage from Seneca, clearly signposted as such in the text, may be considered as a form of quotation; but once one begins to broaden the criterion, one discovers a spectrum of possibilities which passes through translation and paraphrase (acknowledged and unacknowledged) to free imitation or mere distant echoes. The fact that this *is* a spectrum, not a set of distinct categories, is itself an important aspect of the *Essais,* and appears to be in some measure at least the result of a deliberate strategy on Montaigne's part, as will shortly become apparent. But for the purposes of the present analysis, "quotation" will have its narrower sense; "translation," "paraphrase" and "imitation" will cover, with some necessary imprecision, the other possibilities.

Montaigne's love of quotations in the form of sententiae is vividly attested by the fifty-seven "sentences" which he had painted on the rafters of his library ceiling. These inscriptions were made for the most part in the mid-1570s (two-thirds of them are reproduced in the "Apologie"), and correspond precisely with the "florilegium" tradition of which Renaissance readers were so fond. But his insertion of quotations into the *Essais* continued throughout his writing career, and should by no means be considered to be a symptom of an earlier, immature method of composition: their frequency is in fact more or less evenly distributed through the three books, and through the three major layers of the text. Lino Pertile, who makes this point, also draws attention to a striking shift in the practice of quotation in the post-1588 layer. Whereas in the 1580 and 1588 editions Montaigne's quotations from classical authors are virtually without exception taken from the poets, those added after 1588 are overwhelmingly from prose writers such as Cicero, Seneca and Livy. The earlier pattern follows the practice of classical prose writers: Seneca, for example, quotes liberally, but exclusively from poets. Thus the feature which requires explanation is the wholesale grafting of Latin prose (well over 300 quotations) on to the *Essais* in the later years. Pertile's conclusion is that Montaigne deliberately carried out this exercise to increase the unpredictability of his text, to stimulate and provoke the reader who would be over-familiar with the procedure of verse quotation as ornament. The point can be neither proved nor disproved: Montaigne, who so often refers at some point to his own practices, never mentions this one. However, another, if more mundane, explanation is available. In composing the text of the *Essais* for the 1580 and 1588 editions, Montaigne could easily incorporate into his argument translations and paraphrases of the prose writers he wished to quote; this would in fact be normal practice in the sixteenth century. But once the text was at least provisionally complete, it would have been much harder, and above all much more time-consuming, to insert such paraphrases. In other words, Montaigne may, under the pressure of illness and indeed imminent death, simply have taken a short cut. It is even conceivable that, given the time to see a new edition through the press himself, he would have removed this inconsistency.

The Renaissance practice of quotation is comparable with the medieval tradition of citing "authorities" *(auctoritates)*. The role of the quoted material, or of the cited name, in this tradition is to confer weight on an utterance which would otherwise seem personal and arbitrary. Citation links the fragile present with a timeless wisdom. Montaigne is familiar with the procedure, and falls in with it in certain respects. Many of his references to the great men of antiquity and their sayings, and a fortiori his quotations from the Bible, clearly have the function of persuading the reader of the seriousness of the point at issue. When he says in "Des livres" (2.10[a]) that he doesn't trust his own negative judgement of Plato's *Axiochus,* his criterion is "authority"; in "De la phisionomie," (3.12[b]), he concedes that most of our opinions are—and must be—held "à credit"; and again, in a (c)-text at the very end of "De l'experience," he claims: "L'authorité peut seule envers les communs entendemens, et poise plus en langage peregrin [Authority alone has power over common intelligences, and has more weight in a foreign language]" (3.13) (a Latin quotation from Seneca follows).

But none of these three remarks is wholly unequivocal, and one may often detect more than a trace of irony in Montaigne's references to that kind of authority represented par excellence by Aristotle. The whole of the educational method sketched out in "Du pedantisme" and "De l'institution des enfans," like the practice of reading described in "Des livres" and elsewhere, is founded rather on the suspicion of ready-made opinion. The aphorisms of the philosophers appear ineffectual when confronted with the hard facts of experience (3.4; 3.12[c]), and even a parrot could learn to repeat the words of Cicero, Plato or Aristotle (1.25, 136[a]). A bon mot of the historian Philippe de Commynes is found to be already in Tacitus (a post-1588 insertion indicating—ironically enough—parallels in Seneca and Quintus Cicero [3.8]. This last example is part of a larger development on the need to discern, in conversation, whether one's interlocutor really possesses and understands the witty or sententious remarks he makes:

> Aus disputes et conferences, tous les mots qui nous semblent bons ne doivent pas incontinent estre acceptez. La plus part des hommes sont riches d'une suffisance estrangere. Il peut advenir à tel de dire un beau traict, une bonne responce et sentence, et la mettre en avant sans en cognoistre la force. (c) Qu'on ne tient pas tout ce qu'on emprunte, à l'adventure se pourra il verifier par moy mesme.
>
> [in arguments and discussions not all the remarks that seem good to us should be accepted immediately. Most men are rich with borrowed capacity. It may happen to a given man to make a fine point, a good answer and maxim, and put it forward without recognizing its force. That we do not possess all we borrow may perhaps be verified in myself.]
>
> (3.8)

This is a characteristic argument, which embraces also the comment on the difficulty of literary judgement already referred to [earlier in this essay]. A more explicit questioning of belief in *auctoritates* is to be found in "De l'experience":

> Que ferons nous à ce peuple qui ne fait recepte que de tesmoignages imprimez, qui ne croit les hommes s'ils ne sont en livre, ny la verité si elle n'est d'age competant? . . . Il y a bien pour luy autre poix de dire: "Je l'ai leu," que si vous dictes: "Je l'ay ouy dire."
>
> [What shall we do with this people that admits none but printed evidence, that does not believe men unless they are in a book, or truth unless it is of competent age? . . . It carries very different weight with this people if you say "I have read it" than if you say "I have heard it."]
>
> (3.13[b])

Montaigne goes on to state the equivalence between past and present, foreign and domestic, printed and oral—but with a marked leaning towards

the second in each case. To "courir apres les exemples estrangers et scho-
lastiques [run after foreign and scholastic examples]" is to seek "plus
l'honneur de l'allegation que la verité du discours [more the honor of allegation than the truth of discourse]."

If, then, *allégation* is suspect, how does Montaigne present his quotations? As the (c)-text indicates in the passage quoted above from "De l'art
de conférer" ("à l'adventure se pourra il verifier par moy mesme"), he had
sufficient self-irony to be aware that his own bons mots may appear as
only superficially assimilated quotations. He will concede that the reader
may take the *Essais* to be an "amas de fleurs estrangeres [heap of alien
flowers]," or that his book is "massonné purement de leurs despouilles
[built up purely from their spoils], [those of Seneca and Plutarch]." A (c)-
text in "Du pedantisme" turns his argument—that "nos pedantes" pillage
books for their superficial knowledge—against himself:

> Je m'en vay escorniflant par cy par là des livres les sentences qui
> me plaisent, non pour les garder, car je n'ay point de gardoires,
> mais pour les transporter en cettuy-cy, où, à vray dire, elles ne
> sont plus miennes qu'en leur premiere place.

> [I go about cadging from books here and there the sayings that
> please me, not to keep them, for I have no storehouses, but to
> transport them into this one, in which, to tell the truth, they are
> no more mine than in their original place.]

> (1.25)

Thus he will at times disclaim responsibility for his quotations, referring to
them for example as a concession to the fashion of his day (3.12[b]).

A particularly interesting instance occurs in "De la præsumption,"
where the (a)-text speaks of the "superficiality" of his reading ("Je feuil-
lette les livres, je ne les estudie pas [I skim through books, I don't study
them]") in relation to his lack of memory: "l'autheur, le lieu, les mots et
autres circonstances, je les oublie incontinent [the author, the place, the
words and other circumstances, I forget them immediately]." A (b)-text extends the remark to cover his own writings, and then reverts to his verse
quotations and *exempla:*

> On m'allegue tous les coups à moy-mesme sans que je le sente.
> Qui voudroit sçavoir d'où sont les vers et exemples que j'ay icy
> entassez, me mettroit en peine de le luy dire; et si, ne les ay
> mendiez qu'ès portes connues et fameuses, ne me contentant

pas qu'ils fussent riches, s'ils ne venoient encore de main riche
et honorable: l'authorité y concurre quant et la raison.

[People are all the time quoting me to myself without my knowing it. Anyone who would like to know the sources of the verses
and examples I have piled up here would put me to great trouble to tell him. And yet I have begged them only at well-known
and famous doors, not content with their being rich unless they
also came from rich and honorable hands; in them authority
and reason concur.]

(2.17)

It will be noted that the concession to authority recurs here, but in a context where the whole activity of quoting and citing is made to appear superficial, and Montaigne's own practice casual: the word "entassez" suggests that he has not only chosen his quotations at random, from whatever
book he happened to be leafing through, but has also simply piled them
up indiscriminately in his own text. The rôle of chance, which emerged as
a theme in relation to Montaigne's practice of reading in general, appears
again here at the level of quotation (see also 2.10[a]: "A mesme que mes
resveries se presentent, je les entasse" [As my fancies present themselves, I
pile them up]").

But chance may be allowed to intervene as part of a strategy. Montaigne may forget where he got his quotations from, but when he allows
them to be printed in his text anonymously, as he habitually does, something more than failure of memory is at stake. Sixteenth-century practice
overwhelmingly bears witness to the preference for identified quotation:
references—often very precise ones—are provided in the margin or the
text, or even both. Montaigne's omission of such references can thus
hardly be otherwise than deliberate, and the disingenuousness of the account in "De la præsumption" is proved by the fact that he offers a different, if no less disingenuous, motivation in "Des livres":

Je ne compte pas mes emprunts, je les poise. Et si je les eusse
voulu faire valoir par nombre, je m'en fusse chargé deux fois
autant. Ils sont tous, ou fort peu s'en faut, de noms si fameux
et anciens qu'ils me semblent se nommer assez sans moi.

[I do not count my borrowings, I weigh them. And if I had
wanted to have them valued by their number, I should have
loaded myself with twice as many. They are all, or very nearly

all, from such famous and ancient names that they seem to
identify themselves enough without me.]

(2.10[c])

The opposition between quantity and quality in the first two sentences
compels an ironic reading of the third. Montaigne's quotations have
"weight," it would seem, because they come from the most famous authors (or authorities). But the device of presenting them anonymously
would seem rather to strip them of their credentials and thus deprive them
of their function as a citation of authority. One could go further and say
that they are released from their allegiance to another text, and thus free
to become incorporated into Montaigne's. This is indeed what is suggested
by the continuation of the passage, where Montaigne speaks not of his
quotations but of his paraphrases:

> Ès raisons et inventions que je transplante en mon solage et
> confons aux miennes, j'ay à escient ommis parfois d'en marquer
> l'autheur, pour tenir en bride la temerité de ces sentences has-
> tives qui se jettent sur toute sorte d'escrits ... Je veux qu'ils
> donnent une nazarde à Plutarque sur mon nez, et qu'ils s'esch-
> audent à injurier Seneque en moy.

> [In the reasonings and inventions that I transplant into my soil
> and confound with my own, I have sometimes deliberately not
> indicated the author, in order to hold in check the temerity of
> those hasty condemnations that are tossed at all sorts of writ-
> ings ... I want them to give Plutarch a fillip on my nose and
> get burned insulting Seneca in me.]

The tricking of the reader is a symptom of the persistent desire to eliminate
the difference between foreign materials and the text of the *Essais*.

The other procedure adopted by Montaigne in order to naturalize his
borrowings is misquotation. To apply a quotation in a new context is already, in a sense, to misquote; but Montaigne goes further than this. In a
(c)-text of "De l'institution des enfans," having quoted Quintilian and Seneca on the vice of twisting one's discourse in order to place a bon mot, he
makes the point in his own way: "Je tors bien plus volontiers une bonne
sentence pour la coudre sur moy, que je ne tors mon fil pour l'aller querir
[I much more readily twist a good saying to sew it on me than I twist the
thread of my thought to go and fetch it]" (1.26). Another (c)-text, from
"De la phisionomie," brings out still more clearly the notion of "deform-
ing" the borrowed text in order to make it less foreign:

Parmy tant d'emprunts je suis bien aise d'en pouvoir desrober
quelqu'un, les desguisant et difformant à nouveau service. Au
hazard que je laisse dire que c'est par faute d'avoir entendu leur
naturel usage, je luy donne quelque particuliere adresse de ma
main, à ce qu'ils en soient d'autant moins purement estrangers.

[I, among so many borrowings of mine, am very glad to be able
to hide one now and then, disguising and altering it for a new
service. At the risk of letting it be said that I do so through failure to understand its original use, I give it some particular application with my own hand, so that it may be less purely someone else's.]

(3.12)

As will be apparent from the use of the word "desguisant," anonymity and
deformation go hand in hand.

These remarks have often been noted, but Montaigne's practice of
misquotation has never been systematically studied. It is most clearly mea-
surable in the domain of verbatim reproduction of the original, but there
are difficulties even here. In "Sur des vers de Virgile," Montaigne quotes a
passage from Lucretius which he then analyses in some detail; but the
reader who checks it against a modern edition of Lucretius will find that
a line is missing. Was it missing in the sixteenth-century edition (or florilegium) that Montaigne knew? was it omitted by Montaigne's printer,
whose version was copied by subsequent printers? was Montaigne quoting
from his defective memory? or did he omit the line deliberately because it
was superfluous to the point he was trying to make (a slightly implausible
hypothesis in this instance, but one that might be pertinent elsewhere)?
Where translated passages or paraphrase are concerned, the margin for
doubt is even greater; but the exercise of examining Montaigne's "deform-
ations" could nevertheless hardly fail to yield insights into his working
methods.

Up to now, I have considered predominantly, in Montaigne's terms,
the negative side of the coin: quotations as alien, superfluous matter; negligent quotation; deformed quotation. But irony is endemic in all of these
accounts, and we might pause here for a moment to consider the relationship between quotation and irony as rhetorical devices. In both, an utterance is offered as being in some way foreign to the speaker: an ironical
statement is a statement in quotation marks, for which the speaker refuses
to take responsibility. In both cases, the status of the "quoted" utterance
may be more or less obscured, so that the reader is unsure whether to take

it at face value; or, still worse, he may be foolish enough to take it on trust as the authentic utterance of the speaker. Both, too, require that speaker and listener, writer and reader, share a common frame of reference if they are to be correctly understood: the listener must have the competence to know that an ironical reading is required, or that the literary game of quotation is being played. Of course, they function differently in that irony necessarily entails a reversal of ostensible meaning, whereas quotation is in most cases corroborative. But the *Essais* are pervaded with a deep fascination for equivocal modes of discourse: "La verité et le mensonge," says Montaigne in "Des boyteux," "ont leurs visages conformes [Truth and falsehood are alike in face]"; and it is precisely in the domain of quotation that discourse may be most equivocal, its truth least clearly anchored in the *moi*. The habit of quoting both invites irony and fosters the ironical manner.

The uses of quotation may often appear in a more positive light: indeed, this is what one would expect if one has read the irony correctly. But it is also necessary to be able to read the quotations: modern readers are at a disadvantage in that they are unlikely to have the firm grasp of Latin and the knowledge of Latin authors shared by all educated sixteenth-century readers, let alone Montaigne's own bilingual facility, which enabled him to read Ovid's *Metamorphoses* in early childhood as his favourite storybook. As Dorothy Coleman points out, Montaigne is one of the greatest of the sixteenth-century masters of allusion. The quotations should not be considered as inert and opaque obstacles to be skirted hurriedly by means of a rapid glance at the translation provided in the notes of modern editions, or even ignored altogether. Nor are they simply attractive ornaments, repeating with a rhetorical flourish the sense of Montaigne's prose. Ideally, each one should be read in the original, replaced in the context from which Montaigne took it; the two contexts (or more, where two or three quotations are given consecutively) should then be compared. Even if all of Montaigne's borrowings were not as carefully and creatively designed as this procedure would seem to imply, it is nevertheless justifiable as a means of bringing out the maximum possible charge of meaning in a given configuration of texts (the minimum, of course, being zero: a piece of language excerpted from a florilegium and tacked on at random by a writer responding to the pressure of fashion).

To take Montaigne's allusiveness seriously in this way is to treat the *Essais* not so much as a repository of more or less conventional wisdom but as a work of art, a work whose richness lies in a complex interweaving of different coloured strands. Dorothy Coleman gives some examples of such reading, stressing the affinity of Montaigne's writing with poetry, and in particular the highly allusive poetry of Horace. A more ample account, and one more specifically concerned with Montaigne's art of verse quotation, is given by Mary McKinley, who describes the ways in which the themes and images of the quotations are absorbed into Montaigne's text, or form a counterpoint to his own themes and images. Two major points emerge from this analysis. One is that Montaigne seems often to have had the quotation in mind well before he actually added it to his text: the Latin verse comes as the culmination of a development which prepares the way for it. At times it seems clear even that a thematic and metaphorical development in the (a)-text already implies a quotation which is not added until a later edition, as if Montaigne felt, in retrospect, that he should disclose his "source." This is of great importance, since it indicates that Montaigne's imagination was saturated with literary allusions which time and again determined the direction of his writing; as this process certainly began long before he started to write the *Essais,* it would have been impossible for him (or us) to know whether a given idea was his own or a literary echo. Perhaps, in a sense, the *Essais* are "simply" the orchestration of a vast reading experience.

The other point is that, in certain cases at least, Pertile's hypothesis that the quotations are primarily a "text of departure" can be shown to be incorrect (which does not, however, invalidate it as a general insight into Montaigne's method of appropriation). The prose surrounding Montaigne's quotation may tacitly allude to the original context of that quotation, thus greatly increasing the charge of meaning for the skilled and attentive reader. One interesting example occurs near the beginning of "De l'amitié," where a single line quoted from Horace's *Ars poetica* interacts with Montaigne's preceding remarks in such a way as to invoke its own context and to suggest a complex set of reflections on Montaigne's art of writing. Or again, a quotation from Ovid's *Metamorphoses* in the "Apologie" implies the story of Pygmalion from which it is taken, without ever mentioning Pygmalion himself or the details of the story; the reader must supply these if the allusion is to have its full reverberation. Indeed, McKinley goes so far as to claim that "the context from which he borrows is often more relevant to his immediate text than the line or lines he actually incorporates.

An example of an oblique—if not quite hidden—allusion occurs on the last page of the *Essais.* Montaigne recommends his old age to "ce Dieu, protecteur de santé et de sagesse, mais gaye et sociale [that god who is the protector of health and wisdom, but gay and sociable wisdom]" (3.13(b) ).

The god is Apollo; some of his attributes—health, wisdom, joy—are present in Montaigne's text; but the specific reference is carried only by the metonymy "Latoe" in the quotation from an ode of Horace which follows. One of his most celebrated attributes, moreover, although not mentioned by Montaigne, is evoked in the last words of the quotation, which are thus also the last words of Montaigne's book. Apollo is the god of music and poetry, and Horace prays that the lyre will not be absent from his old age. Montaigne's own love of and admiration for poetic beauty thus sounds, in the lines of a favourite poet, the final note of the *Essais*.

The quotations, then, serve to multiply the strata of meaning of Montaigne's text, an effect which may also be accompanied by an aesthetic enrichment, although—as some of Pertile's examples show—the piling up of disparate quotations may at times disconcert the reader rather than giving him aesthetic satisfaction. Montaigne is seldom a bland writer: he likes to surprise and provoke, and can do this in many ways. But whether one considers his quotations as turned back towards their own context, or forward into Montaigne's own, the cumulative effect is that of a dialogue of many voices, past and present; or of a series of windows opened on the not quite forgotten pages of Montaigne's library.

In the light of these practical examples, we may now review the general problem of Montaigne's borrowings and his attitude towards them. We have seen that he may be dismissive, ironical, self-deprecating with regard to his habit of quoting and paraphrasing: he presents his work at times as little more than a heap of borrowed fragments, flung together more or less at random. But the note of irony already suggests that such statements are not to be taken unequivocally, and there are a number of extended passages in the *Essais* where he vigorously defends his practice, distinguishing it from that of mere compilers (e.g., 1.26; 3.5; 3.12). He claims that his material is truly his own: either he had an idea first, and then found it corroborated by the "authorities" (2.12[c]); or he has fully appropriated a borrowed idea, forgetting its origin and adapting it to his own purposes: "Je ne dis les autres, sinon pour d'autant plus me dire [I do not speak the mind of others except to speak my own mind better]" (1.26[c]); "Ce n'est non plus selon Platon que selon moy, puis que luy et moi l'entendons et voyons de mesme [It is no more according to Plato than according to me, since he and I understand and see it the same way]" (1.26[c]).

It is possible to accept these remarks as broadly true, and thus to consider Montaigne's self-deprecation simply as a preliminary strategy, a disarming gesture. But I believe it is more fruitful to give full weight to the shifts and conflicts of perspective. In psychological terms, one might well detect a note of unease in several of these passages: Montaigne's mental library threatens to overwhelm him, to infiltrate all his thoughts, to take possession of his writings. The response to this invasion of foreign bodies is precisely the (at times somewhat nervous) affirmation of the self and its mastery of the materials it is said to deploy. Montaigne is both a Pygmalion, bringing to life the dead texts with which he works, and an Actæon, overtaken by an alien form and fragmented by the very materials he was supposed to control.

Or again, in a historical perspective, one could argue, as Compagnon does, that Montaigne's practice of quotation coincides with a transitional phase between the medieval veneration of *auctoritates,* whose writings the modern writer humbly glosses, and a later ("classical") view according to which the writer is responsible for his every utterance. Instead of a master text, surrounded by fragments of commentary, we have in Montaigne and some of his contemporaries the inverse: namely, fragments of classical and other texts absorbed into an autonomous discourse which asserts its own priority. According to this account, the *Essais* are both a symptom of, and a major contribution to, the formation of the notion of the writer as a subject, a first-person-singular agent who has annexed and mastered all the "thoughts" (sententiae) which he has necessarily borrowed. The advantage of a hypothesis such as this is that it does not assume the project of self-portraiture to be as it were a timeless possibility, a solution a writer might have adopted in any age. It suggests that the relationship between reading, writing and the concept of the self is an intricate one, subject to historical change; and that, when we take for granted the idea of an authentic self, able to distinguish between the utterances which do and do not belong to it, our presuppositions are themselves the product of that change of which the *Essais* are an early but striking example.

## THE *ESSAIS* AND THEIR READER: "ET PUIS, POUR QUI ESCRIVEZ VOUS?"

It will already be clear that the way in which Montaigne presents his readings in the *Essais* is an important aspect of the way in which he presents his text as a whole to be read by others: indeed, there are few works in which the problems of reading so clearly have this double character. It is as if the text were situated exactly at the mid-point between the writings it echoes and its potential readers, looking in both directions simultaneously; or as if it were the catalyst in a chain reaction which displayed some of the characteristics of reading and rereading as a perennial activity.

Broadly speaking, Montaigne's directions to the reader, whether explicit or implicit, may be divided into two categories. The first consists of those which bear on the response to the book as a whole, and in particular on the notion of a self-portrait; the second, of those concerning meaning and form in the *Essais*, the intellectual and aesthetic character of the text. In one case, Montaigne speaks as a man exposing himself, with some irony and not a little anxiety, to the public gaze; in the other, he draws attention to features of his writing such as digression, ellipsis, obscurity, obliqueness, in order to encourage an intelligent and productive reading of his text.

The reader's attitude to the 1580 edition is of course most cogently affected by the preface "Au lecteur," a text which may be regarded as a sharply ironic extension of the "humility topos," by means of which the author disclaims any lofty ambitions for his book. Erasmus's *Praise of Folly* had been presented in this way, as the work of idle moments spent on a journey to England; Du Bellay's *Regrets*, too, are proffered in this spirit. The topos is not meant to be taken literally: it is above all a generic indication, assigning the work loosely to the domain of satire, miscellanies, epistles and the like. It may be particularly useful in an age of repressive censorship, where the author may thus conventionally avoid being read as a serious contributor to theological or political debate; in Montaigne, it rather has the function of excluding the text from the realm of systematic philosophical or pedagogical writing, and distracting attention from what is said to the way it is said. When in the concluding sentence Montaigne tells the reader that he needn't waste his time on the *Essais*, he is attempting to discourage, not all readings, but conventional or pedantic readings.

Even when one takes account of the crucial reference in it to self-portraiture, the preface as a whole has a primarily emblematic function: it is designed to indicate the angle from which the text should be viewed, rather than to give a literal account of its contents. In order to test this, one need only attempt to read the first twenty or so chapters of the 1580 version as if one had never seen the preface or the later versions, as if Montaigne had never said "Ainsi, lecteur, je suis moy-mesmes la matiere de mon livre [Thus, reader, I am myself the matter of my book]." Once the reader has been given appropriate instructions, he will compose the "self-portrait" for himself as he reads; if he—like many of the book's earlier readers—ignores the instructions, he will no doubt treat the *Essais* as a more or less attractively composed miscellany.

The reader's construction of the self-portrait will consist in his giving special attention to the writer's first-person observations, whether in the form of opinions, self-analysis, or familiar anecdote, and however sporadic they may be. Passages which echo the preface, such as the extended development in "Du dementir" on the *Essais* as a memento for friends, will appear as particularly significant and serve to reinforce the construction. Widely scattered passages will have to be drawn together and treated as parts of a coherent whole. Chapters like "De l'amitié," "De l'exercitation," "De la præsumption," will be singled out as focal points and their themes extrapolated to give meaning to other quite different chapters. My point here is not that the notion of the self-portrait is less significant than is normally believed, nor that one is mistaken in accepting Montaigne's instruction to read the *Essais* as if its author were the "matter of his book." I would simply insist that the participation of the reader, his collusion with the author, is an indispensable factor in the elaboration of such a reading.

In the later editions, the perspective is somewhat different. The project of self-portraiture is now clearly formulated in advance and will determine major features of presentation such as the placing of "De l'experience" at the end as a final conspectus of the self-portrait, or the inclusion of a chapter ("Sur des vers de Virgile") which seems to put into practice Montaigne's remark in "Au lecteur" that he would have liked to present himself naked to the reader (and which takes up again a topic explicitly dropped in the opening passage of 2.17). The author's habits, tastes and experiences become a much more pervasive theme of the book, infiltrating the chapters of the 1580 edition in order to create a retrospective unity. Furthermore, by 1588 Montaigne knew that the *Essais* were a success: the earlier editions had been widely read and had already conferred a degree of fame on their author.

The image of the *Essais* as a "private" text presented to a circle of intimates persists, but its figurative character becomes increasingly evident:

> J'escris mon livre à peu d'hommes et à peu d'années. Si ç'eust esté une matiere de durée, il l'eust fallu commettre à un langage plus ferme . . . Pourtant ne crains-je poinct d'y inserer plusieurs articles privez, qui consument leur usage entre les hommes qui vivent aujourd'huy, et qui touchent la particuliere science d'aucuns, qui y verront plus avant que de la commune intelligence.

> [I write my book for few men and for few years. If it had been durable matter, it would have had to be committed to a more stable language . . . Therefore I do not fear to insert a number of personal items, whose usefulness will not extend beyond this generation, and which touch on things particularly known to

some who will see further into them than those of ordinary understanding.]

(3.9[b])

This special group of readers now diminishes almost to vanishing-point
amid the public at large, a public whose anonymity appears at times as a
source of anxiety for the writer: in "Consideration sur Ciceron," having
said that he might have published his thoughts in letter form if he had had
someone "à qui parler," he continues: "J'eusse esté plus attentif et plus
seur, ayant une addresse forte et amie, que je ne suis, regardant les divers
visages d'un peuple [I would have been more attentive and confident, with
a strong friend to address, than I am now, when I consider the various
tastes of a whole public]" (1.40[c]). The need to assess the function and
value of self-portraiture at this level becomes much more acute: the difficulty of the enterprise, its bizarre and extravagant character, the good faith
of the writer and his trust in the reader's judgement, the writer's admission
of his own fluctuating judgement of his book—all of these are signs to the
reader that his normal reading habits are inadequate here. Even the pro-
nouncements which would seem to emerge from the depths of the author's
psyche—"Je suis affamé de me faire connoistre," "je crains mortellement
d'estre pris en eschange [I am hungry to make myself known, I have a mortal fear of being taken to be other than I am]" (3.5[b])—may also be taken
as provocative signals, alerting the reader to the singularity of the enterprise, and inviting him to understand it as a probing reassessment of the
nature of self-knowledge. Thus, when Montaigne says that he hopes his
book may attract to him, during his lifetime, a new friend who shares his
"humours," who will be in complete sympathy with him, he is offering an
emblem of the perfect reader, who is also a rare (if not nonexistent) reader.
This imaginary figure would no doubt play the rôle assigned to Montaigne's lost friend La Boétie, with whom he claimed to enjoy mutual comprehension (1.28). Once again, Montaigne is no longer writing for the figure of a casual friend or relative. His book invites the reader to separate
himself from the anonymous crowd by the application to the text of an
especially rigorous and sustained insight. A singular reader is required for
this singular enterprise.

   In a brief early chapter of the *Essais,* Montaigne describes his father's
suggestion that every town should have a register in which people could
announce their reciprocal needs and thus contact one another, as for example "(c) Je cherche à vendre des perles, je cherche des perles à vendre.
(a) ... tel s'enquiert d'un serviteur de telle qualité; tel d'un maistre [I want
to sell some pearls; I want to buy some pearls. ... so-and-so is looking for
a servant with such-and-such qualifications; so-and-so wants a master]"

(1.35). He even uses the word "advertir," thus anticipating verbally as well as by the general conception the system of advertisement. Like an entry in the personal columns of a modern newspaper, the *Essais* is a text in search of exactly the right reader.

Many other features of the book may be seen as inviting, however obliquely, the reader to reflect on his own status and attitude. Montaigne is acutely sensitive to the ways in which language is proffered and received: he writes about conversation, oratory, storytelling, lying, diplomacy, letter writing, eyewitness reports and above all, of course, *essai*-writing. The treatment of such themes helps the reader to clarify the view he should adopt of the equivocations and paradoxes which are endemic in the *Essais:* they motivate the use of a mode of writing which might otherwise seem gratuitously elusive. Or again, the passages in which Montaigne refers now to his cultivation of solitude, now to his sociability and love of conversation (see especially 3.3 and 3.8), provide a framework within which the reader may comprehend the presentation of a highly personal book for public consumption. When at the end of "De trois commerces" Montaigne says that he returns to his books as his most faithful friends, he is not excluding his own reader; on the contrary, he is endorsing precisely the activity that his reader is engaged in.

While waiting for the ideal reader, Montaigne himself reads and rereads the *Essais.* This activity appears in the same light as his reading of other books in at least one important respect: just as he forgets where he has found his quotations and examples, or fails to discover on rereading the qualities of a book he once found attractive, so in reviewing his own text the original meaning may escape him:

> (c) Ceci m'advient aussi: que je ne me trouve pas où je me cherche; et me trouve plus par rencontre que par l'inquisition de mon jugement. J'aurai eslancé quelque subtilité en escrivant . . . Je l'ay si bien perdue que je ne sçay ce que j'ay voulu dire; et l'a l'estranger descouverte par fois avant moy. Si je portoy le rasoir par tout où cela m'advient, je me desferoy tout.

> [This also happens to me: that I do not find myself in the place where I look; and I find myself more by chance encounter than by searching my judgment. I will have tossed off some subtle remark as I write . . . Later I have lost the point so thoroughly that I do not know what I meant; and sometimes a stranger has discovered it before I do. If I erased every passage where this happens to me, there would be nothing left of myself.]

> (1.10)

(b) En mes escris mesmes je ne retrouve pas tousjours l'air de
ma premiere imagination; je ne sçay ce que j'ay voulu dire, et
m'eschaude souvent à corriger et y mettre un nouveau sens,
pour avoir perdu le premier, qui valloit mieux.

[Even iñ my own writings I do not always find again the sense
of my first thought; I do not know what I meant to say, and
often I get burned by correcting and putting in a new meaning,
because I have lost the first one, which was better.]

(2.12)

These passages form a complex variant of the rule discussed earlier, according to which a reader may legitimately find more in a text than the
author was conscious of inserting. In one sense, the notion of an original
"correct" sense is preserved; but the author's own loss of contact with that
sense, its appropriation by other readers who can quote Montaigne himself
or tell him what he meant, calls into question the very notion of a single
correct sense. Perhaps the first sense was *already* a particular reading, to
which the author brought his own momentary preoccupations, and which
was dissipated as the author-reader shifted his perspective. There would
thus be no moment of perfect unity of text and meaning, presided over by
a godlike author, only a set of words that can be read in various different
ways by different readers.

No doubt Montaigne does not go quite as far as this. But the equivalence between writer and reader which at certain moments he is prepared
to entertain is none the less striking. As will shortly become apparent, it
might seem to invite the reader reciprocally to "rewrite" the text. For the
moment, however, one may observe from the second passage quoted that
Montaigne's reading of the *Essais* is intimately linked with is own rewriting of the text. He claims on more than one occasion that he never corrects
the *Essais,* only adds to them (2.37; 3.9). But this is not quite true, even in
the literal sense: minor alterations, over and above the verbal adjustments
demanded by the insertion of a new development, are quite frequent (one
of the disadvantages of the modern "three-layer" presentation of the text
is that it obscures them).

More centrally, the addition of new material can and does affect the
meaning. In "Du parler prompt ou tardif," the writer's own spontaneity in
speech or writing is never directly mentioned in the (a)-text. It is perhaps
hinted at in "Je cognois, par experience, cette condition de nature [I know
by experience this sort of nature]" (1.10), but this could equally be a reference to his experience of others. A (b)-text inserted immediately before the

final sentence attaches the topic unambiguously to the first person singular, and in the process shifts the balance of the preceding passage from observation of others to personal experience; furthermore, it adds a new charge of irony to the final sentence: the reader is in this version made acutely conscious that the writer gives oral spontaneity priority over the more laborious and "prepared" mode of writing. The (c)-addition which imposes a new ending on the chapter [quoted earlier in this essay] picks up the theme of writing and twists it in an unexpected direction: the reader himself appears on the stage as the "estranger" who may more easily recognize Montaigne's meaning than Montaigne himself. The result (for the reader who can identify the three layers) is a complex interaction between the first text, Montaigne's rewritings, and the explicit theme of the author's discontinuous self-reading. Similar effects may be observed throughout the *Essais*, although not always with this degree of overt reflection on the processes involved.

A crucial question must be touched on here, although its implications exceed the scope of the present study. Montaigne reads his book not just as a literary work to be presented to an eventual public but as a means of self-interpretation. As a record of his trials of judgement over a long period of time, it supplements his supposedly weak memory and provides a history or story which confers some degree of unity on an otherwise fragmented self. The story makes every allowance for the effects of "le passage" as they are described, for example, at the beginning of "Du repentir": the words *réciter* and *raconter* are used here in the sense of "to give a running commentary," without any implication of fictional or aesthetic coherence. Or again, in "De l'inconstance de nos actions" (2.1), man's character (and the writer's) is seen as a random sequence of fragments, on which it would be wrong to impose any order. Nevertheless, Montaigne's self-reading *is* a search for coherence at some level, a level which Montaigne would himself designate by references to "nature," and which he admits to be immensely difficult to perceive and recover. Leaving aside the more problematic aspects of the relationship between the "real" Montaigne and the image presented by the book of its author, it may be observed that the ethical value of the *Essais* for Montaigne depends on his ability to discern in the "registre des essais de [s]a vie" a linking thread. He claims at one point that the publication of his book has had the unhoped-for advantage of providing a "rule" for his actions: having made his image known, he has a strong motive for remaining faithful to it (3.9[b]). This could only be valid if the image were seen to have internal consistency. Even in "De l'inconstance de nos actions," we find the phrase

"Voyla pourquoy, pour juger d'un homme, il faut suivre longuement et curieusement sa trace [That is why, to judge a man, we must follow his traces long and carefully]" (2.1[a]), which suggests that something may emerge if the investigation is long enough and penetrating enough; and most readers would be willing to acknowledge having the intuitive sense of a characteristically Montaignian manner, which would have to be defined in terms of the recurrence of certain themes and stylistic devices. Yet, in the last analysis, one might argue that the unity of the *Essais* does not reside in a human physiognomy imprinted on the multiple fragments of which the book is composed: the "linking thread" is itself produced by the shadow of a writer reading and rereading his text in search of a linking thread. We may now turn from the issue of self-portraiture to the way in which the *Essais* characterize the intellectual and aesthetic (rather than moral and personal) problems of reading. Montaigne's preferred discourse is one which discards theoretical preambles, prefatory apostrophes and rhetorical padding, and in consequence requires an alert reader:

> Je veux qu'on commence par le dernier point . . . il ne me faut point d'alechement ny de sause: je menge bien la viande toute crue; et, au lieu de m'esguiser l'apetit par ces preparatoires et avant-jeux, on me le lasse et affadit . . . [Plutarch and Seneca] et Pline, et leurs semblables, ils n'ont pas de "Hoc age"; ils veulent avoiv à faire à gens qui s'en soyent advertis eux mesmes.
>
> [I want to begin with the conclusion . . . I need no allurement or sauce; I can perfectly well eat my meat quite raw; and instead of whetting my appetite by these preparations and preliminaries, they pall and weary it . . . [Plutarch and Seneca] and Pliny, and their like, have no *Hoc age;* they want to have to do with men who themselves have told themselves this.]
>
>                                                                      (2.10[a])

We return here, in a different context, to the stringent demands Montaigne makes on his reader. Just as, in conversation, he claims to be intolerant of "beginners," so in his writing he makes few allowances for the naïve or inattentive reader (3.8[c]). A remark such as "J'aimeray quelcun qui me sçache deplumer [I will love anyone that can unplume me]" (2.10[c]) (in this case, someone who can distinguish Montaigne's own "propos" from his disguised borrowings) will convey something of the vigorous dialogue he expects to engage with his reader.

But the most astringent definitions which Montaigne provides of his ideal reader are to be found in "Des vaines subtilitez" and a (c)-text of

"De la præsumption." "Des vaines subtilitez," providing illustrations of the principle known as *coincidentia oppositorum* (the meeting of two antithetical extremes), concludes as follows:

> Si ces essays estoyent dignes qu'on en jugeat, il en pourroit advenir, à mon advis, qu'ils ne plairoient guiere aux esprits communs et vulgaires, ny guiere aux singuliers et excellens; ceux-là n'y entendroient pas assez, ceux-cy y entendroient trop; ils pourroient vivoter en la moyenne region.

> [if these essays were worthy of being judged, I think they might not be much liked by common and vulgar minds, or by singular and excellent ones; the former would not understand enough about them, the latter too much. But they might get by in the middle region.]

>                                                                    (1.54[a])

Although the "coincidence of opposites" does not quite have the effect of excluding the middle term, the readers who inhabit the "moyenne region" might appear to be a rather circumscribed group; in "De la præsumption," the same antithesis is made to exclude all but a nameless few:

> (c) Et puis, pour qui escrivez vous? Les scavans à qui touche la jurisdiction livresque, ne connoissent autre prix que de la doctrine, et n'advouent autre proceder en noz esprits que celuy de l'erudition et de l'art . . . Les ames communes et populaires ne voyent pas la grace et le pois d'un discours hautain et deslié. Or ces deux especes occupent le monde. La tierce, à qui vous tombez en partage, des ames reglées et fortes d'elles-mesmes est si rare, que justement elle n'a ny nom, ny rang entre nous: c'est à demy temps perdu d'aspirer et de s'efforcer à luy plaire.

> [And then, for whom do you write? The learned men to whom it falls to pass judgment on books know no other value than that of learning, and admit no other procedure for our minds than that of erudition and art . . . Common, ordinary minds do not see the grace and the weight of a lofty and subtle speech. Now, these two types fill the world. The third class into whose hands you come, that of minds regulated and strong in themselves, is so rare that for this very reason it has neither name nor rank among us; it is time half wasted to aspire and strive to please this group.]

>                                                                       (2.17)

Montaigne's "suffisant lecteur" is thus not only one who, as we saw earlier, brings to bear on the text the sympathy and insight of a uniquely close friend; he is also an unusually skilled reader, and above all an active (as opposed to passive) one.

The characteristics of Montaigne's own writing, as he sees them, which chiefly disqualify a mediocre reader are density, discontinuity and obliqueness. These features are described at the greatest length, and with the most explicit reference to the problems of reading, in a passage from "De la vanité" (greatly expanded in the (c)-text). Having admitted that his preceding remarks were a digression from his central topic, Montaigne adds: "Je m'esgare, mais plustost par licence que par mesgarde. Mes fantasies se suyvent, mais par fois c'est de loing, et se regardent, mais d'une veuë oblique [I go out of my way, but rather by license than carelessness. My ideals follow one another, but sometimes it is from a distance, and look at each other, but with a side-long glance]" (3.9[b]). Digression is thus qualified not as a sign of negligence but as one element in an oblique or interrupted continuity; and the (b)-text continues in similar vein with a reference to the indirect relationship between the name of Montaigne's chapters and their subject matter. The (c)-text, after a reference to Plutarch's spontaneous and random manner, puts the ball firmly in the reader's court: "C'est l'indiligent lecteur qui pert mon subject, non pas moy; il s'en trouvera tousjours en un coing quelque mot qui ne laisse pas d'estre bastant, quoy qu'il soit serré [It is the inattentive reader who loses my subject, not I. Some word about it will always be found off in a corner, which will not fail to be sufficient, though it takes little room]." Thus the reader needs finesse in order to perceive hidden relations or allusions within the text, to bring out through his own activity the closely woven pattern which lies beneath the apparently random surface.

Subsequently, in another (c)-text, Montaigne claims that he dropped his earlier preference for short chapters because the reader's attention was thereby broken:

> En telle occupation, à qui on ne veut donner une seule heure, on ne veut rien donner. Et ne faict on rien pour celuy pour qui on ne faict qu'autre chose faisant. Joint qu'à l'adventure ay-je quelque obligation particuliere à ne dire qu'à demy, à dire confusément, à dire discordamment.
>
> [In such an occupation, if you will not give a man a single hour, you will not give him anything. And you do nothing for a man for whom you do nothing except while doing something else.

Besides, perhaps I have some personal obligation to speak only
by halves, to speak confusedly, to speak discordantly.]

One might be struck by the fact that, whereas Montaigne often affects to
read other books hastily and unsystematically, he expects the reader of his
own book to be unusually alert and persevering. There is no serious contradiction here. The dismissive gesture towards books is part of a more
general view of purely formal learning as pernicious; the venerable, monumental institution of literature must be broken down and adapted to the
individual's needs. Montaigne wants his reader to pay attention in order
to see that the *Essais* are not just another amalgam of *auctoritates*.

   This passage from "De la vanité" implies, then, that the *Essais* are ultimately coherent, even if their coherence has to be reconstructed by the
reader. In a rich (c)-passage from "Consideration sur Ciceron," the density
and discontinuity of the text are presented from a somewhat different
angle:

> Si suis je trompé, si guere d'autres donnent plus à prendre en la
> matiere; et, comment que ce soit, mal ou bien, si nul escrivain
> l'a semée ny guere plus materielle ny au moins plus drue en son
> papier. Pour en ranger advantage, je n'entasse que les testes.
> Que j'y attache leur suitte, je multiplieray plusieurs fois ce vo-
> lume. Et combien y ay-je espandu d'histoires qui ne disent mot,
> lesquelles qui voudra esplucher un peu ingenieusement, en pro-
> duira infinis *Essais*.

> [Yet I am much mistaken if many other writers offer more to
> take hold of in their material than I do, and, whether for better
> or for worse, if any writer has sown his materials more substan-
> tially or at least more thickly on his paper. I order to get more
> in, I pile up only the headings of subjects. Were I to add on
> their consequences, I would multiply this volume many times
> over. And how many stories have I spread around which say
> nothing of themselves, but from which anyone who troubles to
> pluck them with a little ingenuity will produce numberless es-
> says.

(1.40)

This striking image of the almost infinite extensibility of the *Essais* in the
reader's hands is closely bound up with the function of Montaigne's *exempla,* quotations and citations, as the continuation makes clear:

> Ny elles, ny mes allegations ne servent pas tousjours simplement d'exemple, d'authorité ou d'ornement. Je ne les regarde pas seulement par l'usage que j'en tire. Elles portent souvent, hors de mon propos, la semence d'une matiere plus riche et plus hardie.
>
> [Neither these stories nor my quotations serve always simply for example, authority, or ornament. I do not esteem them solely for the use I derive from them. They often bear, outside of my subject, the seeds of a richer and bolder material.]

The "borrowed" elements, then, instead of referring back to an authoritative corpus, become the seedbed of new and unforeseen meanings to be generated by the reader himself. Likewise, the discontinuous, densely packed fragments of Montaigne's own text as a whole—which of course includes all the *exempla* and quotations—signal, as it were, not to one another but to other invisible texts and contexts in the reader's mind.

We thus come to the point at which the *Essais* move beyond the writer's control: the image of the self-portrait now begins to dissolve, since the perfect reader is the one who, in following the traces of the self-portrait and understanding their function, learns that whatever of value he is to gain from the text must be organized in terms of his own experience, not Montaigne's. The sceptical argument of the "Apologie," it will be recalled, proposes that meaning is the product of the reader's subjective awareness rather than an essence residing in the text. In "De l'experience," the point is more moderately, but still very strikingly, put in the formulation "La parole est moitié à celuy qui parle, moitié à celuy qui l'escoute [Speech belongs half to the one who speaks, half to the one who listens]" (3.13[b]). Whether expressed in terms of a dialogue or of an extension or regeneration of meaning, this theme is one which allows for a dynamic and expansive conception of the act of reading. The text remains perpetually an open question; the reader embarks on an endless quest.

The writer's intermediary rôle between his readings and his readers is powerfully embodied in a reworking, in the "Apologie," of the commonplace image of the bear which licks its young into shape:

> Les sciences et les arts ne se jettent pas en moule, ains se forment et figurent peu à peu en les maniant et pollissant à plusieurs fois, comme les ours façonnent leurs petits en les lechant à loisir: ce que ma force ne peut descouvrir, je ne laisse pas de le sonder et essayer; et, en retastant et pétrissant cette nouvelle matiere, la remuant et l'eschaufant, j'ouvre à celuy qui me suit

quelque facilité pour en jouir plus à son ayse, et la luy rends plus souple et plus maniable.

[The sciences and arts are not cast in a mold, but are formed and shaped little by little, by repeated handling and polishing, as the bears lick their cubs into shape at leisure. I do not leave off sounding and testing what my powers cannot discover; and by handling again and kneading this new material, stirring it and heating it, I open up to whomever follows me some facility to enjoy it more at his ease, and make it more supple and manageable for him.]

(2.26)

The communication between writer and reader is part of a chain of metamorphoses; meaning passes along the chain as one text after another assembles itself, then disintegrates to be reassembled in a new form by a new generation.

The ideal paradigm of what one might call the transformational energy of the *Essais* is provided, appropriately and even necessarily, by a text other than Montaigne's: Pascal's reading of Montaigne. In a single-sentence *pensée*, Pascal writes: "Ce n'est pas dans Montaigne mais dans moi que je trouve tout ce que j'y vois [It is not in Montaigne but in myself that I find all that I see in it]" (Lafuma No. 689). His theme is one to which Montaigne himself frequently returns; his phrasing recalls Montaigne's "Ce n'est non plus selon Platon que selon moy, puis que luy et moi l'entendons et voyons de mesme [It is no more according to Plato than according to me, since he and I understand and see it the same way]." Likewise, Pascal is familiar with passages such as the one in "De l'art de conférer" where Montaigne distinguishes between bons mots which are simply borrowed and those that the user has fully grasped and can develop on his own account. Pascal reads Montaigne, and rewrites him, precisely on the subject of reading as appropriation: the sense moves on down the chain of texts, shifting as it moves. And when one looks at the broader perspective of Pascal's reading of the *Essais,* one discovers the very process of absorption and adaptation to quite different ends that the quasi-theoretical remarks would lead one to expect. Pascal is a very abrasive reader of Montaigne—hardly the sympathetic friend Montaigne hoped his text might conjure up. The self-portrait is torn to shreds, indeed reversed, in an argument which denies any content, let alone any value, to the self. The *Essais* take their place among other texts, other and quite different readings. Yet in the *Pensées,* they are transformed and rewritten according to a principle which they themselves advocate.

The topic of reading opens an avenue of approach to all of the central features of the *Essais:* their sources, themes, structure and style, their character as a self-portrait, their literary self-consciousness, as well as the question of the reader's image as projected by the text. One might even say that the intrinsic interest of Montaigne's book is more intimately bound up with the question of what reading is and how it is done than with any other. And if reading is, for Montaigne, always a stage to be transcended, we as readers are none the less incessantly drawn back to the *Essais* in an attempt to make visible the linking thread.

When regarded in a historical context, the fact that Montaigne should have reflected at such length and in such complex ways on the problems of reading is in itself of considerable importance. The gradual fragmentation and dissolution of the humanist ideal of an encyclopedia of knowledge based on classical literature and thought may be perceived at an advanced stage in the *Essais;* at the same time, questions of the utmost historical significance—the status of "authorities," the relationship between a text and its gloss, the capacity of a text for generating an indefinite range of meanings—reemerge in Montaigne's writing in a literary form which changes their character. The change, it may be argued, had been anticipated by Erasmus, Rabelais and others; the Renaissance love of dialogue, enigma, paradox, emblems and adages provides many of the threads which Montaigne wove into his *contexture.* But the fluidity of the *Essais,* their intrinsic capacity for revealing different aspects of a topic and suggesting far more than are revealed, goes beyond anything one finds in Montaigne's forerunners.

Likewise, the acute and many-sided view the *Essais* give of reading as a preeminently difficult activity (while yet not a metaphysically obscure one) would be hard to match from any work, ancient or modern. Perhaps only Pascal has in this respect ever taken Montaigne up at his own pitch. Modern theorists would no doubt have little difficulty in detecting inconsistencies and deficiencies in Montaigne's account: he does not, for example, fully face the problem of where, if texts can be reread and reinterpreted indefinitely, we draw the line between legitimate and illegitimate readings. How far is the original, intended sense recoverable, and if at all recoverable, how far does it determine the limits of what a text can mean? But, once again, Montaigne is not a theorist. What the *Essais* demand of the reader is not passive assent to a set of propositions or to a body of doctrine, but his active engagement: they define him by manipulating and provoking him, by preempting his rôle. It is in this sense that they invite nothing less than a reassessment of the whole activity of reading.

IRMA  S.  MAJER

# Montaigne's Cure:
# Stones and Roman Ruins

*Montaigne, le spirituel, le curieux Montaigne, voyageait en
Italie pour se guérir et se distraire vers 1580. Quelquefois, le
soir, il écrivait ce qu'il avait remarquait de singulier.*

[*Montaigne, the witty, the curious Montaigne, was traveling in
Italy to cure and entertain himself about 1580. Sometimes, at
night, he would write down what he had noticed that was
singular.*]

—STENDHAL, *Promenades dans Rome*

In 1580 Michel de Montaigne left his home and family to take a trip to
Italy and we do not know why. Montaigne never told us, not in the whole
of his voluminous and intimate *Essais,* nor in the few remaining letters of
his correspondence, nor even in the record of the trip, the *Journal de voyage en Italie par la Suisse et l'Allemagne.* Various explanations can be
gleaned from Montaigne's general remarks on travel in the *Essais,* namely
in "De la vanité" (bk. 3, chap. 9), but even so, the trip is one whose specific motives remain unexplained. So we are left to conjecture: Montaigne's
poor health and his desire to seek treatment at various spas; the unstable
state of affairs in France; a desire to leave the everyday cares and problems
of family and estate; an undying curiosity; the desire to experience the
new—all these seem to have had a hand in his decision to leave the château
de Montaigne.

From *MLN* 97, no. 4 (May 1982). © 1982 by the Johns Hopkins University Press,
Baltimore/London.

The circumstances of the voyage, the preparations for departure and the very motives of it are left open to scholarly investigation and informed speculation. For Montaigne's voyage is a curious one with no beginning; and this not only because he does not tell us specifically his reasons for leaving, but as well because the text of the *Journal de voyage* is one with no "first" page, or rather, no page one. The manuscript was not discovered until about 1770 by the abbot Prunis who had found the original to be missing the first two pages, wherein Montaigne perhaps made clear all that is now so puzzling to readers.

So neither the voyage nor the journal of it have a "real" or clear beginning, since there seem to have been many factors at play in determining Montaigne's decision to venture from the security of his château. It has been said as well that the voyage had no particular end either (or it had many); or similarly, that the sole reason for the voyage was the voyage itself: "Le but n'est rien, le voyage est tout [The goal is nothing, traveling is everything]." It follows, then, that if Montaigne's only goal was to travel, he had no goal; and therefore, there is as much of a mystery at the end as there is at the beginning. But I am inclined to agree with Albert Thibaudet, who muses that "le voyage pour le voyage n'est pas un but, c'est l'absence de but [traveling for traveling's sake is not a goal, it is the absence of a goal]." Besides implying that all goals, such as a cure or self-edification, bow to the simple pleasure of traveling about, a philosophy of travel for travel's sake suggests as well that Montaigne had no particular destination either, or one in name only, Rome. And Rome, as it turns out, is something more than just a name or just a destination. Rome is that ultimate goal which is both a geographic destination and a personal, philosophic goal.

Coming to Rome is not for Montaigne simply a voyage of twenty-nine weeks, the readying of pack horses and the bidding farewell to wife and child. It is for Montaigne the affair of a lifetime and for the sixteenth century it is a well-established cultural tradition. Coming to Rome is accomplished by years of formation and learning (a childhood of Latin studies, a library of classical texts). And, of course, by a voyage of months on the road and months of experiencing the *singulier*.

Montaigne's *récit*, or narrative, follows the charted line of the voyage, connecting, as does the physical movement from place to place, two, three or more points on a map. The written journey, the *Journal*, bears the marks of the physical trip and corresponds to a verbal cartographic description of the space traversed by Montaigne on his travels. The reference points of the journal correspond to the landmarks of the journey and the

cities are, in the case of both text and trip, connected by the distances traveled between them:

> Lorette, quinze milles . . .
>
> . . . . . . . . . . . . . . . . . .
>
> Ancona, quinze milles . . .

Meaning of course that Ancona is fifteen miles from Lorette and Lorette is
in turn fifteen miles from some other city, and so on. With the marking of
each new place there comes an indirect spatial reference to the place just
before on the "map," and so the *Journal* is constantly referring back to its
preceding pages to remind us that no city stands alone on this journey,
they are all part of the same itinerary. The sum of the odometric notations
is the actual distance traveled by Montaigne and the sum of the descriptions of the landmarks (what Montaigne calls *singularités*) is the sum of
Montaigne's experience.

This simple locational reference becomes more important, however,
when the cities—like Ancona, Loretta and Basle—begin to repeat one another and become virtually interchangeable. Montaigne's journal illustrates
what Italo Calvino's Marco Polo learned on his journey, that is, in "traveling, you realize that differences are lost: each city takes to resembling all
cities . . . *(Invisible Cities)* This resemblance between cities which makes
Montaigne's *Journal* so repetitive and so tedious at times is a result of the
singularities Montaigne records, which are always the same. Montaigne's
*Journal* is a catalog of, as says Stendhal, "ce qu'il avait remarqué de singulier [what he had noticed that was singular]." The *Journal* is the record of
the New and the Unusual encountered on the road from Bordeaux to
Rome and back again. The singularities Montaigne selects for description
are those same singularities recommended to his ideal student in the essay
"De l'institution des enfants": "Qu'on luy mette en fantasie une honeste
curiosité de s'enquerir de toutes choses; tout ce qu'il y aura de *singulier*
autour de luy, il le verra: un bastiment, une fontaine, un homme, le lieu
d'une bataille ancienne, le passage de Caesar ou de Charlemaigne [Put into
his head an honest curiosity to inquire into all things; whatever is unusual
[*singulier*] around him he will see: a building, a fountain, a man, the field
of an ancient battle, the place where Caesar or Charlemagne passed]"
(1.26; emphasis added).

Not only does Montaigne's itinerary consist of repetitious descriptions
of different singularities; not only do the cities, through the typology of
the *singulier,* becomes images of one another, but they are also variant images of the city which is central in the journey and the *Journal*, Rome.

Rome in its uniqueness seems to cover singly all the categories of the Singular met in the cities preceding and following it on Montaigne's circuit. In describing the places visited along his route to Rome, Montaigne describes places of singularity that are but multiple manifestations of this one city which lies beneath all cities, this one city which determines, defines and epitomizes Singularity. The emblems or signs of the Singular (which are the keys to the knowledge through experience to be gained by students of the world), each "bastiment ... fontaine ... lieu d'une bataille ancienne," translate an interest in Rome, preserve a latinism. The fountains of Schaffouse recall—or announce—the many fountains of Rome; the inscriptions collected from buildings and monuments repeat—or anticipate—those to be found among the vestiges of the half-buried Imperial City. What Montaigne considers to be singular enough to note in his journal are all those localized eruptions of Antiquity, those points of intersection between modern cities and ancient Rome. In light of this tendency of the description of singularities to collapse the récit into one description of Rome, the notation of distances traveled between cities, the marking of textual milestones, can be seen, not as a strategy of connection, but of separation. It is the means by which difference is established through distance in order to allow the point to point narration of the journey.

Traveling as Montaigne does, by way of singularities, necessitates traveling by way of detours. The *Journal de voyage* follows the general direction of the trip, moving first towards Rome and then doubling back, documenting the side trips made along the way (apparently annoying occurrences for Montaigne's travel companions who, according to Montaigne's secretary, would have preferred a more direct route). Hence, the journal, though following chronologically the progress of the trip, does not follow a straight line, but meanders and serpentines its way along from city to city. Montaigne the traveler and Montaigne the keeper of the *Journal* share the same motto: "je ne trace aucune ligne certaine [I trace no sure line]" (3.9). And indeed it is the writer who is at the mercy of the traveler's whim: "Il faut que j'aille de la plume comme des pieds" (2.9). Whither go his feet, so goes his pen; Montaigne writes as he travels, allowing for and creating detours, and following fancy and circumstance rather than a program. This is the case as well in the *Essais* where Montaigne's digressions are far from infrequent.

In the *Essais*, Montaigne questions by quoting Virgil his own practice of the detour: "Quo diversus abis?" (2.9), and offers an answer in the *Journal:* "Toutes choses sont einsin aisées à certeins biais, et inaccessibles par autres [All things are easy in this way from certain angles, and inaccessible from others]." And perhaps the best way to gain access to Rome is to make detours, to see all the singularities one possibly can.

Most of Montaigne's deviations from the direct path to Rome are just that, short side trips or excursions to see something as it became known to him. A few times he even returns to where he has been once before, seemingly contradicting his basic rule of travel mentioned in the *Journal:* "[ne pas] retumber sur mesme voie et revoir deus fois mesme lieu [[not] to fall back on the same road and see twice the same place]." In fact, Montaigne returns to see only what he missed the first time around; he retraces his steps only for the sake of something new. And since Montaigne's world is a book (1.26), he is wise to reread so as not to miss anything.

By far the longest detour made by Montaigne is that one made to return to Rome once he had started the return voyage to the château de Montaigne, and this detour which makes a loop in the circuit of the trip is a singular return to that city Montaigne had to see once more before returning to France. So right in the middle of Montaigne's journey stands a formidable pile of stones—Rome. Just what is Rome for Montaigne?

Besides marking the center of both the journey and the *Journal*, besides delaying—despite what he says about not wanting to see the same place twice—his return voyage to the château de Montaigne, and besides being the source and the epitome of Singularity, Rome is a city for its many citizens whose ranks Montaigne yearned to join. This community and communality of Rome are perhaps its greatest Singularity; not only singular, but eternal and universal as well, Rome is the city par excellence, the city of cities and every man's city: "c'est la plus commune ville du monde, et ou l'étrangeté et différance de nation se considere le moins; car de sa nature, c'est une ville rapieciée d'etrangiers; chacun y est comme chez soi [it is the most universal city in the world, a place where strangeness and differences of nationality are considered least; for by its nature it is a city pieced together out of foreigners; everyone is as if at home]." This universality, along with Montaigne's early training and his experiences on the journey, allowed him to feel at home there. He came to Rome a visitor and left a citizen.

Montaigne considered himself from childhood of Roman culture. He expressed a lifelong wish to make this tie with Rome legal as well as academic and so sought to become a citizen of the Eternal City with, for some time, little success: "Je recherchai pourtant et amploiai tous mes cinq sans de nature pour obtenir le titre de citoyen romain, ne fut-ce que pour l'an-

cien honur et religieuse mémoire de son authorité. J'y trouvai de la diffi-
culté [I therefore sought, and employed all my five natural senses, to obtain
the title of Roman citizen, were it only for the ancient honor and the religious memory of its authority. I found some difficulty in this]."

Montaigne is not speaking figuratively when he says he employed all
his five senses to obtain the long-desired citizenship. Montaigne exercised
these senses on the way to Rome and back on all the singularités encountered in order to know them and, in so doing, know all that is Roman by
nature, history, or structure; to become more versed in Rome's everyday
illustrations, rather than knowing it only through books. Montaigne now
looks not for that abstract, contemplative *science,* but for the knowledge
of the everyday, common Rome:

> Des choses qui sont en quelque partie grandes et admirables,
> j'en admire les parties mesmes communes. Je les visse volontiers
> diviser, promener, et soupper! Ce seroit ingratitude de mes-
> priser les reliques et images de tant d'honnestes hommes et si
> valeureux, que j'ay veu vivre et mourir, et qui nous donnent
> tant de bonnes instructions par leur exemple, si nous les sçavi-
> ons suivre.

> [Of things that are in some part great and admirable, I admire
> even the common parts. I would enjoy seeing them talk, walk,
> and sup! It would be ingratitude to despise the remains and im-
> ages of so many worthy and most valiant men, whom I have
> seen live and die, and who give us so many good instructions
> by their example, if we only knew how to follow them.]

(3.9)

The sight of Rome was as necessary to Montaigne as the study he had
made of it as a youth. He could never have known Rome completely, never
have so felt its spirit, had he not traveled there. The experience of Rome
as a real geographic place rather than as a literary and historical topos fulfills for Montaigne an emotional as well as an instructional need:

> L'estat de cette vieille Romme, libre, juste et florissante . . .
> m'interesse et me passionne. Parquoy je ne sçauroy revoir si
> souvent l'assiette de leurs rues et leurs maisons, et ces ruynes
> profondes jusqu'aux Antipodes, que je ne m'y amuse.

> [The state of that ancient Rome, free, just, and flourishing . . .
> interests me passionately. Therefore I cannot revisit so often the

site of their streets and houses and those ruins stretching deep
down to the Antipodes, that I do not muse over them.]

(3.9)

This sight of Rome conjures up the spirit of place:

> Est-ce par nature ou par erreur de fantasie que la veuë des
> places, que nous sçavons avoir esté hantées par personnes des-
> quelles la memoire est en recommendation, nous esmeut au-
> cunement plus qu'ouïr le récit de leurs faicts ou lire leurs es-
> crits?
>
> "Tanta vis admonitionis inest in locis. Et id quidem in hac
> urbe infinitum: quacunque enim ingredimur in aliquam histor-
> iam vestigium ponimus."
>
> [Is it by nature or by an error of the imagination that the sight
> of the places we know were frequented and inhabited by people
> whose memory is held in honor, somehow stirs us more than
> hearing the story of their deeds or reading their writings?
>
> "Such is the power of places to call up memories. And in this
> city this is infinite; for wherever we walk we set our foot on
> history."]

(3.9)

So Montaigne could have come to Rome no other way. Both his way
of traveling and the stuff of his experience, the *singulier,* were requisite for
his information as a true Roman and made him merit even more the cher-
ished title of citizen of Rome. It was an honor that he may have never received had he not personally made the trip to Rome, for he had sought it
many years without success. The essay "De la vanité," the whole of which
serves as a prelude to the decree of citizenship reproduced at the end, testifies to the importance of this event.

> Parmy ses [la Fortune] faveurs vaines, je n'en ay poinct qui
> plaise tant à cette niaise humeur [vanité] qui s'en paist chez
> moy, qu'une bulle authentique de bourgeoisie Romaine, qui me
> fut octroyée dernierement que j'y estois, pompeuse en seaux et
> lettres dorées, et octroyée avec toute gratieuse liberalité.
>
> [Among [Fortune's] empty favors there is none that so pleases
> that silly humor in me which feeds upon it, as an authentic bull
> of Roman citizenship, which was granted to me lately when I

was there, pompous in seals and gilt letters, and granted with
all gracious liberality.]

(3.9)

The document is then faithfully transcribed at the close of this same essay
and Montaigne follows with this comment: "N'estant bourgeois d'aucune
ville, je suis bien aise de l'estre de la plus noble qui fut et qui sera onques
[Being a citizen of no city, I am very pleased to be one of the noblest city
that ever was or ever will be]" (3.9). Montaigne in effect trades his "lyai-
son nationale à l'universelle et commune [national bond for the universal
and common one]" and demonstrates in this way, through his voyage, his
search for the *singulier* and his visits to Rome that he is, indeed, as says
the bull: "Romani nominis studioissimus"—"très zélé pour le nom romain
[most zealous for the Roman name]" (3.9).

Rome for Montaigne is decidedly dual in nature; simply, the ancient
Rome of the Empire and "modern" Rome of the Renaissance. That Rome
is of two layers is certainly not an idea unique to Montaigne for one can
find it in the works of other visitors to Rome; for example, in Du Bellay,
Chateaubriand and Freud who all shared Montaigne's passion for the Eternal City.

Montaigne's descriptive "map" of Rome in the *Journal* reflects the
doubled image of two Romes, combining the planes of the ancient and
modern cities, where ancient Rome serves as the structural base of the
modern city. Montaigne reads the physical relation of modern-ancient
Rome from bottom to top, following in his text the chronological order of
events, discussing first the ancient Rome which interests him passionately
and then the modern Rome above it.

Ancient Rome, or more precisely its sepulchre, serves as the hidden
infrastructure for the modern city we can see, hear and visit. According to
Montaigne, ancient Rome was destroyed and the very idea of it was sup-
pressed and repressed by the modern world out of fear. The city itself was
buried and even its tomb, the monument to its life, was not spared inter-
ment. Doubly hidden then beneath layers of rubble, ancient Rome was
purposely disfigured; its very structure, plan and form altered to such a
degree that even an ancient Roman would not recognize it as his city.

Hidden, but not completely destroyed, some parts of the ancient
world show through and some even remain intact, though buried; for instance, a column found complete and standing in its usual vertical position, which is an indication of the strength of ancient Rome and that mod-

ern Rome had tried unsuccessfully to suppress. This column and the Roman ruins (though possibly the least grand of all of Roman antiquity in Montaigne's eyes) are, like the inscriptions, the remains of the old Roman road and, in short, all that is to Montaigne *singulier*, examples of instances when such traces of ancient Rome show through the modern veneer: "Encore retient-elle [Rome] au tombeau des marques et image d'empire [Even in the tomb [Rome] retains some marks and the picture of empire]" (3.9).

The two Romes are much like a palimpsest gone bad, perhaps too old, but at any rate one on which the previous writing keeps showing through the new. So there are times and places where some of Roman antiquity finds a place in the light of Montaigne's day. These points of coincidence of the two worlds belong to both the present and the past; they are points of synchrony singled out as *rare, notable* or *singulier*. They are ruins, or inscriptions, or monuments, or buildings, and they occur not only in modern Rome, but in Florence, or Naples or Innsbruck as well.

Montaigne's historical topography of Rome reflects an apparently simple dichotomy of past and present; of antique and modern Rome. Montaigne's vision of Rome, however, is not a mere superposition of new on old, but a (re-)doubled image where the layers are bound together by certain moments of past-in-presence. Montaigne's map of Rome, like the whole of his journal-itinerary, is punctuated by these singular points of coincidence, by present repetitions of a past.

Now, I shall take a detour of my own through time to the voyages, real and psychoanalytic, of Freud who, coincidentally, is also wandering around Rome. His well-known passage on this city in *Civilization and Its Discontents* runs parallel to Montaigne's:

> Historians tell us that the oldest Rome was the *Roma Quadrata*. . . . Then followed the phase of the *Septimonium* . . . after that came the city bounded by the Servian wall; and later still . . . the city which the Emperor Aurelian surrounded with his walls. We will not follow the changes which the city went through any further, but we will ask ourselves how much a visitor, whom we will suppose to be equipped with the most complete historical and topographical knowledge, may still find left of these early stages in the Rome of today. Except for a few gaps, he will see the wall of Aurelian almost unchanged. In some places he will be able to find sections of the Servian wall where they have been excavated and brought to light. If he knows enough—more than present-day archeology does—he

may perhaps be able to trace out in the plan of the city the whole course of that wall and the outline of the *Roma Quadrata*. Of the buildings which once occupied the ancient area he will find nothing, or only scanty remains, for they exist no longer. . . . Their place is now taken by ruins, but not by ruins of themselves but of later restorations made after fires or destruction. It is hardly necessary to remark that all these remains of ancient Rome are found dovetailed into the jumble of a great metropolis which has grown up in the last few centuries since the Renaissance. There is certainly not a little that is ancient still buried in the soil of the city or beneath its modern buildings. This is the manner in which the past is preserved in historical sites like Rome.

Freud's Rome sounds, or looks, rather much like Montaigne's; were they to be drawn, the two maps might be nearly identical (perhaps something like the one Raphael was reported to have drawn). But Freud's Rome is not a simple repetition of an age-old idea common to Montaigne, Chateaubriand and others. Freud goes on to imagine a Rome which is Montaigne's *points de singularité* taken to a fantasmatic extreme:

Now let us, by a flight of imagination, suppose that Rome is not a human habitation but a psychical entity with a similarly long and copious past—an entity, that is to say, in which nothing that has once come into existence will have passed away and all the earlier phases of development continue to exist alongside the latest one. This would mean that in Rome the palaces of the Caesars and the Septimonium of Septimus Serverus would still be rising to their old height on the Palatine and that the castle of S. Angelo would still be carrying on its battlements the beautiful statues which graced it until the siege by the Goths, and so on. But more than this. In this place occupied by the Palazzo Caffarelli would once more stand—without the Palazzo having to be removed—the temple of Jupiter Capitonus; and this not only in its latest shape, as the Romans of the Empire saw it, but also in its earliest one, when it still showed Etruscan forms and was ornamented with terracotta antefixes. . . .

There is clearly no point in spinning our phantasy any further, for it leads to things that are unimaginable and even absurd. If we want to represent historical sequence in spatial terms we can only do it by juxtaposition in space: the same space cannot have two different contents.

The extreme to which Freud's imaginative theorizing takes us is beyond the palimpsest of Montaigne's vision to something much like a photograph of multiple exposures, where images are superimposed, yet distinct; where they coexist. It is at this extreme where his analogy breaks down under its own weight and becomes but "an idle game"; where he admits that a city is unsuitable for comparison to the mechanism of preservation of ideas, thoughts and images in the mind. The past of a city is not preserved intact. That is, it suffers from destruction, demolition, changes. Like the wall of Aurelian in Rome, every city has its gaps. But not the healthy mind, in which "all earlier stages [exist] alongside of the final form."

But perhaps Freud was too quick to cast aside his analogy, and perhaps thought should be given to reclaiming at least some of the comparison, for in the city, even with all the "destructive influences" of the passage of time, there are instances of the past being preserved alongside the present, the old and new forms coexisting. And these are, after all, the instances of interest to us and to Montaigne. The mind-city analogy offered by Freud allows us to approach Montaigne's Rome as a "psychical entity," or at least, as a "phantasy" much like Freud's own. Rome is a singularité and depends upon the traveler's desire to see, which is a function of "fantasie": "Qu'on luy mette en fantasie."

Says Calvino: "Cities, like dreams, are made of desires and fears, even if the thread of their discourse is secret." The thread of Rome's discourse is that thread which seams the two layers, that makes present for Montaigne and for Freud a buried past, a history. It is what allows Montaigne to see amid the ruins of the ancient city and the palaces of the new, a heritage that is, by adoption, his.

In writing his journal as a catalog of all the singularities he sees, Montaigne is writing a history of sorts of the place which is his destination. I understand history in its most common sense and more specifically, in the sense of the Greek *historia,* an inquiry or search. All along the way, Montaigne is on the lookout for what recalls and repeats Roman sights, Roman structures; he seeks an antiquity, a lost time, a classicism, the old in the new.

These monuments and inscriptions and ruins are not, however, the only stones passed along the way. The trip is made not only by a Montaigne in search of history but as well by a Montaigne in suffering, seeking a cure at various spas for his colicky illness and stones. Montaigne's stones cause him excrutiating pain, cause him to try the waters of many spas to rid himself of what blocks the flow of his waters. It is what determines to some extent the circuitous itinerary; it causes Montaigne to change direction and head for a new source of relief. His illness is of no small concern to him, the subject of a good many entries in the journal which at times reads like a medical chart describing the stones in detail: size, color, frequency and consistency. And a painful morning at the Bains della Villa ends finally one morning:

> Enfin, le 24 au matin, je poussai une pierre qui s'arrêta au passage. Je restai depuis ce moment jusqu'à dîner sans uriner, quoique j'en eusse grande envie. Alors je rendis ma pierre non sans douleur ni effusion de sang avant et apres l'éjection. Elle estoit de la grandeur et longueur d'une petite pomme ou noix de pin, mais grosse d'un côté comme une fève, et elle avoit exactement la forme du membre masculin. Ce fut un grand bonheur pour moi d'avoir pu la faire sortir.

> [On the 24th, in the morning, I pushed down a stone that stopped in the passage. I remained from that moment until dinnertime without urination, in order to increase my desire to do so. Then I got my stone out, not without pain and bleeding, both before and after: as big and long as a pine nut, but as thick as a bean at one end, and having to tell the truth, exactly the shape of a penis. It was a very fortunate thing for me to be able to get it out.]

The discomfort, the traveling to spas, the accounting of stones and sand and waters are not the only consequences of this affliction, for Montaigne's illness has affected his life in other ways: "O que n'ay je la faculté de ce songeur de Cicero qui, songeant embrasser une garse, trouva qu'il s'estoit deschargé de sa pierre emmy ses draps! Les miennes, me desgarsent estrangement! [Oh, why have I not the faculty of that dreamer in Cicero who, dreaming he was embracing a wench, found that he had discharged his stone in the sheets! Mine extraordinarily diswench me]" (2.37). Montaigne suffers the impossibility of intercourse, a drastic *coitus interruptus*.

Like the historical markers of the roadside, Montaigne's stones block a passage, not only of his urine, but of his semen as well. It might be wise to ask whether or not these stones, like those landmarks he passes on his trip, do not also carry some message. What is inscribed on Montaigne's stones? This is a question to be considered, by way of an excursus; for the moment, let it be recalled that where there is a blockage, there is often as well a repression.

Both dreams and cities are spun on the wheel of the unconscious. To see precisely what desires and fears are concealed in the rebus-city Rome, it is necessary to back up; to back up to Bordeaux, to the château de Montaigne, and to a place in this text where a brief allusion is made to Montaigne's family. For in Rome, several lines come together; Rome may indeed be the scene of a struggle having ultimately to do with self and identity. It seems, too, that the crumbled remains of Rome that block for Montaigne the path back to his château (la maison de son père), are also connected with a blockage of another sort.

As mentioned before, Montaigne's early life was imposed on him by his father, who instilled in him the love of another, or of an "other culture," in the sense Lionel Trilling has given the expression: "the ideal culture, the wonderful imagined culture of the ancient world no one but schoolboys, schoolmasters, scholars, and poets believed in (Lionel Trilling, "Freud: Within and Beyond Culture" in *Essays on Literature and Learning*). Montaigne is—if not by birth, at least by formation and in spirit—a Roman. And he is so, in a sense, before he is a Frenchman. Witness the following passage in his *Essais:*

> Or j'ay esté nourry dès mon enfance avec ceux icy [les Romains]; j'ay eu connoissance des affaires de Romme, long temps avant que je l'aye eue de ceux de ma maison: je sçavois le Capitole et son plant avant que je sceusse le Louvre, et le Tibre avant la Seine. J'ay eu plus en teste les conditions et fortunes de Lucullus, Metellus, et Scipion que je n'ay d'aucuns hommes des nostres.

> [Now, I have been brought up from childhood with these dead. I was familiar with the affairs of Rome long before I was with those of my own house. I knew the Capitol and its location before I knew the Louvre, and the Tiber before the Seine. I have had the abilities and fortunes of Lucullus, Metellus, and Scipio more in my head than those of our men.]

(3.9)

The ties he feels with Rome are so strong that he cannot align himself with the present:

> Cette accointance dure encore entre nous [entre Montaigne et les Romains]; les choses presentes mesmes, nous ne les tenons

que par la fantasie. Me trouvant inutile à ce siècle, je me rejecte
à cet autre, et en suis si embabouyné que l'estat de cette vieille
Romme, libre, juste et florissante (car je n'en ayme ny la nais-
sance, ny la vieillesse) m'interesse et me passionne.

[This friendship still endures between us [Montaigne and the
Romans]; even present things we hold only by imagination.
Finding myself useless for this age, I throw myself back upon
that other, and am so bewitched by it that the state of that ancient Rome, free, just and flourishing (for I love neither her
birth nor her old age), interests me passionately.]

(3.9)

Montaigne's infancy, that period before language acquisition (*infans:*
which does not speak) was marked by two telling separations: from his
mother tongue, because according to his father's wish, Latin was substituted for French; and from his mother's breast (and consequently the culture that comes to us from "mother's milk"), since he spent his infancy
with a wet nurse. These two initial replacements of the mother seem to
have resulted in a permanent displacement, and Montaigne's mother
makes virtually no appearance in the whole of his *Essais*.

It is not without interest that the part of Montaigne's body that suffers most from the sickness is his penis and that the stones themselves
sometimes resemble the inflicted member. Montaigne's colic easily brings
up questions and problems of procreation and heredity, since Montaigne's
sexual activity is negatively affected and because Montaigne's illness is a
repetition of one fatal to his father:

Il est à croire que je dois à mon père cette qualité pierreuse, car
il mourut merveilleusement affligé d'une grosse pierre qu'il
avoit en la vessie; il ne s'apperceut de son mal que le soixante-
septiesme an de son aage, et avant cela il n'en avoit eu aucune
menasse ou ressentiment aux reins, aux costez, n'y ailleurs; et
dura encores sept ans en ce mal, trainant une fin de vie bien
douloureuse.

[It is probable that I owe this stony propensity to my father, for
he died extraordinarily afflicted with a large stone he had in his
bladder. He did not perceive his disease until his sixty-seventh
year, and before that he had had no threat or symptom of it, in
his loins, his sides, or elsewhere . . . and he lasted seven years

more with this ailment, painfully dragging out the last years of
his life.]

(2.27)

Montaigne's stones are a memorial or testi(s)monial to his father. So
if they are inscribed at all it is with none but the *nom du père,* as well as
the prohibitive *non du père,* forbidding, in this case, sex. If this is so, the
father, then, is the agent of this illness symbolic of castration.

Now, Montaigne travels to Rome, the Spa of spas, in order to rid
himself of a painful biological heritage, his stones. But could his trip to this
city, so bound up with personal relationships, be the search for a cure of
a different sort? It is bound with his father because only through the trip
can he legitimize the cultural heritage and identity his father imposed on
him. At the same time, it could be a voyage in search of a substitute for
that person who is so conspicuously absent from Montaigne's life and
works, his mother. Rome, dubbed by Erasmus the "Mother City," is the
place of Montaigne's "second" birth. And, for someone like Freud, the
meaning is clear: "It may be added that for a man who is impotent (that is,
who is inhibited by the threat of castration) the substitute for copulation is
a phantasy of returning into his mother's womb" ("Inhibitions, Symptoms
and Anxiety").

The trauma of separations from the mother and the mother tongue; a
part of the body injured by the father; the anxiety of impotence; the attempt at flight from the father's house, only to return and take the father's
place; the flight which is repression. . . . Rome and the *Journal* are structured by detours and a fantasy. A trip to the Mother City; the confirmation of an adopted birthright—is this not a fantasy about origins?

Montaigne, in his trip to a fantasmatic Rome, seems to "comble[r] . . .
les lacunes de la vérité individuelle [to fill in . . . the lacunae of individual
truth]" (Freud, "The Paths to the Formation of Symptoms," in *The General Theory of the Neuroses*). Rome can be likened perhaps to the "censored chapter" that is for Lacan the unconscious. It is a chapter long denied that can nevertheless be read elsewhere, reconstructed through its
scattered fragments:

> L'inconscient est ce chapitre de mon histoire qui est marqué par
> un blanc ou occupé par un mensonge; c'est le chapitre censuré.
> Mais la vérité peut être retrouvée; le plus souvent déjà elle est
> écrite ailleurs: à savoir:
>     —dans les monuments: et ceci est mon corps . . .

—dans les documents d'archives aussi: et ce sont les souve-
nirs de mon enfance . . .
—dans les traditions aussi, voire dans les légendes qui sous
une forme héroïsée véhiculent mon histoire;
—dans l'évolution sémantique: et ceci répond au stock et aux
acceptions du vocabulaire qui m'est particulier, comme au
style de ma vie et à mon caractère;
—dans les traces, enfin, qu'en conservant inévitablement les
distorsions, nécessités par le raccord du chapitre adultéré
dans les chapitres qui l'encadrent, et dont un exégèse ré-
tablira le sens.

[The unconscious is that chapter of my history that is marked
by a blank or occupied by a falsehood: it is the censored chapter. But the truth can be rediscovered; usually it has already
been written down elsewhere. Namely:
—in monuments: this is my body . . .
—in archival documents: these are my childhood memories . . .
—in semantic evolution: this corresponds to the stock of
words and acceptations of my own particular vocabulary,
as it does to my style of life and to my character;
—and, lastly, in the traces that are inevitably preserved by the
distortions necessitated by the linking of the adulterated
chapter to the chapters surrounding it, and whose meaning
will be reestablished by my exegesis.]

To read the story of Montaigne's *singulier* and Montaigne's Rome is
to read the marks of the unconscious, to read its missing chapter written
elsewhere: in stones of monuments and of the body, in documents which
are the memories of childhood, in words and in the traces left by seams.
The unconscious and the study of its discourse, and the study of the discourse of cities, are both the stories of a *non-écrit,* of an adulterated chapter; or perhaps, of a chapter of adultery, an infidel blank.

Montaigne's journey has less to do with the topography of real and
historical places than with images formed in history and the unconscious.
Montaigne's paradigm of the Singular, Rome, is like its many manifestations a flight of fantasy. It is a fiction (*fictio,* to create, to make). Rome,
however, is not fashioned out of thin air as an unreal tale might be, but
rather, takes shape—"par erreur de fantasie"—in specific contexts, both
cultural and personal. It is a construct of the mind.

Montaigne discovers in Rome the traces of buried pasts: that of a city and a culture, and that of a man with no city and no culture. He comes, by way of traveling, to write the story that was written, not in the *Essais,* but in the singularities of Rome. The censored *moi* who could not speak in the *Essais* finds his voice in Rome, and speaks the language of the unconscious in his discourse of the *singulier.* Now, despite their loss, the missing pages of the *Journal* can be read.

Montaigne has filled in the gaps of his own history. Only this allows him to return to the château de Montaigne and his family, and to Bordeaux to take up the post of Mayor. Only this route allows him to take up where his father left off and to identify with him. Montaigne's *Journal* of Singularities and his "fantasy" of Rome are meant, like the dream of Cicero's *songeur,* to expel the stone.

CATHERINE   DEMURE

# The Paradox and the Miracle:
## Structure and Meaning in
## "The Apology for Raymond Sebond"
## (Essais 2.12)

From this essay to the *Essays,* there is neither any shortcut possible nor
any implication from a principle to a consequence: the refusal of an organizing system in this fundamentally open work makes the circle which goes
from the whole to its parts interminable. But doubtless it is not unimportant, nor without implications for the reading of the entire work, to be
able to show, throughout a text as considerable as the "Apology," the coherence of a system of thought which is the rigorous expression of the possibilities and limits of the philosophical enterprise at the dawn of modern
times.

The goal of this study is to bring to light the structure of one chapter
of the *Essays,* the "Apology for Raymond Sebond," whose importance the
most divergent readings acknowledge in spite of the conflict of interpretations. We know that Villey sees in the "Apology" the high point of a
"skeptical crisis" which Montaigne was then to transcend and repudiate;
as for Brunschvicg, he uses the "Apology" as a constant, central reference
point for his reading of the *Essays,* but he blurs its tension in order to demonstrate the powers of balance and happiness of a moral subject on the far
side of skepticism. We have been obliged to recall these conclusions before
proposing a structural reading of the "Apology," that is, very simply, a
reading which bases meaning on the formal organization of the text in its
literalness and integrality.

We shall show, thus, counter to a "humanist" or moderate reading,
that the coherence of Montaigne's thought appears here in the rigor of a
maintained contradiction: the model of this paradox, which makes up the

From *Yale French Studies* 64 (1983). © 1983 by Yale University.

very heart of the text, is constituted by the status of theology, a knowledge which is both necessary and impossible.

But inversely, against an "antihumanist" reading such as Jean-Yves Pouilloux's, we affirm the existence of an "ideological content": in dealing with knowledge and action, Montaigne affirms both the distinction and contradiction of the two orders, and, with a dual fidelity to Christianity and Socrates, asserts that true knowledge is awareness of ignorance: a goal to regain, where all the possibilities of philosophical endeavor are inscribed.

## I. IN ORDER TO READ,
## ONE MUST READ EVERYTHING

We know that, following his presentation of the "Apology," Villey proposes an outline of it. Without going into detail, we can note from the start that the opening of the text is excluded from the outline, which Villey thereby relegates to the inessential; now, this opening is a rapid presentation of Montaigne's relationship to knowledge and of the conditions of his access to Sebond's text. Speaking in it of knowledge in general, of "letters," Montaigne indeed writes here: (a) "Moy, je les ayme bien, mais je ne les adore pas [Myself, I like them well enough, but I do not worship them]."

Even if we reserve an understanding of this text, it is clear that it has a slightly different ring from certain affirmations of a total, definitive rejection of knowledge which the ulterior text will present. But Villey also presents the end of the text as a mere prolongation, without connecting it in any way with the context; as for Pouilloux, he says nothing about this ending. Is it innocuous, then, or repetitive? Not at all: what is involved is a quotation from Seneca which is difficult and paradoxal in itself: (a) "O la vile chose, dit-il, et abjecte, que l'homme, s'il ne s'esleve au dessus de l'humanité! ['O what a vile and abject thing is man' he says, 'if he does not raise himself above humanity!']" and which Montaigne's commentary takes up again—especially strengthening its paradoxical, even contradictory, aspect—in two additions dating from the (c)-manuscript; the two moments of this commentary are in fact the following: the first moment: (c) "Voylá un bon mot, et un utile desir, mais pareillement absurde [That is a good statement and a useful desire, but equally absurd]"; and the second moment—and this sentence definitively closes the text of the "Apology": (c) "C'est à nostre foy Chrestienne, non à sa vertu Stoique, de pretendre à cette divine et miraculeuse metamorphose [It is for our Christian faith, not for his Stoical virtue, to aspire to that divine and miraculous metamorphosis]." Here again, this difficult text—a real appeal to understanding and a quite manifest return to the problematics of the "Apology" as to the true place of man and his powers in the world—cannot be evaded.

Without anticipating the ulterior reading of the text, we can then already affirm that these two texts, the opening and closing of the "Apology," must be understood within and through the context, which will doubtless be illuminated by them in its turn. Limits of a very long text which they enclose, these passages may find in it their meaning, or perhaps a confirmation of their meaning by reflection. One must affirm, then, the absolute necessity of first respecting the external form of the text, which really begins with this opening and which really ends with this conclusion. *In short, in order to read, one must read everything.* No matter what the "situation" of a text which it claims to reveal and activate, no rigorous reading can abandon what constitutes the material boundaries of that text.

This methodological requirement, moreover, is not based only on these criteria of the exhaustiveness of the reading. Every partial reading reaches a second stopping point when it encounters a new difficulty, in this case one so obvious that it is all but forgotten in the most precise readings, and this difficulty will also lead us to problems of meaning.

## II. WHY THIS SUBJECT:
### "THE APOLOGY FOR RAYMOND SEBOND"?

We know that Pouilloux shows, rightly, that for Montaigne there is "an intellectual, philosophical innovation which makes all subjects possible for him." Granted, all subjects are possible for him, but: the longest *Essay* on a text which Montaigne literally destroys! On a text about which he says (a strange compliment for a theological work) that he finds "belles les imaginations [the ideas of this author fine]" and that "beaucoup de gens s'amusent à le lire, et notamment les dames [many people are busy reading it, and especially the ladies]"; on a text which he judges doubly vain, first because no theology is possible for man—a sufficient argument in itself!—and secondly because reason is particularly unsuitable for this task (which is impossible, besides . . .). There is, at the very least, a problem here: why then does Montaigne devote such a long discourse to this work which he could sufficiently refute in a few lines? In other words, *why* "The Apology for Raymond Sebond"? How can we not see an anomaly, an incoherence, in taking as the object of his reflection a text of which Montaigne will show only the weaknesses, when we know that, no matter how critical, even subversive, his thought may be, it is never polemical?

It seems that on one level, however, this contradiction may be, if not completely removed, at least made comprehensible by its presuppositions. First of all, Montaigne tells us, the text is dear to him because he translated it and worked on it, which confers upon it at least a subjective importance, especially since this work was undertaken for Montaigne's father, and at his request:

> Or, quelques jours avant sa mort, mon pere, ayant de fortune rencontré ce livre soubs un tas d'autres papiers abandonnez, me commanda de le luy mettre en François.

> (Now some days before his death, my father, having by chance come across this book under a pile of other abandoned papers, commanded me to put it into French for him.)

This father had died several years before (in 1568), and Montaigne loved him. This is what permits us to understand his choice of Sebond's text among other theological essays. But there is more. In this era of conflicts and religious wars (and we know how overwhelmed Montaigne was to learn of their atrocity, and that this atrocity appealed on both sides to evangelical truth), and even though in other respects Montaigne believes theology to be impossible and dangerous, he still thinks that after the "nouvelletez de Luther (innovations of Luther)" Sebond's text could reasonably appear capable of combatting "un execrable atheisme (an execrable atheism)" which the "maladie (malady)" of free examination "aysément (easily)" risked bringing about.

But if Montaigne's choice of Sebond's text becomes comprehensible in this way, the essence of the difficulty remains, since the text, dear to Montaigne's heart and possibly useful on the religious and social plane, will nevertheless be totally ruined by him. But this is because we had only seen a superficial difficulty, so to speak historical, which masked a *contradiction that will dominate the whole text, to which we shall have to refer the text in its entirety.*

This dominant contradiction is announced and confirmed by the opening and closing texts of the "Apology," whose importance we have already emphasized. Radical and definitive, it is presented in the sixth paragraph of the "Apology" when Montaigne takes up an examination of the theological project.

What does Montaigne affirm in fact? First of all (and this thesis will be abundantly developed in the continuation of the text, notably at the criticism of anthropomorphic conceptions of God) *the radical impossibility of all theology;* it is a knowledge which is absolutely out of our power and grasp:

Toutefois je juge ainsi, qu'à une chose si divine et si hautaine, et surpassant de si loing l'humaine intelligence, comme est cette verité de laquelle il a pleu à la bonté de Dieu nous esclairer, il est bien besoin qu'il nous preste encore son secours, d'une faveur extraordinaire et privilegée, pour la pouvoir concevoir et loger en nous; et ne croy pas que les moyens purement humains en soyent aucunement capables.

(However, I think thus, that in a thing so divine and so lofty, and so far surpassing human intelligence, as is this truth with which it has pleased the goodness of god to enlighten us, it is very necessary that he still lend us his help, by extraordinary and privileged favor, so that we may conceive it and lodge it in us. And I do not think that purely human means are at all capable of this.)

Human intelligence, therefore, cannot gain access to God or theology; only faith in the revealed word enables us to attain the mysteries of religion, but not to understand them, or perhaps even to express them. And this determining thesis will weigh on the whole text. Montaigne will conclude his account of philosophical contradictions concerning the soul's immortality with these words: "Confessons ingenuement que Dieu seul nous l'a dict, et la foy: car leçon n'est ce pas de nature et de nostre raison [Let us confess frankly that God alone has told us so, and faith; for a lesson of nature and of our reason it is not]," words which he had founded earlier with the affirmation that "c'est à Dieu seul de se cognoistre et d'interpreter ses ouvrages [it is for God alone to know himself and to interpret his works]."

Why then doesn't Montaigne stop there, why this detour through Sebond's theology, through the conflict of philosophical and religious beliefs? Why, if only to demonstrate its inanity, pursue at such length the road of theology? Because this impossible knowledge is nevertheless necessary to man; it is even the highest, most valorized human enterprise; so that *after* having posited the impossibility of theology, Montaigne affirms that

[c'est] une tresbelle et tresloüable entreprinse d'accommoder encore au service de nostre foy les utils naturels et humains que Dieu nous a donnez. Il ne faut pas douter que ce ne soit l'usage le plus honorable que nous leur sçaurions donner.

(it is . . . a very fine and very laudable enterprise to accommodate also to the service of our faith the natural and human tools that God has given us. There can be no doubt that this is the most honorable use that we could put them to.)

Therefore we see Montaigne conclude the paragraph in this way, by legitimating the attempt at thought about the divine which must "accompaigner nostre foy [accompany our faith]" even though he knows that "ny . . . nos efforts et arguments puissent atteindre à une si supernaturelle et divine science [our efforts and arguments can[not] attain a knowledge so supernatural and divine]."

In such a way is this fundamental contradiction stated. It refers to a paradox of which neither term will be removed or modified. The whole development of the "Apology," as it has often and truly been said, aims at ruining any claim to establish certain knowledge; the senses and reason, experience and discourse (discours), are deceptive, and human privilege doubtful. Like any other realm of knowledge and more than any other, theological knowledge is impossible. What has been seen less often is the situation of this apology for skepticism in a paradoxical problematics: even if it is impossible, knowledge about God is still necessary. The whole "Apology" testifies relentlessly to the vanity of human knowledge, but *we shall only be able to understand this "apogee of skepticism" by enclosing it within the paradox which governs the whole text and which alone permits it to function.*

This schema of a paradoxical thought is close to the one which Lucien Goldmann presented as constitutive of Pascal's philosophy in *Les Pensées* and which he related to the notion of "tragic vision" borrowed from the young Lukács. The proximity of Montaigne's and Pascal's approaches and the difference between them thus become the instrument of a vaster theological enterprise seeking to reveal, before and after the emergence of the Cartesian system, the meaning of this contestation of a rationalist vision of man and the world.

### III. STRUCTURE AND MEANING IN "THE APOLOGY FOR RAYMOND SEBOND"

#### 1. The "Apology" Fits into a Criticism of Learning: More Restricted Than Limited

Montaigne's reflection begins with an affirmation of principles whose bearing could be vague or could betray an inconsequential "skepticism" were it not for the context and argumentation which support it:

> C'est à la verité, une tres-utile et grande partie que la science, ceux qui la mesprisent, tesmoignent assez leur bestise; mais je n'estime pas pourtant sa valeur jusque à cette mesure extreme qu'aucuns luy attribuent, comme Herillus le philosophe, qui logeoit en elle le souverain bien, et tenoit qu'il fut en elle de nous rendre sages et contens.

> (In truth, knowledge is a great and very useful quality; those who despise it give evidence enough of their stupidity. But yet I do not set its value at that extreme measure that some attribute to it, like Herillus the philosopher, who placed in it the sovereign good, and held that it was in its power to make us wise and content.)

Such are the first lines of this essay which situate us, it seems, in that moderation, that equilibrium to which it would be Montaigne's mission to bear witness. Will he not reinforce his moderate and somewhat distant attitude towards "letters," which are the very body of all knowledge, by writing at the end of this same paragraph: "Moy, je les ayme bien, mais je ne les adore pas [Myself, I like them well enough, but I do not worship them]"? But do we understand the text correctly? It is a question here of nuances, of moderation, of equilibrium? Can one accept a flat, anodyne reading of these lines of exordium when they lead to one of their author's most important essays?

Let us go back. And first of all, in order to point out the unexpectedness of this praise of knowledge on the threshhold of one of Montaigne's most violently skeptical texts; what is written (l'écrit) remains, as well as the totality of the text. Being ignorant of knowledge is "bestise (stupidity)"; loving philosophy and knowledge, on the contrary, goes without saying; to be unaware of them is to deprive oneself of thought itself. *No matter what the limits of factual knowledge, they are contested by a movement of thought which is a philosophy and a search for a possible learning.* It is the manifest character of the statement—Montaigne being the intellectual that he is—and not any scorn or irony on his part, which makes it so brief and so little argued here: the "will to know (le vouloir-savoir)" is legitimate if not in its results, at least in its intention to learn and to organize learning into a body of knowledge. Thus when the text turns back upon itself and Montaigne refuses to take this love of knowledge to the "extreme," it is not in order to exhibit a skeptical argumentation on the impotence of reason or the opacity of reality. If he refuses the type of life which will be Descartes's, the one which the true moral maxim of the *Discours de la Méthode* expresses: "to spend my whole life in cultivating my reason, and to advance as much as I can in the knowledge of truth," it is not at all that he "moderates" adoration into simple affection; the difference is not quantitative, but qualitative. To love the sciences rather than to worship them, no matter how great the effort which leads Montaigne toward intellectual reflection, is not to be moderate but divided. The postulate which underlies Montaigne's reticences here is neither methodological nor skeptical: it refers to the irreducible difference of orders. What Montaigne refuses is adoration owed to God, to the signifying totality of the world; and he is gently ironical toward his father, infatuated with learned personages;

> recueillant leurs sentences et leurs discours comme des oracles, et avec d'autant plus de reverence et de religion qu'il avoit moins de loy d'en juger, car il n'avoit aucune connoissance des lettres.
>
> (collecting their savings and discourses like oracles, and with all the more reverence and religion as he was less qualified to judge them; for he had no knowledge of letters.)

More versed than him in letters and intellectual life, Montaigne does not ask for moderation, but the distinction of genres: life cannot be inscribed in a single register which would be that of knowledge. Science—no matter what its scope, rigor, and possibilities are in other respects—cannot "nous rendre sages et contens [make us wise and content]"; he does not believe, he says, "ny ce que d'autres ont dict, que la science est mere de toute vertu, et que tout vice est produit par l'ignorance [what others have said, that knowledge is the mother of all virtue, and that all vice is produced by ignorance]."

Such is the postulate of Montaigne, who refutes what one may call the search for a theoretical confirmation, an epistemological legitimation of action. Happiness and virtue remain real finalities of human life, different from knowledge. This postulate is clear, and its understated formulation should not deceive us: its position preliminary to the whole development of the chapter marks a refusal of rationalism—if one means by the word, in its Cartesian sense, not the belief in a possible and necessary usage of rigorous reason, but the affirmation of the homogeneity of the world as knowable reality, and hence, the homogeneity of learning (*connaissance*) itself, completely identified with knowledge (*savoir*), whose model is mathematical science.

Thus for Montaigne, beyond any skeptical argumentation, including

the one which he himself will develop in the "Apology," the first insufficiency of all knowledge is that it is *only* knowledge, and for this reason
never concerns us entirely as such. For the rupture between orders is first
of all a rupture in me; I am a being of mobility and conflict, diverse in the
long run *(durée)* as well as during the moment, and a being whose unity
is always in question; so much so that in the first chapter of the second
book, Montaigne writes:

> Cette variation et contradiction qui se void en nous, si souple,
> a faict qu'aucuns nous songent deux ames . . . une si brusque
> diversité ne se pouvant bien assortir à un subjet simple.

> (These supple variations and contradictions that are seen in us
> have made some imagine that we have two souls . . . for such
> sudden diversity cannot well be reconciled with a simple sub
> ject.)

Montaigne discovers this shattered subject in himself, such that

> je n'ay rien à dire de moy, entierement, simplement, et solide
> ment, sans confusion et sans meslange, ny en un mot. DIS
> TINGO est le plus universel membre de ma Logique.

> (I have nothing to say about myself absolutely, simply, and sol
> idly, without confusion and without mixture, or in one word.
> *Distinguo* is the most universal member of my logic.)

This is why learning *(connaissance)* is not knowledge *(savoir)* here, but
first of all description, "recitation"; and it is because I am—like the
world—a "branloire perenne [perennial movement]" (bk. 3, chap. 2); that
"je ne puis asseurer mon object [I cannot keep my subject still]." Located
here is the origin, in Montaigne, of resistance to (rather than refusal of)
the rationalist hypothesis: for the truth can be contradictory: "Tant y a
que je me contredits bien à l'adventure, mais la verité . . . je ne la contredy
point [So, all in all, I may indeed contradict myself now and then; but
truth . . . I do not contradict]."

  One sees where this modest introductory paragraph leads us and what
a permanent counterpoint it will bring to bear on the whole ulterior argumentation of the text; under no circumstances can the skeptical argumentation of the "Apology" be considered the sole foundation of Montaigne's
criticism of knowledge. The refusal to worship letters, the (real) distance
with regard to organized knowledge, are not primarily skeptical attitudes
putting the quality of knowledge into question, but the expression of a
mistrust whose foundation is *practical;* wisdom and happiness are of a dif-

ferent order, which nothing permits me to reduce or subordinate to that of knowledge. If it is conceivable, such a dependence is at least "subject à une longue interpretation [subject to a long interpretation]." Montaigne, for his part, does not believe in it, and the skeptical argumentation will have to be reread in this perspective, which allows us to save the interest of the text beyond that of a rather superficial criticism of organized knowledge which one century would render obsolete. Pascal's thought will also violently express this mistrust and this affirmation of the heterogeneity of orders without the slightest intrusion of skepticism. Copernicus, Galileo, Descartes will produce a new, rigorous knowledge; but this triumphant reason will stir up in Pascal (who is, however, a beneficiary of its rise) a protestation all the more forceful in that it is more divided: he goes so far as to write against Descartes: "And even if that were true, we do not consider all philosophy to be worth one hour of pain."

This introduction allows us then to affirm that the criticism of knowledge in Montaigne cannot be reduced to mere skepticism: the plurality of human finalities and the impossibility of reducing the subject to unity are here, explicit or implicitly, the point of departure of the reflection. And this contradiction prepares and grounds the paradoxical structure of the text: it is a divided subject, perhaps even rife with conflict, which touches upon his entire relationship to knowledge in general, and to theology in particular. This major contradiction organizes the argumentation of the whole ulterior development; it will establish the coherence of a thought which is necessarily in conflict with all unifying dogmatisms. Skeptical argumentation properly speaking—multiform and uneven, besides—is thus only second in relation to this first, irremediable break of which the subject is the bearer.

## 2. Theology, Exemplary Knowledge

Thus we can understand the strange series of reversals which Montaigne effects in his evaluation of the theological enterprise, which is the knowledge under consideration here. Montaigne's whole art here consists in encountering theology through personal paths, thereby merging reflection on an essential knowledge with his own story—which seems to be the inessential, the anecdotal, or even the insignificant.

For therein, first of all, lies the privilege of theology in relation to Montaigne's project: history confronted him and his father, like all men of their time, and much more than others, with religious problems. Faced with the reality of contrary arguments, and with the reality of actions which take their inspiration from these arguments or which claim to, theology becomes a personal matter for Montaigne. By choosing Sebond's theological work as the theme of a text as long and important as the "Apology," Montaigne chooses first of all, in accordance with his philosophical project, to speak himself *(de se dire lui-même)*, a theme which is doubly his, both through his personal history and through History itself. No matter what the difficulties or the impossibility for me to invest myself totally in an enterprise of knowledge, I feel myself (me, Montaigne, a Christian, a Catholic and a politically responsible figure) entirely concerned by a problem to which, beyond the properly intellectual interest which it can inspire, the necessities of action and the attempt to live happily lead me back incessantly, and often tragically. The first privilege of theology resides then in the fact that this "knowledge" is, in the sixteenth century, like the locus where all the possibilities of action and happiness converge—or from which they arise. And even though this is not the place to speak of "Montaigne's religion," let us simply remember that the historical reality of the religious wars, the strange metamorphoses of the legitimacy throughout the relationships between the royalty and the Catholic and Protestant religions, only serve to dramatize the fundamental importance of the religious question for the whole sixteenth century, and force us—us, belated readers—to take this question into consideration as a constant horizon of this century, as Lucien Febvre has admirably shown in *Le Problème de l'incroyance au XVIᵉ siècle.*

But theology is privileged in another way—theology which causes Montaigne to choose it as the model of knowledge for and against which he will argue. This privileged status is not made any more explicit than the preceding one and, unlike the other, is not even alluded to. We feel it necessary, however, to bring it to light because it allows us, among other things, to perpetuate a contemporary reading of this text of Montaigne, and not just a historical one.

What is theology for Montaigne, at least the one he discusses, and which he judges here in order to illustrate, let us not forget, a reflection on knowledge? It is a work of reason, entirely separate from the revelation and faith which certainly ground it, give rise to it, and control it, but which never mingle with it. Theology is a human science, an implementation of "utils naturels et humains [natural and human tools]," of "moyens purement humains [purely human means]"; it is a work of "raison [reason]" by means of "efforts et argumens [efforts and arguments]"; in short, it is the realm of reason, and of human reason alone. It is therefore homogeneous with mathematics or logic and can thus perfectly illustrate the powers and the shortcomings of our capacity for knowledge. But in contrast to the other sciences, it allows us to attribute all its successes and failures to that reason alone; for, unlike all the other sciences, *it has all its possible experience behind it:* no progress to come, no discovery, no accumulation of results can occur to improve it or to modify it. Founded on revelation alone—which came about historically and was handed down to the man completely in definitive texts—it cannot look to the future for anything. Its field is that of reason alone.

This is why skeptical argumentation takes on such a particular tone in this text, one so disdainful of the specific divisions of the sciences. This is not due to a misunderstanding *(méconnaissance)* of these sciences, but justifies rather this argumentation, as we have already said. For what reason cannot do is speak for happiness and the good. If it could, where could we see it better than in theology, a knowledge which, by its very essence, as the French historical context of the sixteenth century demonstrates dramatically, is the constant theoretical referent of men's lives?

Then Montaigne's entire perspective turns back on itself indefinitely, for this impossible knowledge still remains just as necessary, and reason is its only instrument. And this is why Montaigne's attitude will be paradoxical when he chooses—as he does choose to love, not worship, knowledge in general—to attempt this inevitable but unrealizable search for God through reason:

> (a) Il . . . faut . . . accompaigner nostre foy de toute la raison qui est en nous, mais tousjours avec cette reservation de n'estimer pas que ce soit de nous qu'elle dépende, ny que nos efforts et argumens puissent atteindre à une si supernaturelle et divine science.

> (We must . . . accompany our faith with all the reason that is in us, but always with this reservation, not to think that it is on us that faith depends, or that our efforts and arguments can attain a knowledge so supernatural and divine.)

We have sufficiently shown that Sebond's text is not a simple pretext here by linking theology as a model of knowledge to Montaigne's global philosophical project and to the general subject of this essay. The fact still remains that the whole ulterior text will ruin the very claims of Sebond: is it to ridicule him? Could this be the real reason behind Montaigne's choice: a text too naive to resist skeptical argumentation?

Such a hypothesis is necessarily reductive, not only because it shows us a cynical Montaigne including his father in his derision, which is highly improbable and would be somewhat distressing, but especially because it masks the very tension of the text—and therefore its meaning, such as the paradoxical structures already pointed out allow us to foresee. For the truth is that Montaigne is both "for" and "against" Sebond, and not only in the relative, manageable harmony of good and bad arguments or of laudable intentions and mediocre results: even if real, these reasons remain absolutely accessory to Montaigne's observation. He is totally for and against Sebond, throughout, in contradiction and paradox—in the coherent but contradictory affirmation that we must approach the theological quest as perhaps the most urgent, fundamental pursuit, while at the same time we are convinced of the aporetic result of such a quest. So that no theological text other than Sebond's, even if it were infinitely superior to his, could have escaped Montaigne's criticism—nor be destroyed by it, either, however.

In order to see this better, we must take a closer look at the "responses" given by Montaigne to objections to Sebond. We find it particularly interesting to give the text here its complexity and movement against all simplification. Let us follow Montaigne, then:

> La premiere reprehension qu'on fait de son ouvrage, c'est que les Chretiens se font tort de vouloir appuyer leur creance par des raisons humaines, qui ne se conçoit que par foy et par une inspiration particuliere de la grace divine.

> (The first criticism that they make of his work is that Christians do themselves harm in trying to support their belief by human reasons, since it is conceived only by faith and by a particular inspiration of divine grace.)

In answer to this objection, Montaigne gives the response in which he defines the difficult and paradoxical relationship of man to theology. We shall not return to this response except to emphasize that it does not "ridicule" Sebond in any way; it *maintains* the legitimacy of its (theological) attempt even while *affirming* the impossibility of reaching God through human means.

But there is more. For Montaigne's text continues beyond this paragraph upon which we have commented at length; and Montaigne adds to this first response a much more extensive text covering several pages. What we find there is surprising, to say the least: *Montaigne legitimates theology by the very absence in which we find ourselves of any contact with God.* Only revelation can found and give rise to theology, he says, thus clearly defining the distinct fields of religion and theological knowledge. But here this human, rational approach to the subject of God is made all the more urgent and legitimate by the fact that we no longer seem to be able to actualize revelation: theology lets the very essence of the divine escape, but the faith which would exempt us from it, or which is at least able to found it, is no longer in us. Our only personal and present access to God is therefore, undoubtedly, this path of reasoning, the reference to the divine word remaining more historical than personal. For this knowledge of God,

> (a) si elle n'entre chez nous par une infusion extraordinaire; si elle y entre non seulement par discours, mais encore par moyens humains, elle n'y est pas en sa dignité ny en sa splendeur. Et certes je crain pourtant que nous ne la jouyssions que par cette voye.

> (if it does not enter into us by an extraordinary infusion; if it enters, I will not say only by reason, but by human means of any sort, it is not in us in its dignity or in its splendor. And yet I am afraid that we enjoy it only in this way.)

Faith is difficult and rare; does it really exist? Are there men, even among Christians, other than those whom Montaigne divides (in a surprisingly Pascalian expression) into two equally inauthentic categories:

> (c) Les uns font accroire au monde qu'ils croyent ce qu'ils ne croyent pas. Les autres, en plus grand nombre, se le font accroire à eux mesmes, ne scachants pas penetrer que c'est que croire.

> (Some make the world believe that they believe what they do not believe. Others, in greater number, make themselves believe it, being unable to penetrate what it means to believe.)

Thus theology, Sebond's as much as any other, will open up a whole propaedeutic to faith, not by proving the existence of God or by revealing him, but by showing at least "comment il n'est piece du monde qui desmante son facteur [how there is no part of the world that belies its maker]," and in this way theology will serve "d'acheminement et de premiere guyde à un apprentis pour le mettre à la voye de cette connoissance [as a start and a first guide to an apprentice to set him on the road to this knowledge]" so that theological arguments at least

le façonnent aucunement et rendent capable de la grace de
Dieu, par le moyen de laquelle se parfournit et se perfet apres
nostre creance.

(fashion him to some extent and make him capable of the grace
of God, by means of which our belief is afterward completed
and perfected.)

Montaigne, far from ridiculing Sebond in these responses to the first objection made against him, shows that this objection itself gets carried away in
criticizing theology in the name of the powers of a faith which never appears—and which none of us, Christians, including me, Montaigne, can
manifest. And yet, against Sebond, the fact remains that theology is impossible—at least if its object really is God.

It is of capital importance to see here how Montaigne evades the
tragic conflict to which his paradoxical argumentation seems to lead him:
this is because the possibility remains of going around the irreducible opposition between God and man, between faith and reason, between necessary and impossible theology, through action—including the intellectual
act which is theology. Only true faith, which I do not have, leads to God.
And yet, theology is inevitable, de facto and de jure. *Montaigne finds a
way out of this double, contradictory affirmation which he maintains:*

1. by changing the object of theology, which becomes a simple
   account of the marks of the divine in the world, and even
   more modestly, of the marks of the possibility of the divine in
   the world. From knowledge about God we pass then to a
   purely human propaedeutic to possible belief;
2. by recalling a faith in Christian revelation which is certainly
   formal—since it is not acted upon by the subject—but nevertheless real. Faith remains, historical, as an acquisition of humanity, even if each particular man today fails to recapture it
   and live it.

There is, therefore, a displacement between the philosophical—or
metaphysical—aporia which we unmasked and the possibility—minimal,
hazardous, but real—of bridging this gap between the divine and the human, for our forces are not absolutely null, nor God absolutely hidden:

Ce seroit faire tort à la bonté divine, si l'univers ne consentoit
à nostre creance. Le ceil, la terre, les elemans, nostre corps et

nostre ame, toutes choses y conspirent: il n'est que de trouver
le moyen de s'en servir.

(It would be doing a wrong to divine goodness if the universe
did not assent to our belief. The sky, the earth, the elements,
our body and our soul, all things conspire in this; we have only
to find the way to use them.)

One of the actualizations of this precarious path in the search for a way
out of the theological dilemma is precisely the work of Raymond Sebond.

The response to the second objection to Sebond remains to be exam-
ined: "Aucuns disent que ses argumens sont foibles et ineptes à verifier ce
qu'il veut, et entreprennent de les choquer aysément [Some say that his arguments are weak and unfit to prove what he proposes, and undertake to
shatter them with ease]."

Montaigne does not answer this objection, as much as if to say that
he would willingly accept this thesis, and we know moreover that he will
be opposed to Sebond's arguments in favor of the powers of reason and
human supremacy in the world. But this is not the essential point. Montaigne's answer will be a radical argument which to be sure also subverts
Sebond's thesis, but which aims first at the dangerous naiveté of an objec-
tor sure of the powers of his reason. Montaigne's argumentation will in
fact constitute the rest of the Essay. The whole "Apology" will now be
devoted to the criticism of reason, and this so-called "skeptical" development will hold true for the totality of knowledge—thus justifying the
choice of the theme announced by the introduction.

We see what form the paradoxical coherence of Montaigne's thought
takes here: it does not save the value of Sebond's work; it merely confuses
its detractors, who are assimilated to Sebond himself and to all humanity
in a common misery (how can we avoid using the Pascalian term here?).
But this tactical victory is a strategic rout since it carries Sebond with it.
What does it matter? What does it matter if we have read well, if we remember that theology cannot aim at a true knowledge—its object is incommensurate with knowledge, and no progress can bring it closer to this
object; if we also remember that theology was not so much a theoretical
possibility as a practical solution to the conflict between the necessity and
the impossibility of a relationship with God? If we understand, finally, that
theology is valuable for the practice of humility and the search for God
which it initiates, and which can only prepare us to believe? And this is
why the skeptical tornado which follows will sweep away real or possible
knowledge much more than a theology already disproved as theoretical

knowledge. What does it matter whether or not it is rich or even rigorous, if it can be of use to me—or if it can help anyone to reconcile his abstract belief with Christianity through a real faith? The important thing is for me to live in spite of my powerlessness; life implicates me completely, and not only as the subject of knowledge—as a transcendental consciousness or soul: and this is what this theology—a propaedeutic, good or bad—will be useful for: living. Montaigne affirms indeed that

> nous ne nous contentons point de servir Dieu d'esprit et d'ame; nous luy devons encore et rendons une reverence corporelle; nous appliquons nos membres mesmes et nos mouvements et les choses externes à l'honorer.

> (we do not content ourselves with serving God with mind and soul, we also owe and render him a bodily reverence; we apply even our limbs and movements and external things to honor him.)

So that what is under attack is not so much the result of theology—that of Sebond or any other—as its claim to be a science, testifying as much to the powers of man as to divine nature. This is why we must understand the position of Montaigne, who both accepts and refuses theology, and who, even while ruining Sebond's argumentation, considers it just as convincing as any other: for the question no longer has to do with the content—the argumentation and results—of theology, but only with the *need* for theology, which paradoxically stems from a deficiency of faith but derives its value only from its anchoring in faith. From personal—absent—faith to revealed faith—in the form alone of dogma.

Thus we can, at least schematically, situate the problematic "religion" of Montaigne and his religious "conservatism": without this real and personal faith, by which "nous remuerions les montaignes de leur place [we should move mountains from their place]," our belief does not even attain the level of a "simple belief (une simple croyance)" such as one grants a "story (histoire)"; religion is but the never really attained horizon of our acts; only dogma permits us to keep its form and possibility. Let us be conservative, then, but tolerant: we have neither true faith nor the intellectual means of attaining it or ruining it. Playing the role of a Catholic here is neither hypocritical nor facile; it is becoming entirely accustomed to the possibility of encountering personal faith; theology, on the condition that it remains in conformity with dogma, is an element like any other of this preparation of the self for God; all the same, it must know its limits.

## IV. THE PARADOX AND THE MIRACLE

This reading of the first pages of the text of the "Apology for Raymond Sebond" has allowed us to bring out a paradoxical structure, that is, a form accounting for a signification which cannot be reduced to either one of the opposing terms constituting it. We have shown that this structure also governs the conclusion of the essay—thus giving shape to a homogeneous and coherent text through the additions of the manuscript. We shall not return to the quotation from Seneca or to the commentary which Montaigne makes on it, "utile desir, mais pareillement absurde (useful desire, but equally absurd)," which now allow us to encompass in a concise form, the very movement of the text. Let it suffice to point out that Montaigne's so-called disorderly writing demonstrates here a masterful—and durable—organization of free reflection: there is nothing more satisfying, on the level of esthetics as well as on the level of meaning, than this conclusion which offers, in the form of a maxim, the model of the whole preceding argumentation and which strengthens the expression both of the contradictions justifying the opening's reservations—to "love," not "worship" knowledge—and of the particular paradox at the very heart of the text: necessary and impossible theology. Neither our personal faith nor the powers of reason enable us to go beyond humanity:

> Car (a) de faire la poignée plus grande que le poing, la brassée plus grande que le bras, et d'esperer enjamber plus que de l'estanduë de nos jambes, cela est impossible et monstrueux. Ny que l'homme se monte au dessus de soy et de l'humanité.

> (For (a) to make the handful bigger than the hand, the armful bigger than the arm, and to hope to straddle more than the reach of our legs, is impossible and unnatural. Nor can man raise himself above himself and humanity.)

But we can seek to rejoin the impossible, the living God who must ground revealed texts, so that the paradox moves towards a transcendence: I cannot raise myself above the human condition, either by my faith or by my reason. And yet the whole meaning of the text refers back to this desire which is unrealizable except through the miraculous intervention of God: man

> s'eslevera si Dieu lui preste extraordinairement la main; il s'eslevera, abandonnant et renonçant à ses propres moyens, et se laissant hausser et soubslever par les moyens purement celestes.

(will rise, if God by exception lends him a hand; he will rise by abandoning and renouncing his own means, and letting himself be raised and uplifted by purely celestial means.)

Man is not himself the subject of the transcendence, but is acted upon by God. The paradox is due to the personal and collective displacement between the particular and the historical which traverses this "form" of the human condition from one end to the other, causing man to hope beyond his human possibilities; and therein, for Montaigne, lie man's fragile humanity and his emergence—purely potential—out of nature and animality.

Dogma renders such a transcendence, if not comprehensible, at least expressible. The illusion lies in believing that it is humanly or even intellectually realizable. Against Seneca—but also against all theology which believes it is speaking of God—and against all rationalism which would mask our immersion in nature and its multiple orders, Montaigne, to conclude, appeals therefore "à nostre foy chrétienne (to our Christian faith)" for this true "métamorphose (metamorphosis)" which he describes as "divine" and "miraculeuse" ("divine" and "miraculous") in order to show fully that we are perhaps its beneficiaries, but under no circumstances its origin or author.

Only a miracle, then, permits us to get out of the paradox. Only dogma affirms—and founds—the irruption of the miracle in the order of nature. So that the very situation of paradox is paradoxical, which is to say, human: necessary and impossible for man and for him alone, theology becomes possible and useless if he surpasses himself, if God frees him from his contradictions and his limits, which "la foy chrestienne (Christian faith)" allows us to hope (and maybe even forces us to hope).

THOMAS M. GREENE

# Dangerous Parleys— Essais *1.5 and* 6

Tout ce qu'on peut dire de la plupart de ces chapitres-la, c'est qu'il n'y a rien à en dire.

—PIERRE VILLEY

The opening page of the *Essais* introduces the reader to terror—the massacre of a city's inhabitants by the Black Prince, who has taken it by force and who is finally deterred only by the exemplary heroism of three defenders. This first essay continues with anecdotes instancing other examples of cruelty and compassion, most of them involving a military siege: Conrad III at Guelph, Dionysius at Rhegium, Pompey at the city of the Mamertines, Sylla at Perusia, Alexander at Gaza, Alexander at Thebes. The concluding paragraph records the slaughter of six thousand Thebans and the enslavement of the remaining thirty thousand. This terror at the opening of the book is anything but rare. The elements of horror and cruelty in the earlier essays of Montaigne have been insufficiently noted and insufficiently explained. Their presence is all the more remarkable in view of their comparative infrequence in the mature essays. It is equally remarkable that the ubiquitous military anecdotes in the very earliest essays (most of them preceding bk. 1, chap. 1 in the chronology of composition) tend to involve the siege of a city or fortress. The siege is the locale of peculiar menace, the contest which exacerbates cruelty and, when successful, conventionally authorizes the harshest carnage.

---

From *Yale French Studies* 64 (1983). © 1983 by Yale University.

Specific anecdotes add substance to these impressions. For the defender, even the limited choice of military options can be perilous. Essay 1.15 ("On est puny pour s'opiniastrer à une place sans raison [One is punished for defending a place obstinately without reason]") cites a number of recorded massacres victimizing those foolhardy enough to resist too long. Yet the succeeding essay ("De la punition de la couardise [Of the punishment of cowardice]") cites examples of those commanders who exposed themselves to the charge of cowardice by yielding too easily and who were justly punished by degradation. The defender, it appears, must walk a fine line, if indeed one exists. The next essay but one ("De la peur [Of fear]") opens with examples of self-destructive madness which overwhelms terrified men under siege. 1.34 offers a series of miracles: walls of invested cities which fall by divine will without attack, or the more recent case, truly wonderful, of a wall blown up which settled down neatly into place again. 1.47 cites the case of the Roman commander Vitellius whose siege of a city was repelled because his troops taunted the defenders too caustically. 2.3 ("Coustume de l'isle de Cea [A custom of the island of Cea]") in its long catalogue of recorded suicides, individual and communal, returns again and again to the city reduced to despair by an encircling army. 1.24 narrates an incident clearly analogous to these others which Montaigne witnessed as a child: the governor of a city walks out from a secure building to address a frenzied mob and is killed. Miracles aside, all of these stories evoke an intensity of violence whose narrow spectrum runs from peril to nightmare. As a set, they outdo in brutality the other military anecdotes which accompany them.

I have not yet mentioned one more early essay, or rather two twin essays, whose organizing situation is the siege. These are 1.5 ("Si le chef d'une place assiégée doit sortir pour parlementer [Whether the governor of a besieged place should go out to parley]") and 1.6 ("L'heure des parlemens dangereuse [Parley time is dangerous]"). These are apparently among the earliest of all (1571–72), and in the 1580 edition they are among the very simplest in structure: a bare series of brief stories scarcely mortised by minimal commentary. Although they mute to a degree the explicit brutality of their companion essays, they offer a useful focus for the study of the motif or the obsession which unifies them. They also introduce a distinctive element missing elsewhere, a third tactical option—the possibility of a parley, a verbal negotiation, between the opposing forces. This element complicates the primitive oppositions of the other anecdotes and confers a special interest on these crude and laconic texts.

For all their ostensible simplicity, however, they do not lack their puzzles and reversals. First reversal: 1.5 opens not with the decision of the defending commander posed by the title but with the corresponding decision of the investing commander (should he win an advantage by faking a truce to negotiate?).

(a) Lucius Marcius legat des Romains en la guerre contre Perseus roy de Macedoine voulant gaigner le temps qu'il lui falloit encore a metre en point son armée, sema des entregets d'accord, desquels le roy endormi accorda trefve pour quelques jours, fournissant par ce moyen son ennemy d'opportunité & loisir pour s'armer: d'ou le roy encourut sa dernier[e] ruine. Si est ce que le Senat Romain, a qui le seul advantaige de la vertu sembloit moyen juste pour acquerir la victoire trouva ceste praticque laide & des-honneste, n'ayant encores ouy sonner a ses oreilles ceste belle sentence, *dolus an virtus quis in hoste requirat?* [*Aeneid,* 2.390] Quand a nous moings superstitieux, qui tenons celuy avoir l'honneur de la guerre, qui en a le profit, & qui apres Lysander, disons que ou la peau du lyon ne peut suffire, qu'il y faut coudre un lopin de celle du renard, les plus ordinaires occasions de surprinse se tirent de ceste praticque: & n'est heure, disons nous, ou un chef doive avoir plus l'oeil au guet, que celle des parlemens & traites d'accord. Et pour ceste cause c'est une reigle en la bouche de tous les hommes de guerre de nostre temps, qu'il ne faut jamais que le gouverneur en une place assiegée sorte luy mesmes pour parlementer.

(Lucius Marcius, legate of the Romans in the war against Perseus, king of Macedonia, wishing to gain the time he still needed to get his army fully ready, made some propositions pointing to an agreement, which lulled the king into granting a truce for a few days and thereby furnished his enemy with opportunity and leisure to arm. As a result, the king incurred his final ruin. Yet the Roman Senate, judging that valor alone was the just means for winning a victory, deemed this stratagem ugly and dishonest, not yet having heard this fine saying ringing in their ears: "Courage or ruse—against an enemy, who cares?" As for us, who, less superstitious, hold that the man who has the profit of war has the honor of it, and who say, after Lysander, that where the lion's skin will not suffice we must sew on a bit of the fox's, the most usual chances for surprise are derived from this practice of trickery. And there is no time, we say, when a leader must be more on the watch than that of parleys and peace treaties. And for that reason there is a rule in the mouth of all military men of our time, that the governor of a besieged place must never go out to parley.)

There are really two questions at issue: the *ethical* choice of a Lucius Martius, chastised by the senate for his unscrupulous strategem, and the *tactical* choice of the captain who must weigh the advantages of the proffered armistice. In the incident cited, both commanders appear to have selected the wrong alternative; Lucian commits an error of morality and Perseus of prudence. Both errors seem to stem from the ambiguity of a truce which fails to conclude hostilities for good and creates a grey area of ethics and judgment suspending all conventional rules. The polarity attacker defender then yields to a second polarity ancient/modern, since the contemporaneous world is represented as heedless of all promises, ironically "moings superstitieux," less scrupulous regarding good faith than the Roman senate. Yet in another reversal, the integrity of antiquity is blurred by the Virgilian quotation (Courage or ruse—against an enemy, who cares?), which subdivides the ancient member of the polarity by distinguishing republican honesty from imperial deceit. Aeneas's aphorism might be the motto of faithless modernity. He seems to share a grey area of history with the Spartan general Lysander.

Up to this point, the evidence presented would dictate a negative answer to the question of the essay's title; under the given circumstances, negotiation is suicidal. This will also be the conclusion of the sequel essay; the hour of parleying *is* dangerous. But here in 1.5, in another reversal, this implication receives a qualification.

> Du temps de nos peres cela fut reproché aus seigneurs de Montmord & de l'Assigni deffandans Mouson contre le Conte de Nansaut, mais aussi à ce conte celuy la seroit excusable, qui sortiroit en telle facon, que la surté & l'advantaige demeurat de son costé, comme fit on la ville de Regge, le Conte Guy de Rangon (s'il en faut croire Monsieur Du Bellay: car Guichardin dit que ce fut luy mesmes) lors que le seigneur de l'Escut s'en approcha, pour parlementer: car il abandonna de si peu son fort, que un trouble s'estant esmeu pendant ce parlement, non seulement monsieur de l'Escut & sa trouppe qui estoit approchée avec luy se trouva la plus foible, de façon que Alexandre Trivulce y fut tué, mais luy mesmes fust contraint, pour le plus

seur, de suivre le Conte, & se getter sur sa foy a l'abri des coups, dans la ville.

(In our fathers' day the seigneurs de Montmord and de Lassigny, defending Mouzon against the count of Nassau, were blamed for this. But also, by this reckoning, a man would be excusable who went out in such a way that the security and advantage remained on his side; as Count Guido Rangone did at the city of Reggio (if we are to believe Du Bellay, for Guicciardini says it was he himself) when the seigneur de l'Escut approached to parley. For he stayed so close to his fort that when trouble broke out during this parley, Monsieur de l'Escut not only found himself and his accompanying troop the weaker, so that Alessandro Trivulzio was killed there, but was constrained, for greater security, to follow the count and trust himself to his good faith, taking shelter from the shots inside the town.)

Properly managed, a sortie to parley *can* be profitable. The tortuous syntactic convolution of this long sentence and the factual uncertainty (does the credit go to Rangone or Guicciardini?) introduce new types of blurring, but through the distractions one can isolate the crucial tactical factor on the victor's side: he left behind his bastion *only a little*. This crucial calculation not only leads to the death of a prestigious enemy leader but forces a humiliating reverse upon the besieging leader, who ends within the walls dependent upon the defender's good will. We assume, without learning from Montaigne, that the supplicant is accorded grace. The text leads us to question only the word of the outsider, not the insider. The defender tends to appear as a moral virgin; only the attacker is a potential rapist or seducer.

The incident at Reggio throws into doubt the negative answer to the title-question which the Macedonian incident had appeared to imply. It remains for a final incident to obscure the question definitively by providing the one remaining outcome which is theoretically possible.

Si est ce que encores en y a il, qui se sont tres bien trouvés de sortir sur la parolle de l'assaillant: tesmoing Henry de Vaux, Chevalier Champenois, lequel estant assiegé dans le chasteau de Commercy par les Anglois, & Berthelemy de Bonnes, qui commandoit au siege ayant par dehors faict sapper la plus part du chasteau, si qu'il ne restoit que le feu pour acabler les assiegés soubs les ruines, somma ledict Henry de sortir a parlementer

pour son profict, comme il fit luy quatriesme, & son evidante
ruyne luy ayant esté monstrée a l'oeil il s'en sentit singuliere-
ment obligé a l'ennemy, a la discretion duquel apres qu'il se fut
rendu & sa trouppe, le feu estant mis a la mine les estansons de
bois venant a faillir le chasteau fut emporté de fons en comble.

(Yet it is true that there are some who have done very well by
coming out on the attacker's word. Witness Henri de Vaux, a
knight of Champagne, who was besieged in the castle of Commercy by the English. Barthélemy de Bonnes, who commanded
the siege, after having the greater part of the castle sapped from
outside, so that nothing remained but setting fire in order to
overwhelm the besieged beneath the ruins, asked the aforesaid
Henri to come out and parley for his own good; this Henri did,
preceded by three other men. And, convinced by what he was
shown that he would have been ruined without fail, he felt re-
markably obliged to his enemy, to whose discretion he surrendered himself and his forces. After this, the fire was set to the
mine, the wooden props gave way, and the castle was demol-
ished from top to bottom.)

This final reversal ends the original published version of the essay, which
I have now quoted in its entirety. It leaves the hostile parties pacifically
together outside the castle as the previous story left them inside the city,
and here, one gathers, the "discretion" of the attacker is to be trusted as
it could not be earlier. The essay might be said to leave the question
whether to go out to parley permanently up in the air, so to speak, since
the text is void of authorial intervention beyond the sarcasm of the two
phrases: "belle sentence [fine saying]" applied to Virgil, "moings superstitieux [less superstitious]" applied to modern tacticians. Yet even this con-
clusive inconclusiveness will be reversed as we turn to the opening of the
sequel essay. "Toute-fois [However]" it begins, and after a longer catalogue of disastrous sorties by gullible defenders, it in turn ends with a timid
authorial leap onto the shoulders of a Stoic philosopher. The writer's position on the *tactical* question, the options of the besieged, can only be in-
ferred from the ambiguous evidence of the twin but divergent essays. On
the *ethical* question he edges into the second essay through the opposition
of two other voices. We just catch sight of Montaigne as thinker in the
final antithesis of Ariosto and Chrysippus.

Fu il vincer sempremai laudabil cosa

Vincasi o per fortuna o per ingegno, (*Orlando furioso,* 14.1)
disent-ils mais le philosophe Chrisippus n'eust pas esté de c'est
advis: car il disoit que ceux, qui courrent a lenvy doivent bien
employer toutes leurs forces a la vistesse, mais il ne leur est
pourtant aucunement loisible de mettre la main sur leur adver-
saire pour l'arrester, ny de juy tendre la jambe, pour le faire
cheoir.

(To conquer always was a glorious thing,

Whether achieved by fortune or by skill, [*Ariosto*]
so they say. But the philosopher Chrysippus would not have
been of that opinion. For he used to say that those who run a
race should indeed employ their whole strength for speed but
that, nevertheless, it was not in the least permissible for them
to lay a hand on their adversary to stop him, or to stick out a
leg to make him fall.)

This seems to align the essayist with the philosopher, but the alignment is
tacit, merely implicit. And even this tiny, almost imperceptible gesture of
approval is made after the terrible problem of the siege has been elided
into a metaphorical footrace. Later published versions would render the
approval slightly more visible ("le philosophe Chrisippus n'eust pas esté de
cet advis, *et moy aussi peu* [The philosopher Chrysippus would not have
been of that opinion, *and I just as little*]") they would also introduce further incidents, complications, quotations, citations of authority, together
with a fuller though somewhat straddling comment on the ethical issue in
1.6, and in 1.5 a new auto-referential ending affirming the writer's quick-
ness to accept the word of others. This credulity, which cuts against those
prudential concerns present earlier, represents one more reversal in the
form of an afterthought.

Considered as an integral text, this fifth essay might be said to possess
unity only in the persistence of its portentous theme and in the consistency
of its failure to resolve its own questions. Together with its companion, it
stands as a chaos of diverging or conflicting events, quotations, opinions
perspectives, shifts of the issue at hand. All we can ascertain with certainty
as we stand back from the two conflicted texts as from book 1 as a whole
is that the dilemma of the man surrounded and the question whether
speech is of use to him are indeed of pressing concern to the writer.

What remains obscure is the basis of this concern, and given the reticence of these little sketches, especially taciturn in their original form, the interpreter is obliged to turn to the appropriate larger context, which can only be the entire work in which they take their modest place. But this step, though necessary, is problematic, since the *Essais* repeatedly throw out versions of inside/outside antitheses. Many of the antitheses can be read back into the siege motif so as to render it in varying degrees metaphoric. One could then consider the work as a series of explications or unpackings of a dramatic situation transformed into a trope. This becomes problematic only because the potential "explications" are so numerous and entangled that the original obsession will emerge as overdetermined to the point of meaninglessness. If in other words we scrutinize the *Essais* for all the ways in which the siege motif might be understood to "symbolize," we may be left with a blur as inconclusive as the uninterpreted point of departure. To avoid this impasse, the most promising procedure would be to follow those directions which the texts themselves offer most insistently, to privilege those hints whose networks of reinforcement prove densest, without denying the potential relevance of other networks and other metaphoric displacements.

The most obvious extrapolation is biographical. Montaigne is a landowner whose property is walled during a period of civil conflict and routine pillage. He marvels in fact that it has remained intact, (b) "encore vierge de sang et de sac, soubs un si long orage, tant de changemens et agitations voisines [still virgin of blood and pillage, under so long a storm, with so many changes and disturbances in the neighborhood]." The sexual metaphor is not to be disregarded; for the proprietor, the invasion of his house would be experienced as the breaking of a hymen. Domestic anxiety, remarks Montaigne, is the peculiar product of civil war alone. (b) "Les guerres civiles ont cela de pire que les autres guerres, de nous mettre chacun en eschaugette en sa propre maison. . . . C'est grande extremité d'estre pressé jusques dans son mesnage et repos domestique [Civil wars are worse in this respect than other wars, that they make us all sentinels in our own houses. . . . It is a great extremity to be beset even in our household and domestic repose]." A passage toward the end of "De la phisionomie [Of physiognomy]" narrates the attempt by a neighbor to capture Montaigne's house by a ruse, a ruse which fails through the intended victim's trusting manner. This threat of violence is not however altogether distinct from the threat of daily affairs to the man of letters. The significant interior may not be the property as such but the tower library. (c) "C'est là mon siege. J'essaie . . . à soustraire ce seul coin à la communnauté. . . . Miserable à mon gré, qui n'a chez soy où estre à soy. [There is my throne. I try . . . to withdraw this one corner from all society. . . . Sorry the man, to my mind, who has not in his own home a place to be all by himself]." It is impossible to distinguish firmly the military press which threatens the landowner from the press of affairs which threatens the meditative solitary. But the physical withdrawal to a quiet place is impossible to distinguish in turn from the mental withdrawal to an inner quietude. The *coin,* the corner where one can reign alone, already contains in germ a metaphor of psychological space which other contexts will make explicit. (b) "Si je ne suis chez moy, j'en suis tousjours bien pres [If I am not at home, I am always very near it]." This metaphoric dimension of the "chez moy" in the *Essais* emerges so commonly and spontaneously that the reader almost overlooks its figurative force.

In a passage justifying his failure to fortify his house against marauders, Montaigne writes that "any defense bears the aspect of war" and invites attack, then remarks of his house: (c) "C'est la retraite à me reposer des guerres. J'essaye de soubstraire ce coing à la tempeste publique, comme je fay un autre coing en mon ame [It is my retreat to rest myself from the wars. I try to withdraw this corner from the public tempest, as I do another corner in my soul]." This internal corner clearly corresponds to the "arriereboutique [back shop]" of the essay on solitude (1.39) (a) "en laquelle nous establissons nostre vraye liberté et principale retraicte et solitude [in which to establish our real liberty and our principal retreat and solitude]." The evocation of this internal withdrawal does not lack military imagery. (a) "Nous avons une ame contournable en soy mesme; elle se peut faire compagnie; elle a dequoy assaillir et dequoy defendre, dequoy recevoir et dequoy donner [We have a soul that can be turned upon itself; it can keep itself company; it has the means to attack and the means to defend, the means to receive and the means to give]." But the most powerful image at the close of the essay suggests a defensive cunning and contracted force still more absolute: (a) "Il faut faire comme les animaux qui effacent la trace, à la porte de leur taniere [We must do like the animals that rub out their tracks at the entrance to their lairs]." It was this profound impulse to lie still in a spiritual center, beleaguered, alert, solicited but cautious, which brought Montaigne home from the Bordeaux *parlement,* and it is this impulse, more than any other, which seems to underlie the obsession with the siege.

The experience of the *parlement* may not be irrelevant to the twin essays that concern us, since the title of 1.6 ("L'heure des parlemens dangereuse") contains the word and the title of 1.5 a cognate form ("parlementer"). A useful gloss on these essays can be found in the opening pages of "De l'experience [On experience]" (3.13), where legal abuses bring into focus the capacity of language for obliquity, ambiguity, treachery, and self-subversion. (b) "Cette justice qui nous regit . . . est un vray temoignage de l'humaine imbecillité, tant il y a de contradiction et d'erreur [This justice that governs us . . . is a true testimony of human imbecility, so full it is of contradiction and error]." Jurisprudence is (b) "generatrice d'altercation et division [generating altercation and division]." Law does not offer (b) "aucune maniere de se declarer qui ne tombe en doubte et contradiction [a way of speaking (one's) mind that does not fall into doubt and contradiction]." The wish for an absolute intercourse beyond ambiguity and contradiction is already present in 1.5, which begins by positing a Roman purity betrayed both by event (Lucius Marcius's stratagem) and by quotation ("Dolus an virtus"). The military *parlement,* like the judicial, places the heaviest pressure on direct language since, as we have seen, there is no time when a commander must be more wary. The quotation from Virgil that closes 1.6 (added in 1588) can be read as an expression of Montaigne's fantasized escape from the verbal and the equivocal.

> (b) Atque idem fugientem haud est dignatus Orodem
> Sternere, nec jacta caecum dare cuspide vulnus:
> Obvius, adversosque occurrit, seque viro vir
> Contulit, haud furto melior, sed fortibus armis
>
> (Nor did he deign to knock down from the rear
> Fleeing Orodes with an unseen spear:
> He passes, veers, and man to man, in fight,
> He proves the better, not by stealth but might.)
>                                    (*Aeneid* 10.732–35)

To attack from behind would savor of linguistic obliquity, would be analogous to the tricky indirections of negotiations; the ideal struggle is silent, face to face, on a plain outside a city, as here in the *Aeneid.* It matters little if even this fantasy, having descended to language, is faintly undermined by our remembrance that it depicts the brutal tyrant Mezentius. The only alternative would be mutual confidence, *fiance,* which the opening of 1.6 has ruled out in modern times. (a) "Ne se doit attendre fiance des uns aux autres, que le dernier seau d'obligation n'y soit passé: encore y a il lors assés affaire [parties should not trust one another until the last binding seal has been set. Even then there is plenty of room for wariness]." The final seal of commitment (real or metaphorical?) points back again to a judicial parallel; the effect of the analogy is to imply a nostalgia for a finality which is supradiplomatic, suprajudicial, supralinguistic. Even after the ostensibly final seal, one must be on one's guard. In effect there is no conclusion to a conflict; that might only be produced by the frontal, mute assault of a Mezentius, slugging it out hand to hand—a kind of salvation. The Mezentius quotation is immediately preceded by an anecdote wherein Alexander refuses a lieutenant's advice to (b) "se servir de l'avantage que l'obscurité de la nuit luy donnoit pour assaillir Darius [to take advantage of the darkness of night to attack Darius]." It is tempting to extend this obscurity metaphorically to evoke that dimness of indirect, verbal engagement which the writer wants to evade.

Thus these apprentice essays seem to condone indirectly their author's choice to withdraw from a parliament into his tower bastion. Here one might suppose that there would be fewer *heures des parlemens dangereuses*. Yet if we look to the early essays as products of pure interiority, we will of course be disappointed. The first versions of 1.5 and 6 appear to be almost entirely the contrary, a collection of actions by other men reported in other writers' books, bearing as we have noted only the barest traces of authorial commentary. What is besieging the mind on these pages are the words, experiences, and opinions of cultural memory, to the degree that the writer's own voice seems scarcely audible. Montaigne has opened his text as Montmord and Assigni opened their gates, and seems to have suffered something of their fate, a fate he fails to specify though we gather it to have been unpleasant. Even in this essay's later versions, where the authorial voice can intermittently be made out, it merely makes one in a somewhat cacophonous chorus. The self is hedged about by all those who solicit entrance to the allegedly self-defining text; the self is exposed to the wounds, the subversions, the variances of opinion, the linguistic and moral codes pressing about it. In the final versions of 1.5 and 6 the writer's own outlook, to the degree that it is felt at all, is jostled by that of the Roman senate, the Achaians, the ancient Florentines, contemporaneous Frenchmen, of Virgil (or Aeneas), Cleomenes, Xenophon, Ariosto, Alexander. There is no "arriereboutique," no untraceable lair, although the yearning for one might well be a reasonable consequence of the crowded page. Montaigne, one might say, has taken a step which is called in "L'heure des parlemens dangereuse" a "pas de clerc."

> A Yvoile seigneur Iullian Rommero *aiant fait ce pas de clerc* de sortir pour parlementer avec monsieur le Conestable, trouva au retour sa place saisie.

(At Yvoy, Signor Giuliano Romero, having made the novice's blunder of going out to parley with the Constable, on his return found his place seized.)

Modern French has lost this idiom, which associates the clerkly with the naive, but we understand it here with more clarity than its author may have intended. A cleric may, in certain situations, be reasonably associated with the unworldly; the question hovers whether this handicap extends to all who have taken it upon themselves to write.

Thus if we consider the essays themselves, we have no difficulty in making out a textual equivalent to the military drama. Wherever else in Montaigne's experience the threat of invasion lies, it can be found unmistakably upon the pages he is beginning to produce. In a later essay he would confront clairvoyantly the aggressive dimension, the *murderous* dimension of this solicitation from outside.

> (b) Or j'ay une condition singeresse et imitatrice: quand je me melois de faire des vers . . . ils accusoient evidemment le poete que je venois dernierement de lire; et, de mes premiers essays, aucuns puent un peu à l'estranger. . . . Qui que je regarde avec attention m'imprime facilement quelque chose du sien. Ce que je considere, je l'usurpe: une sotte contenance, une desplaisante grimace, une forme de parler ridicule. . . .
>
> (c) Imitation meurtriere comme celle des singes horribles en grandeur et en force que le Roy Alexandre rencontra en certaine contrée des Indes.

(Now I have an aping and imitative nature. When I used to dabble in composing verse . . . it clearly revealed the poet I had last been reading. And of my first essays, some smell a bit foreign. . . . Anyone I regard with attention easily imprints on me something of himself. What I consider, I usurp: a foolish countenance, an unpleasant grimace, a ridiculous way of speaking. . . .

A murderous imitation, like that of the horribly big and strong apes that King Alexander encountered in a certain region of the Indies.)

The anecdote that follows tells how these apes were led to hobble or strangle themselves by men who exploited their imitative bent. The murderous capacity of compulsive imitation can apparently be directed either at one's models or at oneself. Montaigne finds it both in his nature ("condition") and his book, malodorous and destructive. The early essays which stink of others are those precisely haunted by the terror of the siege. Perhaps the younger Montaigne fears the fate of those captains in 1.16 who surrendered their bastions too quickly and suffered for it. Perhaps he fears (or envies?) the fate of Henri de Vaux; he might, through the act of writing, pass outside himself altogether, yield to his besiegers, turn around and see his self explode forever.

To write at any rate is to face the risk of invasion, capture, destruction, murder. Perhaps the struggle between inside and outside is the struggle imposed by the composition of the *Essais*. We can follow this struggle *metaphorically* through the various implications of Montaigne's intersecting images and anecdotes, or we can follow it *intrinsically,* through the unevenly developing power of assimilation, the absorption of anecdote, allusion, and quotation by a unique, recognizable voice, a distinctive moral style. One allows oneself to be conquered, one surrenders one's tower, one's city, if one reads and writes credulously, obsequiously, without independent judgment. One has to learn how to speak without leaving the gate behind.

In view of the felt risk, one may wonder how the first essays ever came into being. Two or three answers can be made. One can point first of all to the freedom of reception as a mark of underlying assurance. The apparently humble and gullible hospitality may mask a secret pride, a reserve which is not hospitable, a confidence on the writer's part that he can be strengthened by his chosen and willed vulnerability. From this miniscule egoism, almost invisible in the first version of 1.5, would grow the bulk of the *Essais*. The caution, the wariness, the ambivalent receptiveness of these early sketches would remain in their denser and more poised successors; we can watch the interplay in simpler form at the outset, where we are given a radical metaphor with which to trace the intertextual drama.

But aside from this nascent confidence, Montaigne seems sometimes to perceive the act of writing not as exposure but protection, not as centrifugal but centripetal. This at least is the basis of the apology in the brief but fascinating "De l'oisiveté [Of idleness]" (1.8), where writing involves the exorcism of wild and disorderly fantasies, just as the cultivation of a field removes weeds and just as the fertilization of a woman by an alien seed ("une autre semence") produces normal offspring rather than shapeless lumps. Here it is the mind abandoned to reverie, undisciplined by writing, which runs off like an escaped horse ("faisant le cheval eschappé"). Writing centers and fortifies the mind, even if it admits a little of the alien. In this formulation the writer maneuvers like Guy de Rangon, emerging just a little to make his capture and then retire. We remember that in 1.15 those who defend their cities *too* stubbornly are exposed to terrible vengeance.

In still other formulations of the apprenticeship phase, we find repeated images of tremendous pressures unhealthily bottled up. Too much sexual desire can make a man impotent.

> (a) De là s'engendre par fois la défaillance fortuite, qui surprent les amoureux si hors de saison, et cette glace qui les saisit par la force d'une ardeur extreme, au giron mesme de la joüyssance.

> (From that is sometimes engendered the accidental failing that surprises lovers so unseasonably, and that frigidity that seizes them by the force of extreme ardor in the very lap of enjoyment.)

The news of bad fortune can paralyze response, until relief comes in an outpouring of tears and speech (1.2). Too much eagerness to write well hampers composition, just as water in a full bottle is hampered by its own pressure from issuing through the neck (1.10). Images like these bespeak terrific expansive energy acutely in need of release. But there is also a recognition that the release must be guided by an authentic external resistance.

> (a) L'ame esbranlé et esmeuë se perde en soymesme, si on ne luy donne prinse: et faut tousjours luy fournir d'object où elle s'abutte et agisse.

> (The soul, once stirred and set in motion, is lost in itself unless we give it something to grasp; and we must always give it an object to aim at and act on.)

The essay from which this is quoted (1.4—"Comme l'ame descharge ses passions sur des objects faux, quand les vrais luy defaillent [How the soul discharges its passions on false objects when the true are wanting)"] fails to specify what the *object vrai* would be; one might presume it to be the thought and writing of another man. Here the *prinse*, the clutch of otherness, is not dangerous but necessary, a tonic encounter which saves the soul from its unbridled solitude.

The conflict of the siege then is both life-threatening and life-preserving. We cannot miss in any case the debate just below the surface of the apprentice essays over the prudence, the ethics, and the hygiene of their composition. The question whether or not to parley contains the question whether or not to write. To use language is to be invaded and to invade.

To parley is to assume the vulnerability of a writer, to enter the grey area of language, of interchange, of the prinse of oppositions. Montaigne was by no means insensitive to this contingent, dialogic, oppositional character of discourse.

> (c) Nous raisonnons hazardeusement et inconsidereement, dict Timaeus en Platon, par ce que, comme nous, nos discours ont grande participation au hazard.

> ("We reason rashly and inconsiderately," says Timaeus in Plato, "because, like ourselves, our reason has in it a large element of chance.")

We hear in this remark the appeal and the safety of silence, which is opposed to speech and perhaps more authentic.

> (a) Le nom, ce n'est pas une partie de la chose ny de la substance, c'est une piece estrangere joincte à la chose, et *hors d'elle* [my italics].

> (The name is not a part of the thing or of the substance, it is an extraneous piece attached to the thing, and outside of it.)

This exteriority of the name is the exteriority, and thus the inferiority, of all words, artificially and arbitrarily connected to the thing, the true, valid, inner, voiceless substance, the silent *res*. Between this authenticity and hazardous expression lie the crucial thresholds of the lips and the page. Any utterance or act of writing is a sortie, a leaving behind the bastion of the private self. A *parlement* is an *essai*, a hazardous initiative, a lowering of defenses. Speech will betray the beleaguerment of those forces which only silence can hold at bay. Speech is already an acceptance of infiltration and contamination, because language to have meaning has always already been used, because Montaigne's language in particular is composed of external examples, opinions, tropes, sentences. One defines one's position in relation to others (Chrisippus, the Roman senate) and against others (Xenophon, Cleomenes, Ariosto). The alternative is that refusal of contact which is seen intermittently as sterile, as producing shapeless lumps, and as sustaining: (a) "Ce n'est pas pour la montre que nostre ame doit jouer son rolle, c'est chez nous, au dedans, où nuls yeux ne donnent que les nostres [It is not for show that our soul must play its part, it is at home, within us, where no eyes penetrate but our own]." In writing this tribute to the *chez nous,* Montaigne is of course exposing it to others; he is violating that pure interiority which he entrusts to paper (and thus violates) so often. The muteness of pure interiority, of the beast in its den, is often praised but in the very praising subverted. Elsewhere he resigns himself to the dialogue within all discourse.

> (c) Je propose les fantasies humaines et miennes, simplement comme humaines fantasies, et separement considerées, non comme arrestées et reglées par l'ordonnance celeste, incapables de doubte et d'altercation: matiere d'opinion, non matiere de foy; ce que je discours selon moy, non ce que je croy selon Dieu.

> (I set forth notions that are human and my own, simply as human notions considered in themselves, not as determined and decreed by heavenly ordinance and permitting neither doubt nor dispute; matter of opinion, not matter of faith; what I reason out according to me, not what I believe according to God.)

Here an implication emerges which anticipates Bakhtin, that human discourse necessarily contains "altercation."

We have noted the oddity of an essay whose titular concern is with the prudence of a defender but whose opening paragraph, among others, deals with the ethics of the besieger. These two pairs of options, ostensibly so different in military terms, begin to approach each other in discursive terms. Once one has made a verbal foray from one's bastion, one is already on the road to becoming an invader, if not a seducer. Montaigne is alert to the risk.

> (b) Il y a tant de mauvais pas que, pour le plus seur, il faut un peu legierement et superficiellement couler ce monde. (c) Il le faut glisser, non pas s'y enfoncer. (b) La Volupté mesme est douloureuse en sa profondeur.

> (There are so many bad spots that, for greatest safety, we must slide over this world a bit lightly and on the surface. We must glide over it, not break through into it. Even sensual pleasure is painful in its depth.)

> (b) J'essaie à tenir mon ame et mes pensées en repos. . . . Et si elles se desbauchent à quelque impression rude et penetrante, c'est à la verité sans mon conseil.

> (I try to keep my soul and my thoughts in repose. . . . And if they sometimes veer under some rough and penetrating attack, it is in truth without my consent.)

Both passages betray a certain ambiguity which blurs the image of penetration. Is the writer's sensibility male or female? Perhaps it partakes of both. The element of aggression is present in any case, and it is subject to considerations of both prudence and ethics. There is the risk of penetrating too far; there is also the risk of attacking too much. (b) "Nous empeschons . . . la prise et la serre de l'ame à luy donner tant de choses à saisir [We impede the mind's grasp and grip by giving it so many things to seize]." The last of the essays seems to attribute a certain "animosité [animosity]" and "aspreté [bitterness]" to all writing. And the "Institution des enfans" will discuss the risk of assaulting the classics too directly. (c) "Je ne luitte point en gros ces vieux champions là, et corps à corps: c'est par reprinses, menues et legieres attaintes [I do not wrestle with those old champions wholesale and body against body; I do so by snatches, by little light attacks]." Even for the post-Humanist that Montaigne became, engagement with antiquity involved a circumspect struggle. Thus beneath the concern for the threatened center, one distinguishes an interest in the policy of attack. To go out to parley is already to begin to take the offensive.

Revisions of the first paragraph of 1.5 will suggest subtly that speech and action lie upon a single spectrum. The Roman senate, disapproving the stratagem of Lucius Marcius,

> (a) "accuserent cette pratique de leur *stile* (c) antien. . . . C'estoient les *formes* vrayment Romaines. . . . (a) Il appert bien par le *langage* de ces bonnes gens qu'il n'avoient encore receu cette belle sentence: 'dolus an virtus quis in hoste requirat?' "

> ("condemned this practice as hostile to their old style. . . . These were truly Roman forms. . . . It clearly appears from the language of these good men that they had not yet accepted this fine saying: 'Courage or ruse—against an enemy, who cares?' ")

Here the word *stile* adumbrates a moral code. Today we may feel the word as a metaphor, since a rhetorical term seems to have replaced a normative one. But for Montaigne there may have been no sense of transferal; for him ethics and language interpenetrate each other, as they do for most Renaissance writers. Each utterance and each act of writing possess a moral character, so that soldier, legislator, and writer can be judged by a single criterion. Each is governed by a moral style. In the gradual emergence of a moral style lies the interest of the earlier essays, and also their achievement. In the apprentice essays, one feels the resistance the composed self has to overcome in order to declare itself. One cannot really speak of subtexts, since the appropriations lie on the surface; one can only speak of a subself which gradually reveals itself through its power to absorb, which is to say rewrite, Seneca, Plutarch, Lucretius, Diogenes Laertius. We come progressively to respect this composed self precisely because it has accepted its vulnerability, its engagement in discourse, and has struggled with the resistance of alterities.

The siege may fade from the mature essays because Montaigne acquires confidence in his own moral style and its capacity for assimilation without risk. The self-destructive reception without assimilation is what Montaigne calls *pedantisme*.

> (a) Nous prenons en garde les opinions et le sçavoir d'autruy, et puis c'est tout. Il les faut faire nostres. . . . (b) Nous nous laissons si fort aller sur les bras d'autruy, que nous aneantissons nos forces.

> (We take the opinions and the knowledge of others into our keeping, and that is all. We must make them our own. . . . We let ourselves lean so heavily on the arms of others that we annihilate our own powers.)

As Montaigne matures, the danger of this annihilation, this pillage or rape, tends to diminish without altogether disappearing. A posthumous addition to "L'heure des parlemens dangereuse" signals a new willingness to enter the equivocal play of diplomacy.

> (c) Il n'est pas dict, que, en temps et lieu, il ne soit permis de nous prevaloir de la sottise de nos ennemis, comme nous faisons de leur lascheté. Et certes le guerre a naturellement beaucoup de privileges raisonnables au prejudice de la raison.

> (It is not said that, at a given time and place, it is not permissible for us to take advantage of the stupidity of our enemies, as we do of their cowardice. And indeed war has by nature many privileges that are reasonable even at the expense of reason.)

With the passing of years, parleying became less dangerous and less reprehensible, the siege motif less relevant, because the self could allow itself to be permeable. A passage in the essay 1.50 ("De Democritus et Heraclitus") constitutes a kind of manifesto of the soul's transformative energy.

> (c) Les choses à part elles ont peut estre leurs poids et mesures et conditions; mais au dedans, en nous, elle [l'ame] les leur taille comme elle l'entend. . . . La santé, la conscience, l'authorité, la

science, la richesse, la beauté et leurs contraires se despouillent
à l'entrée, et recoivent de l'ame nouvelle vesture, et de la tein-
ture qu'il lui plaist: brune, verte, claire, obscure, aigre, douce,
profonde, superficielle, et ce qu'il plaist à chacune d'elles: car
elles n'ont pas verifié en commun leurs stiles, regles et formes:
chacune est Royne en son estat.

(Things in themselves may have their own weights and measures and qualities; but once inside, within us, she [the soul] al-
lots them their qualities as she sees fit. . . . Health, conscience,
authority, knowledge, riches, beauty, and their opposites—all
are stripped on entry and receive from the soul new clothing,
and the coloring that she chooses—brown, green, bright, dark,
bitter, sweet, deep, superficial—and which each individual soul
chooses; for they have not agreed together on their styles, rules
and forms; each one is queen in her realm.)

Each soul has its stile, regle, and forme, which not only render matter profound or superficial, but also brown or green; the style tinctures matter
with its own indissoluble shading. This is the victory of the soul and preeminently of the writer, since it liberates him from beleaguering hostilities.
It is not too much to say that the ultimate subject of the *Essais* is this transformative stile of their author's soul. "(a) Qu'on ne s'attende pas aux ma-
tieres, mais à la façon que j'y donne [Let attention be paid not to the matter, but to the shape I give it]." This indeed is what essentially he seeks in
other writers. "(c) Tous les jours m'amuse à lire en des autheurs, sans soin
de leur science, y cherchant leur façon, non leur subject [Every day I amuse
myself reading authors without any care for their learning, looking for
their style, not their subject]." If one neglects this progressive discovery of
the façon as his own final accomplishment as well as others', one is likely
to misunderstand Montaigne's book. If one reduces this stile to a purely
linguistic or rhetorical comportment, then one misses anachronistically its
energy and breadth. As Montaigne writes, his trust grows in the integrity
of his own façon and its power to negotiate with his classics.

There remains to be sure a certain wariness.

(b) Quand j'escris, je me passe bien de la compaignie et souvenance des livres, de peur qu'ils n'interrompent ma forme. Aussi
que, à la verité, les bons autheurs m'abattent par trop et rom-
pent le courage.

(When I write, I prefer to do without the company and remembrance of books, for fear they may interfere with my style. Also

because, in truth, the good authors humble me and dishearten
me too much.)

The impulse to withdraw remains a temptation, but each page belies this
alleged surrender of the literary memory; the *souvenance* is not so easily
or perhaps so willingly abandoned. The strongest defence against marauders, we learn from the careful householder of "De la vanité [Of vanity],"
is not to lock one's gates. The third book bears witness to a less private
conception of solitude.

(c) Qui ne vit aucunement à autruy, ne vit guere à soy.

(He who lives not at all unto others, hardly lives unto himself.)

(c) Ma forme essentielle est propre à la communication et à la
production: je suis tout au dehors et en evidence, nay à la société et à l'amitié.

(My essential pattern is suited to communication and revelation. I am all in the open and in full view, born for company
and friendship.)

It is true that a yearning emerges in "De l'experience [Of experience]" for a
purely uninterpreted experience, for pure and absolute knowledge without
commentary and without a secondary voice. But this desire, which remains
active, can be balanced against the willing acceptance of linguistic duality
in the same essay: each word belongs equally and rightfully to its speaker
and its auditor. (b) "La parole est moitié à celuy qui parle, moitié à celuy
qui l'escoute [Speech belongs half to the speaker, half to the listener]."

Terence Cave discerns a vacuum at the center of the *Essais,* which
constitute a failed attempt to compensate for the loss of La Boétie.

As they proliferate around the space left by the absence of La
Boétie—like decorative motifs around a missing painting—they
can only designate with greater and greater intricacy their own
condition of exile and *écoulement,* so that finally the focal absence reveals itself to be that of Montaigne himself.
                        (The Cornucopian Text: Problems of Writing
                        in the French Renaissance)

Each reader of Montaigne will find the metaphor that suits best his own
impressions. But Cave's focal absence at the center fails to account for that
tincturing of the external as, in Montaigne's own metaphor, it enters and
crosses the threshold of the soul. This stylization or coloring of things by

a central sensibility is the dominant activity of the *Essais;* it defines that human façon which brings us to them as it brought Montaigne to his preferred masters. If in place of the Renaissance vocabulary one substitutes the terms of post-Saussurian linguistics, one skirts anachronism. Cave writes:

> Discourse can never be a transparent vehicle for a given content. Asserting its own presence, it contaminates, obscures, and renders invisible its reference; the resolution of meaning is deferred to some future articulation which will never occur.

This contamination and postponement constitute the text's "diseased nature." But if Renaissance rhetoric approves the technique of *contaminatio,* if discourse pretends neither to transparence nor to reference but to a tincturing stile, then there is no pathology of obscurity or deferral; the creation of a transformative moral style is everywhere achieved. Cave cites effectively the myth of the Danaids, whose leaking buckets forestall plenitude, but Montaigne's predilections lead more frequently to images of solid centers and surroundings which encroach upon each other as the center expands or contracts, negotiates or withdraws, stiffens or softens. Each alternative might be regarded as "a movement toward death," but only if it is understood always to stop short. Death would lie in the collapse of centric resistance, in the suicidal *imitation meurtriere,* or it would lie antithetically in the absolute resistance of silence, the permanent closing of the gate, the refusal of speech. We know that there is a living self when there is a locus of dialogic "altercation." Speech contaminates Montaigne as it contaminates everyone, but for the cunning negotiator, speech saves as well as threatens; it preserves the fortress-self from the two mortal tactical extremes.

The neighbor who invades Montaigne's estate by a ruse of murderous intent is disarmed finally by his host's trustfulness, an apparent simplicity which is spontaneous but not naive. "(b) Je suis peu deffiant et soubçonneux de ma nature," he remarks [I am by nature little given to distrust and suspicion]," and it is this clear-eyed credulity that preserves his life. The essay with which we began (1.5) ends on the same note, in an addition of 1588.

> (b) Je me fie ayseement à la foy d'autruy. Mais mal-aiseement le fairoy je lors que je donnerois à juger l'avoir plustost faict par desespoir et faute de coeur que par franchise et fiance de sa loyauté.

(I put my trust easily in another man's word. But I should do so reluctantly whenever I would give the impression of acting from despair and want of courage rather than freely and through trust in his honesty.)

Trust seems both spontaneous and tactical; it may coexist with fear, but not so as to reveal fear. This partial and qualified trust is Montaigne's response to the problem of these twin essays, "l'heure des parlemens dangereuse." His book reveals his cautious, gradual extension of faith to the voices who encircle him on its pages, as he gained faith that his own quirky, placid voice could be heard through theirs and above theirs and *in* theirs. The *Essais* might be said to adumbrate a textual theology like one their author hated: Lutheranism. A man accepts both the estrangement of the word and its promise of engagement; in a grey area without rules, he is saved by his *fiance*. But here this perennial interchange is embraced with a secular temperance: (b) "Celuy qui se porte plus moderéement envers le gain et la perte, il est tousjours chez soy [He who bears himself more moderately toward winning and losing is always at home]."

JEAN STAROBINSKI

# "And Then, for Whom Are You Writing?"

### THE QUESTION OF IDENTITY

The dilemma (or crisis) to which the 1571 retreat provided a decisive response . . . involved a choice of *identity,* of a stable relationship to one-self—in conscious opposition to the world and its theater of illusion.

It is customary to regard the first chapters that Montaigne wrote (between 1572 and 1574) as "impersonal" texts, in contrast to subsequent chapters which mark the entrance of the ego and of the desire to paint a self-portrait. It must be granted, however, that the "painting of the self" is merely a belated development of a philosophy that is from the first oriented toward personal life; the question of the ego is raised from the start. Montaigne first tried to answer it by traditional means, and it was because he found those means incapable of satisfying his expectations that he later adopted a different method, essaying a wholly different attitude.

One has only to read the texts of the first period to see that Montaigne is particularly susceptible to arguments from moral philosophy (of the Stoics as well as Epicurus) counseling self-reliance and self-possession. He repeats and paraphrases these arguments to himself, he rehearses them with variations—and what is more, he will continue to make them his own to the end of his days.

Reread, for example, the chapter entitled "Of solitude" (bk. 1, chap. 39), the argument of which is frequently echoed in other passages; what Montaigne is seeking is a place in this world which is truly his own, unlike other men who, allowing themselves to be carried away by their own

From *Montaigne in Motion,* translated by Arthur Goldhammer. © 1985 by the University of Chicago. University of Chicago Press, 1985.

imagination, presumption, or vanity, take leave of themselves, desert, in order to conquer imaginary honors or riches. Montaigne, in subscribing to this argument, includes himself in the collective *we* of the remonstrance: "Among our customary actions there is not one in a thousand that concerns ourselves. . . . Who is there that will not readily exchange health, rest, and life for reputation and glory, the most useless, worthless and false coin that is current among us?" In this way we become subject to the power of other people's words. It is impatience, or the need to cut a striking figure on another stage, that drives men to abandon their true place, thus giving rise to the comedy of the world with its proliferation of masks. For men arm themselves with the expressions and accoutrements that transport them, before the fact, into the chimerical future to which they aspire. And so inevitably a creature fallen prey to the temptations of the imagination is transformed into a man of deceit, a wearer of masks. Having bestowed false visages on all things, he cannot appear before them except concealed behind a mask or grimace. He is hypocritical because he is *alienated* (as a later vocabulary would have it): he has made his being dependent on opinion, esteem, on the *words* by which others (the "world," "society") confer "reputation" and "glory." (Rousseau's formation of the first count in his indictment of society scarcely differs from this in its language.)

Everything that belongs to the order of the project, every anticipation in which the individual takes the future for granted, becomes suspect in the eyes of this morality, which holds that it is a culpable weakness for one to set one's sights *elsewhere*. Montaigne refers to this in the title of one of his early chapters (1.3): "Our feelings reach out beyond us." There he writes: "We are never at home, we are always beyond. Fear, desire, hope, project us toward the future." This apothegm takes a negative view of the enthusiasm that causes us to transcend the present and reach out toward the future, an enthusiasm over which the shadow of uncertainty always hangs. Even the quality of providence comes in for criticism, for providence jeopardizes the individual's cohesion and constancy, which can only rest on a continuous *here* and *now*: providence presupposes a morality of *restraint* (in every sense of the word), which prevents a man from dispersing himself and commits him to breviloquence, sententiousness, and, so far as the objects of desire are concerned, to *continence* (of which Montaigne will repeatedly insist he is incapable).

Withdrawal from desire: this is the universal error which Montaigne, following Seneca, stigmatizes, and from which he hopes to escape. "My professed principle . . . is to be wholly contained and established within myself." He vows, or at any rate advises his readers, to resist the temptations that Pascal would later subsume under the synthetic noun *divertissement* (amusement): "It is here in us, and not elsewhere, that the powers and actions of the soul should be considered. . . . We must reserve a back shop all our own, entirely free, in which to establish our real liberty and our principal retreat and solitude." To focus one's thoughts *here* (as opposed to elsewhere) is to bring the maximum possible attention to bear on the place actually inhabited by consciousness, on the identity assigned thereto, and on the powers that are unlocked through this conversion to self *(conversion à soi-même)*. (The animal's inability to foresee the future will thus become, for Montaigne, a claim to superiority.)

Effective teaching and healthy moral choice dictate unequivocal responses to a series of alternatives, all of which involve choosing between concentration and disintegration of the self. It is immediately obvious which alternative is correct as between *being* and *appearance, here* and *elsewhere, self* and *others, mine* and *alien, natural* and *artificial, spontaneous* and *learned, interior* and *exterior, profound* and *superficial.* Each of these antitheses contains, or resonates with, all the others. All are interchangeable or equivalent. The decision is taken in advance: the antitheses in question do not allow suspense or hesitation. All indicate a choice to be made, and advocate turning inward, regaining self-possession, autonomy, and autarchy.

What does philosophy's ancient teaching have to say? That man, subjected to outside forces, squanders his being: he is passion and passivity, the pleasures he pursues disappoint him in the end, he dissipates his substance, his will flags, and he becomes a slave. Yet life regains its solidity and value to the extent that man is willing to plumb his inner depths and take refuge in the fortress of the self. To do so is to regain one's health, to recover one's natural vigor. Once he has gotten rid of all that is alien, man can enjoy his true strength, purely possessed. At one with himself, he forbids his energies to reach out toward a chimerical future or an external objective and thus prevents the self's substance from draining away. When he acts, he chooses a point of exertion as close as possible to the agent himself. In the limit, the ideal action will consist in total self-reflection, in the reaffirmation of a persistent identity and nothing else; turned back on itself, action does not extend beyond the limits of the *here* and *now,* but fills them, consolidates them, inhabits and possesses them in possessing itself, in pulling itself together. Now, here: this instant and this place will from now on be *contained* and preserved in the decision to be oneself and to belong only to oneself. Time and space are no longer endured as destructive forces but produced from within by the voluntary decision that affirms the *here* and *now* by its own decree. Thus consciousness may hope never to be distracted from the self. It husbands an unexpended reserve of energy that perpetuates itself from moment to moment, without aiming at anything other than itself and hence without seeking to invest anything outside itself. This action of the self on the self striving for completion must be wary of flattery and inducements from outside. One must remain constantly on one's guard, perpetually suspicious, ready to fend off any temptations that might distract the attention or drain energies needed for taming the self and defending it against its enemies. This suspicion extends even to the subject himself: solitude does not free us from our vices, weaknesses, or "concupiscences": "It is not enough to have gotten away from the crowd, it is not enough to move; we must get away from the gregarious instincts that are inside us; we must sequester ourselves and reappropriate ouselves." This overinvestment in the ego ideal is not without peril for the ego itself, to use the language of contemporary psychology. Montaigne will make the point in his own way, however.

Montaigne's interpreters have in general been clearly aware of how this kind of "turning inward," derived from the teachings of the Greek and Latin philosophers, differed from that urged by Christian piety and especially by Augustinian preaching: the latter advised turning inward in order to heed the voice of God and submit to his judgment, internalizing the individual's submission to the transcendental. By contrast, the withdrawal desired by Montaigne has as its only purpose the discovery of a conversational mirror within oneself; it aims to restore full powers of judgment to the mortal individual, dividing the self between two equal powers and rejecting the claims of any outside authority. Although humanism and religion both recommend interior "conversation" and *reappropriation,* from the standpoint of the believer this is but a first step, to be followed by obedience to divine authority and the hope of salvation. For the humanist who has taken his distance from religion, the inner reappropriation, if successful, is sufficient unto itself. The solitude sanctioned by humanism is not to be confused with the traditional *vita contemplativa,* which in the religious scheme of things was opposed to the *vita activa,* or life in the world. The humanist attitude would later be denounced, by the moralists of Port-Royal and after them by Malebranche, as culpable self-indulgence. Montaigne was perfectly aware that his choice was not that of religious vocation. He begs pardon for this, offering weakness as his excuse while indicating his reverence for those capable of true devotion: "They set God before their eyes, an object infinite both in goodness and in power; in him the soul has the wherewithal to satisfy its desires abundantly in complete freedom. . . . And he who can really and constantly kindle his soul with the flame of that living faith and hope, builds himself in solitude a life that is voluptuous and delightful beyond any other kind of life." But denial of the flesh and a radical rupture with the realities of the world Montaigne declares to be beyond his reach; while seeming to praise asceticism, he declares himself incapable of it: "Wiser men, having a strong and vigorous soul, can make for themselves a wholly spiritual repose. But I, who have a commonplace soul, must help support myself by bodily comforts." At times he shows himself more severe toward those who carry contempt for the world to the point of "dissociating themselves from their bodies": "They want to get out of themselves and escape from the man. That is madness: instead of changing into angels they change into beasts; instead of raising themselves, they lower themselves. These transcendental humors frighten me, like lofty and inaccessible places." This is to shatter life's recaptured unity: it is again to succumb to the evil of exteriority, to stand "outside oneself." Montaigne saves his most vigorous disapproval for those who seem to break with the world only to reform what they have abandoned and subject it even more strenuously to God's commandments, to which they claim to be privy; in Montaigne's eyes such fanatics are themselves merely actors wearing masks, the first victims of the opinions they wish to impose on others.

If Montaigne opts for inward *identity,* for a stable and equal relationship of the segments of the self, he does so while continuing to focus his gaze on the world, with which he maintains ties that do not impair his self-possession. From the windows of his library he looks out onto court and bailey. He intends to maintain as much *presence* in the world as is compatible with his refusal of servitude (because the freest personal existence includes the life of the flesh, and the body is a "piece" of the world, a part of nature).

By recapitulating in this way several of the major themes of ancient moral philosophy, Montaigne is in fact taking up ambiguous arguments which can be used, in the name of speaking the whole truth, on behalf of either commitment or withdrawal from commitment, action or the shunning of action. When he contrasts the solidity of *acts* with the futility of *words,* he accepts the traditional moral teachings and opts for acts. What Friedrich calls his "aristocratic pretensions" are thereby bolstered: a well-born gentlemen disdains to give precedence to style, to eloquence, to the blandishments of cunning words (see 1.51, "On the vanity of words"). In the moral order, the traditional antinomy *res/verba* militates in favor of the solidity of things over the wind of rhetoric. But when it comes to the contrast between the *inside* and the *outside,* which harks back to another traditional antithesis and moral injunction, he refuses to be dragged into action, which belongs to the fraudulent realm of the "outside": just a moment ago I mentioned his views concerning those who opted for action in their zeal to reform religious dogma or civil law, in the name of a truth they claimed to possess. The only activity that does not deceive is the inner action of an individual: the activity of judging the world, or oneself. Ultimately it will be the action of which the ego is both source and target, an action expressed in terms of reflexive verbs: to essay oneself, to examine oneself, to paint oneself—*self-referential* movements to which we shall be paying particularly close attention in what follows. In the end, both words and acts regain their validity, but guaranteed by reflective consciousness and apathy. The identity that will finally be offered to us in the work of the self-portraitist is different from the identity that Montaigne originally sought in the strict and tacit equality between the segments of the self. Our task will be to follow Montaigne's progress from one concept of identity to the other. The *movement* that I shall try to describe is nothing other than the effort of a man who, starting from a concept of identity based on the principles of constancy, stability, and self-consistency (a goal that turns out to be impossible to achieve), begins to develop a new concept of identity without abandoning the original one, but nonetheless altering its content and meaning.

## THE THEORETICAL LIFE AND THE FUNCTION OF THE EXAMPLE

The relation to the world that Montaigne initiated from his refuge of reading and repose was what the ancients called *theoria,* or the theoretical life, i.e., comprehension of the world as it offers itself to the contemplative gaze. In a passage added to the manuscript by Montaigne's own hand (subsequent to 1588) we find one of many classical *topoi* justifying *theoria*: "Our life, Pythagoras used to say, is like the great and populous assembly at the Olympic games. Some exercise their bodies to win glory in the games, others bring merchandise to sell for gain. There are some, and not the worst, who seek no other profit than to see how and why everything is done, and to be spectators of the life of other men in order to judge and regulate their own." This is not merely a "chrie," or rehearsal of an *authorized* opinion, an opinion worthy of approval, but even more a statement of the attitude that Montaigne himself intends to adopt in the face of contemporary reality: "As I seldom read in histories of such commotions in other states without regretting that I could not be present to consider them better, so my curiosity makes me feel some satisfaction at seeing with my own eyes this notable spectacle of our public death, its symptoms and its form. And since I cannot retard it, I am glad to be destined to watch it and learn from it. Thus do we eagerly seek to recognize, even in shadow and in the fiction of the theaters, the representation of the tragic play of human fortune."

Gazing upon the agitation of men absorbed by battles and interests of their own, the stationary spectator looks to the causes of things: his concern is to discover the *how* and the *why*, in order to satisfy his *curiosity*. This does not mean that he is disinterested, however; he can, if he wishes (and Montaigne seems to have so wished, at least when he began his work), strive to ensure that the truth revealed in the spectacle of the world is applied in his inner life. To succeed in this he must enlist the aid of his judgment (i.e., the intellectual act in which an individual looks at himself and compares himself with others) and his will (i.e., the formative or transformative act by which an individual *governs* his life).

The aim of the investigation, acutely pursued through the varied spectacle of human action, is to discover regular sequences, which will possess, in addition to explanatory value, direct or indirect *regulative* value. The fortune or misfortune of illustrious men may serve as models or warnings: even the errors of great men disclose principles of conduct and in so doing help to unify our moral lives. A moral truth perceived externally in its universal validity should be capable of being reexperienced internally in the same way; its efficacy should be apparent in the identity of its inner and outer forms, i.e., in the consistency and cohesiveness of the soul. The hope that animates this view is that mimetic fidelity will guarantee inner fidelity. Once the truth has been grasped by the contemplative gaze (i.e., *theoria*), it cannot be changed in any essential way, only repeated; hence the subject who has taken possession of the truth is himself assured of maintaining a stable identity. Internal continuity comes about as a result of fidelity to the external model. In particular, this is the function that the spectator ascribes to exemplary lives: an *exemplum,* or figure that stands apart *(ex-emplum)* and yet stimulates imitation and generalization, can help strengthen the individual through its unique virtue. An individual who constantly strives to resemble an exemplum that is in itself a marvel of constancy is actually striving to achieve an identity of his own. To live up to such a standard, or at least to begin to do so, it ought to be enough merely to *recall* the exemplum or its emblem, an effigy on a medal. The impersonal literature of adages and lessons will be effective to the extent that the reader puts all his personal energy into his response. But *histories* will be even more effective. We have only to fix our gaze upon examples so admirable that we cannot help rehearsing them within ourselves:

> Until you have made yourself such that you dare not trip up in your own presence, and until you feel both shame and respect for yourself, (c) *let true ideals be kept before your mind* [Cicero], (a) keep ever in your mind Cato, Phocion, and Aristides, in whose presence even fools would hide their faults; make them *controllers* of all your intentions; if these intentions get off the track, your reverence for those men will set them right again. They will keep you in a fair way to be content with yourself, to borrow nothing except from yourself, to arrest your mind and fix it on definite and limited thoughts in which it may take pleasure; and, after understanding the true blessings, which we enjoy in so far as we understand them, to rest content with them, without any desire to prolong life and reputation. That is the counsel of true and natural philosophy, not of an ostentatious and talky philosophy like that of Pliny and Cicero.

We must turn our eyes toward exemplary individuals so that we can in turn imagine their eyes fixed on us: under the *scrutiny* of those who are set over us much as teachers and parents are, we are assigned our private truth, we learn the act of reaffirmation that constitutes our personal identity, and we do so purely in confrontation with ourselves *(dans la pure présence à soi)*.

The efficacy of the example depends in large part on its being a completed event; the image of moral perfection that it holds out is conjugated in the past perfect tense. The sharpness of its outline is associated with its remoteness in time. But the past of the example is for those devoted to it secretly inhabited by the future of the must-be. What the exemplary man *was* we must be in our turn, we *shall be* if we apply ourselves with all the energy at our disposal. For the exemplum, as I hardly need point out, is a preexisting cultural form that offers itself for us to emulate: the goal is to construct our own egos, to shape ourselves by surmounting all that is amorphous and vague in everyday life. It is to surround all that is soft and fluid in our "conditions and humors" with a firm outline copied from life in order to gather our substance together and cause it to solidify. A stamp is thus always impressed upon us. (La Boétie, Montaigne says, is a "soul of the old stamp.")

The imitation of the exemplum is a simulacrum, but a simulacrum that aims at identification. It is a role, but a role into which we must pour ourselves by allowing its law to inhabit us. We give ourselves over wholly to the formative power of the example. The latter, by giving us contour and firmness, at first seems either to rob us of our spontaneity or to oblige us to repress it. But before long the example has invaded us fully, pervaded our life. And our second spontaneity will then effortlessly carry out the acts required by the embodied model. To assimilate the exemplary lesson: such is the classical program of a pedagogy whose aim is to inculcate *norms* through imitation of great lives in which those norms have seen actualized. (This is a good point at which to measure the distance that separates the world of humanism from the contemporary cultural situation. In the humanist world, the example stands out against a horizon of achieved perfection—the ancient world; or else it offers itself in the form of a figure that is at once familiar and transcendent—Christ. By contrast, contemporary ideals—heroes, stars, charismatic figures, many of them ephemeral and interchangeable—are usually taken from the contemporary world itself; they are frequently subject to "manipulation," which, since exemplary figures are a powerful means of directing our desires, allows them to be exploited for economic and political ends.)

The ancient exemplum is a figure in a theater that has nothing to do with the theater of the world *(un théâtre absolu)*; it is separated from our world as the "Italian stage" is separated from the hall: the exemplum speaks, it carries the force of an admirable maxim, it is simultaneously maxim and act. Even more: it judges us, for it determines the scale of values, the measuring rod against which our merits and demerits are gauged. Exemplary words and images are too powerful ever to vanish from memory. Their imprint is indelible: for the example, as we shall see more than once, is usually deployed in a memorable scene, in which we are offered the hero's words inextricably intertwined with his life and death. We shall be looking more closely in what follows at [an] important illustration of this point: the death of La Boétie. . . .

## THE EXCEPTION

It is not impossible, as has been asserted, that Montaigne, when he began writing the *Essays,* set out in search of paradigms of many kinds (political, military, and moral) in an attempt to write a manual for the perfect gentleman. But his attention immediately turned, as Hugo Friedrich and Karlheinz Stierle have rightly pointed out, to the exception that contradicts the paradigm, to discrepancies among the lessons implicit in the

great exempla consecrated by tradition, and to the testimony of various
writers that the same behavior may on one occasion yield good results and
on another disaster. In considering many examples, Montaigne saw how
setting one beside another may give rise to contradictions, to mutual destruction. No human act can claim to be a fixed model or universal rule:
there are singular occurrences, remarkable events, and uncommon individuals worthy of our consideration. These do not lend themselves to imitation; and even supposing one wished to imitate them, they turn out to be
inimitable, unsuitable as guides and protectors for our travels. Hence the
past, like the contemporary world, offers a multitude of *facts* worthy of
curiosity, yet none that can claim to exercise full authority over our lives.
To be sure, these facts are far from equivalent to one another; some wear
the aspect of good, others of evil, and in Montaigne the verdict of the
moral conscience generally never wavers. As I said earlier, he never hesti-
ates as to what is *inadmissible*. But it is one thing to ascribe a moral value
to a famous act and another thing to see that act as a value capable of
orienting our own action, as life's polar star, so to speak. In the final analysis, all exempla, no matter how noble, are treated as mere anecdotes (in
the sense of "curious oddities" or, at most, "wonderful stories," certainly
worth the effort of retelling). They testify only to their singular existence;
such-and-such "occurred," according to witnesses worthy of being believed. Thus the only thing exemplified is that a possibility was in fact realized. Nothing is indicated but the occurrence of an event: sometimes quite
unexpected or out of the ordinary and hence worthy of our admiration
*(mirabilia)* but hardly of imitation. Manifesting their own uniqueness, exempla point to a world composed of unique, dissimilar entities, a world of
diversity in which "fabulous testimony" deserves at least a hearing and
perhaps full confidence. Each new event adduced as a specimen adds another dash of color to the picture of a motley world ruled by heterogeneity,
variety, and contradiction, another patch to an enormous patchwork "of
human capacity"—contingent and devoid of normative authority.

No doubt, Montaigne, who was in the habit of selecting and borrowing details—words and actions—from ancient books for use in his own,
was acutely aware of how easily those details could be mobilized, altered,
and permuted: he knew, in a word, how readily they could be decomposed
into *passages,* with all the ambiguity implicit in the term. His reading of
doxographers such as Stobeus encouraged him in this. No longer is the exemplum a fixed beacon shining above the vicissitudes of the corruptible
world. It is simply a piece of this disorderly world, an instant in its ever-
changing state, a figure of universal flux. With the passage of time and the

harm done by repetition, the exemplum is stripped of its preeminence, its privileged permanence. The paradigmatic figure loses the universal authority invested in it and returns to the accidental existence of which it is henceforth just one more manifestation. The would-be rule dissolves and is reabsorbed in the irregularity of the phenomenal universe. By contrast, the spectacle of the historical and natural world, enriched in this (sixteenth) century by innumerable marvels reported from other continents, comes to seem inexhaustible and manifold: possibly insecurity gains the upper hand with the encyclopedic expansion of "tableaux" and "histories" which, despite many efforts to establish enduring systems of nomenclature and classification, refuse to conform to any irrefutable order and contribute to the breakdown of the traditional structures of knowledge. Monsters, sports of nature, claim the same rank as lawful forms, since nature, everywhere the same, cannot distinguish between her legitimate offspring and her bastards. Deviance is henceforth only one possibility among many: its scandalous aspects are abolished with the disappearance of an undisputed right path or goal. "Every example is lame," concludes Montaigne, after instructing us not to hobble ourselves before exemplary men.

Henceforth it becomes impossible to complete the circuit linking the external example to the inner constancy of individual identity. Man must take the risk of living without the protection afforded by the example. Montaigne will even carry this to the point of saying, of his own moral life, that it is "exemplary enough if you take its instruction in reverse." . . .

### THE LOST FRIEND

In 1569 Montaigne published his translation of the *Natural Theology of Raymond Sebond,* thus fulfilling a request of his father, Pierre de Montaigne. The dedicatory letter was deliberately dated Paris, June 18, 1568: this was the day Pierre de Montaigne died (probably at Montaigne, where he was buried). His son was not present when he died, but atoned for his absence by the gift of this book.

In 1570 Montaigne sponsored the publication of two volumes of "booklets" containing material from manuscripts left to him by Etienne de la Boétie, who had died seven years earlier: included were translations of Plutarch and Xenophon, Latin verse, and French poetry. The dedicatory letters accompanying these booklets date from the period April–September 1570. In the same year Montaigne sold his councilorship in the Bordeaux Parlement.

Several months later, in March of 1571, Montaigne dated the votive inscriptions in his library that mark the beginning of this "retirement" from the date of his own birth. Soon thereafter, he began writing the *Essays*, the 1580 edition of which concluded in a postscript (to 2.37) with a dedicatory letter to Mme de Duras; the book begins with the note to the (anonymous) reader analyzed above, which was no doubt written after the book was complete.

Thus a series is formed by Montaigne's manifestations of devotion to beloved individuals (the father and the friend he had lost), his renunciation of public office, and his undertaking to write a work of his own for the benefit of those friends and relatives who would survive him.

Montaigne began his book because he believed he had only a short time left to live. His reasons for writing are reinforced, however, when he thinks of his late friend, whose literary legacy he had saved in its entirety from oblivion: "He alone enjoyed my true image, and carried it away. That is why I myself decipher myself so painstakingly." Thus the connection between death and the act of writing is twofold, for it involves the much earlier death (in 1563) of the friend who has not ceased to haunt Montaigne's thoughts.

It is hardly necessary to recall the many occasions on which Montaigne speaks of the loss of his friend and his subsequent mourning. Among them are the letter of 1563 to his father in which he recounts La Boétie's illness and death; the five dedicatory letters of 1570; and the entire chapter "Of friendship" (1.28) in the 1580 *Essays*: "Since the day I lost him . . . I only drag on in a weary life. And the very pleasures that come my way, instead of consoling me, redouble my grief for his loss." In 1581 he relates, in his *Travel Diary*, how, while taking the waters at the baths of La Villa, a sudden thought plunges him into sadness: "I was overcome by such painful thoughts about M. de la Boétie, and I was in this mood so long, that it did me much harm." Then, in a marginal addition to chapter 2.8 of the *Essays*, which would ultimately be incorporated into the edition of 1595, he wrote. "O my friend. Am I better off for having had the taste of it [friendship], or am I worse off? Certainly I am better off. My regret for him consoles and honors me. Is it not a pious and pleasant duty of life to be forever performing his obsequies? Is there an enjoyment that is worth this privation?" This loyalty, this assiduity in mourning, here turns into "enjoyment," for mourning makes Montaigne feel that he is better off. For this uninterrupted escort, in memory, of his departed friend, these "obsequies" that Montaigne is "forever performing," constitute an element, perhaps the only element of constancy and continuity in a life that knows itself consigned to inconstancy and discontinuity. Here we find avowal of an egocentric interest ("was I better off?") combined with a confession of voluntary dependence on an external object. The attention that Montaigne bestows upon himself and the sorrow for his lost friend, here so singularly mixed, together reveal the close interdependence between the sentiment of the ego and thought turned toward the privileged *other* ("O my friend!"); this conjunction is reflected in the paradoxical experience of simultaneous mourning and "enjoyment." The memory of one who is never finally laid to rest is accompanied by pleasure, attesting to the omnipotence of thought, to an ability to vanquish oblivion wherein the individual becomes conscious of his own strength.

For Montaigne, his friend's regard performed an essential function of moral instruction and direction. His friend was in possession of one version of the complete truth about Michel de Montaigne, a truth that Montaigne's own conscience was unable to carry to a comparable degree of fulness. Reread what he says: "He *alone* delighted in my true image, and carried it away with him." La Boétie's death robbed Montaigne of his only mirror: the loss of his friend effaced forever the image that La Boétie possessed. The fuller, more truthful *copy (double)* was erased. Inward reflection must belatedly come to the rescue: "That is why I decipher myself so curiously." It is important to pay close attention to what substitutes for what in these two parallel sentences. The "I" takes the place of "he alone" and the verb "decipher myself" replaces "delighted in my true image." It is clear that something has been lost in the exchange, that the truth of the image no longer has a possessor, which means starting all over from the beginning. Rather than the "delight" which was the friend's province, rather than the full, direct intuition of the same order as that exercised (according to Neoplatonist doctrine) by the celestial intelligences, Montaigne must resign himself to the laborious effort and partial revelations of introspective decipherment. Instead of the *immediate* knowledge that La Boétie possessed, the only knowledge of Montaigne now available requires a more tentative approach, and is marked by concern (the word he uses, "curiously," derives from *cura* and in the sixteenth century still connoted "concern"). With decipherment, the best that could be hoped for was a series of approximations to the truth, juxtaposing one word with another and thus constituting a *discursive* knowledge by means of a series of discontinuous strokes. But Montaigne has aged since La Boétie's death: thus he will never be able to reconstruct the image that existed in his friend's mind and that was carried with him to the grave: the portrait of the young Michel de Montaigne by Etienne de la Boétie is lost forever. What must be produced—at the cost of considerable effort—for the inspection of other viewers is a different image, as close as possible to the effigy spontaneously made available to his departed friend and just as spontaneously welcomed by La Boétie. In place of the faithful mirror reflecting the "true image," which enabled Montaigne to live two lives, one in himself and one in his friend's regard, there remains only the white page on which the aging Montaigne must tell about himself *(se dire soi-même)*, in words that will remain forever inadequate compared with the reciprocity of life. The perfect symmetry wherein friendship is explained by its individual cause— "because it was he; because it was I"—has become forever impossible. The friend's death has destroyed this tautology which, through mutual encouragement and exhortation, shared projects, and commerce in ideas, culminated in the mute "enjoyment" of brotherly likeness. Henceforth it will be necessary for Montaigne to enter into an asymmetrical relationship with himself and others, to save all that can be saved of this abolished happiness by giving it another body: the written word, the book. To perpetuate what one cannot resign oneself to having lost is to commit oneself to a work of replacement, substitution, translation.

Now we can more readily understand an attitude that Montaigne exhibits in the dedication (to his dying father) of Sebond's *Natural Theology*. Writing is justified primarily as the accomplishment of an assigned mission, a task that one has promised to perform; Montaigne indicates how scrupulously he viewed his role: "Monseigneur, in carrying out the task you set me last year at your home in Montaigne, I have cut out and trimmed with my own hand for Raymond Sebond, that great Spanish theologian and philosopher, a costume in the French style." The translation has dressed the text in a new "fashion." And this transformation offers one great advantage: the book can now "present itself in all good company." Thus it will be able, thanks to the wishes of Pierre de Montaigne and the labor of his son Michel, to do itself credit, now that it has been stripped of its scholastic Latin ("this wild bearing and barbaric demeanor"). The "improvement and correction" go beyond the work's outer dress, however. Pierre de Montaigne (to whom Michel respectfully imputes the paternity of the translation) remains a 'debtor": "For in exchange for his excellent and very religious arguments, his lofty and as it were divine conceptions, it will turn out that you for your part have brought him only words and language: a merchandise so vulgar and so vile that the more of it a man has, peradventure, the less he is worth." Pride in having improved the text by translation becomes humility: compared with the "conceptions" of the philosopher, the translation is nothing but idle words, a mere change of costume. The second life of Sebond's book in no way attests to the value of the person who provided it with "words and language." But who is that person? Michel de Montaigne, the translator of the work, is confounded with the *vous* addressed to his father, whose wish was the prime mover of the translation. The fact that the date of the dedication is the very day of the father's death says that the published work is the *continued* and realized wish of the late Seigneur de Montaigne. The survival of his father's wish will be recalled at the beginning of the "Apology for Raymond Sebond" (2.12) and, on the pretext of defending the ideas of the Spanish theologian, Montaigne will be able, in the "Apology," to secure a new lease on life for his father's last wish:

> (a) Now some days before his death, my father, having by chance come across this book under a pile of other abandoned papers, commanded me to put it into French for him. . . . It was a very strange and a new occupation for me; but being by chance at leisure at the time, and being unable to disobey any command of the best father there ever was, I got through it as best I could; at which he was singularly pleased, and ordered it to be printed; and this was done after his death.

Sebond's book, which was recommended to Montaigne's father for the conservative effect it might exert by winning increased respect for "our old belief," thus bore a double responsibility for prolonging lives threatened with destruction: Montaigne's father, when Pierre Bunel gave him the Spanish theologian's work, had not much time to live; and the old religious "customs" had been shaken by the "innovations of Luther," which Montaigne compares to an "incipient malady." In any case the point is to save what is in danger, to treat the symptoms of ruin. But just as the dedicatory letter ironized about that "base and vulgar commodity," words and language, so the "Apology for Raymond Sebond," in its attack on the book's adversaries (who are indirectly the enemies of Montaigne's father as well), develops arguments for skeptical nominalism so well that it jeopardizes the very authority that Montaigne would like to preserve. He had hoped to culminate his argument with a humble confession of personal "inadequacy," while forcing Sebond's adversaries to make a similar confession. Readers were not slow to notice that Sebond's own thought, far from being protected by this defense, itself succumbed to the implied radical critique of human knowledge. The son, eager in his humility to champion his father's cause, nearly undid it by excess of zeal. This was an undesired result, and perhaps a ruse of the unconscious. So far as his conscious desires are concerned, Montaigne tried his best to keep reminders of his father constantly before him. The list of things he wished to *preserve* in honor of his father's memory is a long one: habits of dress, trivial items, public offices, even pieces of masonry from the family residence.

> (b) My father loved to build up Montaigne, where he was born; and in all this administration of domestic affairs I love to follow his example and his rules, and shall bind my successors to them as much as I can. If I could do better for him, I would. I glory in the fact that his will still operates and acts through me. God forbid that I should allow to fail in my hands any semblance of life that I could restore to so good a father. Whenever I have taken a hand in completing some old bit of wall and repairing some badly constructed building, it has certainly been out of regard more to his intentions than to my own satisfaction. (c) And I blame my indolence that I have not gone further toward completing the things he began so handsomely in his house; all the more because I have a good chance of being the last of my race to possess it, and the last to put a hand to it.

The will of the father, already prolonged by the publication of the Sebond translation, was further prolonged in the work of finishing off the family residence, carried out under the son's direction. Montaigne did not want to fail in the task of continuing and conserving what had been transmitted to him: this, one might say, was the *private* aspect of his political conservatism, and indeed it may have been the latter's secret cornerstone. Here again, self-accusation on Montaigne's part accompanies his vow to safeguard that which was entrusted to him by a dying man: he has discharged his father's wishes well enough, but he might have done more. He blames "indolence" for his inability to carry through the things that his father had "begun so handsomely" to equally handsome conclusions. But he also furnishes an excuse: he has no male offspring to whom he can bequeath both his house and his name. Thus he is able to build his life, his book, while abandoning any thought of "building up Montaigne" apart from the plans that his father had already made. Now by making his book he would be able to ensure that his father's will would survive, whereas the walls of the castle, fated as they were to pass into the hands of others, could no longer guarantee such survival: the same intention of filial piety, the same desire to preserve an "image of life" have merely changed their locus, found new material in which to cast themselves and a new focal point for their expression.

As for Etienne de la Boétie, Montaigne openly proclaims a like desire to perpetuate his memory after death. He proposes to do this first by publishing his friend's works and second by the gift he makes of them in his dedicatory letters to selected readers: to them is entrusted the *safekeeping* of the *reliquiae* that bear witness to the personality of the departed friend. The witness that they bear, however, Montaigne regards as comporting an imperfect image of what La Boétie was, and even more of what he promised. His qualities and his promise remain unknown. He makes the following argument in the first place to M. de Mesmes:

> I think . . . it is a great consolation to the frailty and brevity of this life to believe that it can be *strengthened and prolonged* by reputation and renown. . . . So that, having loved above all else the late Monsieur de la Boétie, the greatest man of our time, in my opinion, I would think I was grossly failing in my duty if I wittingly let a name as rich as his and a memory so worthy of commendation vanish and be lost, and if I did not try, by those same parts of him, to *revive him and bring him back to life.* I do believe that he has some sense of this, and that these services of mine affect him and give him joy. In truth, he is still lodged in me *so entire and so alive* that I cannot believe that he is so irrevocably buried or so totally removed from our communication. Now, sir, because each new revelation I give of him and of his name is a *multiplication of this second life of his,* and, moreover, because his name is ennobled and honored by the place that receives it, it is up to me not only to spread it as much as I possibly can, but also to *entrust it to the keeping* of honorable and virtuous persons.

Later, Montaigne stated to Michel de L'Hospital his opinion that La Boétie was never granted employment commensurate with his abilities on behalf of the *res publica* and that he wrote only "by way of passing the time." He never won recognition for himself; he was "careless about pushing himself into the public eye." La Boétie's Latin verses must be regarded as the point of departure for a prophetic *induction*. Montaigne therefore begs Chancellor de l'Hospital to "*rise* through this work of his to the knowledge of him, and consequently to love and embrace his name and memory. . . . For there was not a man in the world in whose acquaintance and friendship he would rather have been *lodged* than in yours." Montaigne here feels free to argue from what was visible (and sometimes imperfect) to the admirable whole that lacked the opportunity to make itself manifest: "The very sports of great personages reveal to the clear-sighted

some honorable mark of the rank from which they come." In a similar
vein, when he speaks in the *Essays* of Alexander playing chess, he remarks:
"Each particle, each occupation of a man betrays him and reveals him just
as well as any other." La Boétie lacked the time to show what he was
worth: "The true juice and marrow of his worth have followed him, and
all we have left is the bark and the leaves." While saying that he is incapable of making his friend's qualities "visible," Montaigne nevertheless enu-
merates what they are: "the disciplined movements of his soul, his piety,
his virtue, his justice, the liveliness of his mind, the weight and soundness
of his judgment, the loftiness of his conceptions, so far elevated above
those of the vulgar, his learning, the graces that were ordinary companions
of his actions, the tender love he bore to his wretched country, and his
mortal and sworn hatred of every vice, but especially of that ugly traffic
that is hatched under the honorable name of justice." La Boétie deserved
an important mission; he himself, during his final illness (according to
Montaigne's account), regretted that he had not been given one; and Montaigne asks to be taken at his word, for his wishes to secure a "lodging"
for this figure in danger of oblivion, this friend whose writings by themselves are not sufficient to guarantee survival: "I am prodigiously eager
that at least his memory after him, to which alone from now on I owe the
good offices of our friendship, should receive the reward of his merit and
*be well lodged* in the good opinion of honorable and virtuous persons."
Montaigne can act as guarantor of this value because "no spoken or written statement in the schools of philosophy ever represented the rights and
duties of sacred friendship as exactly as did the practice that my friend and
I formed together." He repeats this judgment in the dedicatory letter to M.
de Lansac, in which he asks Lansac to "continue" his "good opinion and
good will" toward the "name" and "memory" of La Boétie, and then adds
the following by way of magnifying the image of his lost friend:

> And to speak boldly, sir, do not be afraid to find your good
> feeling for him somewhat increased; for since your taste of him
> has been only from the public evidence he gave of himself, it is
> my duty to assure you that he had so many degrees of ability
> beyond this that you are very far from having known him
> whole and entire. When he was alive, he did me the honor,
> which I count among my greatest good fortunes, of forming
> with me a bond of friendship so close and tight-knit that there
> was no slant, impulse, or motive in his soul that I was not able
> to consider and judge, at least unless my vision at times fell

short. Now, without prevarication, taken all in all, he was so nearly a miracle that in order not to fly beyond the limits of plausibility and be completely disbelieved, I am obliged, in speaking of him, to restrain myself and say far less good than I know about him.

Writing to M. de Foix, Montaigne relies even more explicitly on what he has been told in confidence in order to justify his claim that La Boétie's greatness is insufficiently reflected in his public record and written work. The "glory" that he wishes to attach to his friend's "virtue" is, he says, not undeserved. What he, Michel de Montaigne, says, moreover, should be believed just as if he were an apostle or a disciple of Socrates, for he is the first to admit how "pernicious" is the "license to toss . . . to the winds as we wish the praises of one and all"; and he offers the judgment that the "vice of lying" is "most unbecoming to a well-born man":

And his bad luck will have it that whereas he has provided me, as well as a man can do, with very just and very manifest occasions for praise, I have just as little means and ability to render him his due—I indeed, *to whom alone he communicated himself to the life, and who alone can vouch* for a million graces, perfections, and virtues which molded idle in the midst of so fair a soul owing to the ingratitude of his fortune. For since the nature of things has allowed, I know not how, that however beautiful and acceptable truth may be of itself, yet we embrace it only if it is infused and insinuated into our belief by the instruments of persuasion, I find myself so very destitute both of the credit that might give authority to my simple testimony and of the eloquence to enrich it and set it off well, that I have come very close to giving up this whole effort, for I have not even anything of his left by which I can worthily present to the world so much as his mind and his learning. . . . But finally I decided that it would be much more excusable for him to have buried with himself so many rare favors of heaven than it would be for me to bury also the knowledge he had given me of them.

Montaigne justifies his arbitrary juxtaposition of the various "booklets" written by his friend on the grounds that it is necessary to spread his memory abroad as widely as possible. This literary legacy, so heterogeneous in nature, is incommensurate with the sovereign personality of the departed: Montaigne deliberately published his friend's work piecemeal, in systematically scattered fashion, in order to increase the number of persons to whom he could address portions (within a volume that resembles an edited anthology):

> And therefore, having assiduously collected everything complete that I found among his *notebooks* and papers *scattered* here and there, the playthings of the wind and of his studies, I thought best, whatever it was, *to distribute and divide it up into as many parts as I could,* in order thereby to take the occasion to commend his memory to all the more people, choosing the most notable and worthy persons of my acquaintance, and those whose testimony might be the most honorable to him.

The diversity of the recipients will presumably help to spread his friend's posthumous renown. On the other hand, in order to preserve the unique image of this unique man, Montaigne, the privileged confidant, offers his own consciousness as the focal point in which the scattered fragments can converge; he is the sole repository, the unique guarantor of his friend's worth, the only person to whom was revealed "how great was his full worth."

> Posterity may believe me if it please, but *I swear to it upon all the conscience I have that I knew and saw him to be such, all things considered, that even in desire and imagination I could hardly reach beyond,* so far am I from assigning him many equals. I very humbly entreat you, sir, to *assume the general protection not only of his name* but also of these ten or twelve French poems, which cast themselves, as if out of necessity, *under the shelter of your favor.*

These lines of French verse are to be read, therefore, as a mere exercise:

> This was neither his occupation nor his study, and ... he hardly put his hand to his pen once a year, witness the little we have left from his whole life. For you see, sir, unseasoned and dry, all of his poetry that has come into my hands, without selection or choice, so that there is even some from his boyhood. In short, it seems as though he put his hand to it only to show that he was capable of doing anything. For as to the rest, thousands and thousands of times, even in his ordinary remarks, we have seen things come from him that were even more worthy of being known, more worthy of being admired.

This superior soul did not, however, have the time or the opportunity to figure on the world's stage. Montaigne, inclined as he is to indict the "vanity of words" (the title of 2.51), feels obliged to note that his own words are the only intermediary between what La Boétie was and the glorious memory of him that he hopes will be sustained, lodged, and taken *in safekeeping* by any number of important personages. Furthermore, when Montaigne addresses his wife in the last of the dedicatory epistles, his purpose is not merely to remind her of the legacy of papers and books that "this dear brother of mine" left her when he died, but even more to recommend that she read, following the death of a daughter "in the second year of her life," La Boétie's translation of a "letter of consolation" that Plutarch wrote to his wife in similar circumstances. What better way to hear the voice of philosophy than to attend to it at a time when "fortune" has subjected us to a similar ordeal? "I am sorry," Montaigne writes, "that fortune has made this present so appropriate for you." In this case it is the mother's suffering that guarantees that his friend's image will be appropriately received or "kept," as he wishes in all his dedications. Once again, La Boétie's voice, which has insinuated itself into Plutarch's thought, cannot fail to be perpetuated. Of the circle of friends whom Montaigne wished to "apprise" of La Boétie's writings (so as not "stingily to enjoy them all alone"), "none is more intimate" than his wife. Once again, Montaigne proposes his own weakness as grounds for effacing himself and allowing La Boétie (who had likewise placed himself at the service of an exemplary ancient text) to speak: "I leave to Plutarch the charge of consoling you and advising you of your duty in this, begging you to believe him for my sake. For he will reveal to you my views, and what can be said in this matter much better than I could myself."

In this latter aspect of his *second life*, La Boétie, the interpreter of Plutarch, is expressly called upon to encourage the work of mourning. Rescued from his first death, the brother resurrected in the form of the book is to help heal the wound caused by the loss of the child, by the continuing lack of offspring.

Here it is worth pausing to reread an important passage in the long letter that Montaigne wrote to his father to inform him of the final hours of La Boétie's life:

> Then, among other things, he began to entreat me again and again with extreme affection to *give him a place;* so that I was afraid that his judgment was shaken. Even when I had remonstrated with him very gently that he was letting the illness carry

him away and that these were not the words of a man in his
sound mind, he did not give in at first, and repeated even more
strongly: "My brother, my brother, do you refuse me *a place*?"
This until he forced me to convince him by reason and tell him
that since he was breathing and speaking and *had a body,* consequently he had *his place.* "True, true," he answered me then,
"I have one, but it is not the one I need; and then when all is
said, I have no being left." "God will give you a better one very
soon," said I. "Would that I were there already," he replied.
"For three days now I have been straining to leave."

The dying man's entreaty, which Montaigne apparently did not comprehend at the time, had since been fully appreciated. La Boétie's place (in
French: *place, lieu*) will henceforth be not only the library to which Montaigne had his departed "brother's" books and papers transported but also
the memory of the important persons to whom Montaigne publicly offered
the "collection of his works" while urging them to take the name of La
Boétie under their protection. Those who read these dedicatory letters in
1570 could hardly ignore the honorable home or "shelter" that an unknown author, Michel de Montaigne, was asking for a man struck down
before his time, while still neglected by the world at large. The task was
not yet complete, for Montaigne set apart the *Discours de la servitude volontaire,* reserving for it a *place* of honor at the center of the first book of
the *Essays.* The *Discours* deserved such a place of honor because it was
like a "rich, polished picture, formed according to art," around which
Montaigne arrayed his own prose in a frame of decorative *crotesques.*
Here again, as in the dedicatory letters, Montaigne proclaims his own inferiority and "inadequacy" although his friend's work was nothing more
than an adolescent exercise, "tentatively" written (*par manière d'essay*).
The essay "Of friendship" (1.28) takes up and freely develops a theme already broached in the dedicatory letters of 1570. Montaigne then recounts
the history of his friendship with La Boétie and compares it to other
friendships in order to justify his contention that this was unlike any other.

Hence Montaigne can, with justice, consider himself to be the faithful
executor of his friend's last wishes. He has preserved La Boétie's image,
given him a place, and made himself the jealous guardian and a trustee of
both: "And if I had not supported with all my strength a friend that I lost,
they would have torn him into a thousand contrasting appearances."

Yet, having safeguarded the name of La Boétie and made his writings
available to the public, Montaigne still feels that he has not done enough

to ensure the survival of one who gave more of himself to the duties of friendship than to the duties of writing or public life (where others failed to use him for the important tasks for which his talents suited him). Was publication of his works enough to give him, in full measure, the "place" for which he asked?

The experience of friendship had been one of a reciprocal "transport" of wills—on both sides, a voluntary alienation. Let us read once more the following celebrated lines:

> (a) It is not one special consideration, nor two, nor three, nor four, nor a thousand: it is I know not what quintessence of all this mixture, which, having seized my whole will, led it to plunge and lose itself in his; (c) which, having seized his whole will, led it to plunge and lose itself in mine, with equal hunger, equal rivalry. (a) I say lose, in truth, for neither of us reserved anything for himself, nor was anything either his or mine.

La Boétie's place was in Montaigne, who in turn "lost" himself in his friend's will. Note, in passing, that this paradigm (of complete reciprocity in total giving) brings to fruition in a pair of friends the same movement that Rousseau, at the beginning of the *Social Contract*, describes as occurring between the individual and the entire community at the moment of foundation: "Each of us makes common property of his person and all his strength." This "total alienation" then becomes constitutive of a new *body* or will—the general will. It would not be unreasonable to argue that Rousseau applied the model of *philia* and *amicitia* (which he might have taken from Aristotle and Cicero, or from Montaigne) to the *polis*, to the City animated by a "common *self*." Nothing in Montaigne's writing stands out more clearly than the image of two bodies inhabited by a single soul ("their relationship being that of one soul in two bodies, according to Aristotle's very apt definition") and of a will which, though based on personal conviction, is confounded with the will of another. Nevertheless, for Montaigne the perfect friendship consists of two friends, no more. Only "common friendships" can be "divided up." The superior friendship can only involve two people, who achieve a form of twinship. Montaigne cites the Roman example of Tiberius Gracchus and Caius Blossius: "(c) Having committed themselves absolutely to each other, they held absolutely the reins of each other's inclination." The result, says Montaigne, is "the complete fusion of our wills," so that "I have no doubt at all about my will, and just as little about that of such a friend." Certainty as to the wants of one's "brother" in friendship is no less complete than certainty as to one's own wants: "It is not in the power of all the arguments in the world to dislodge me from the certainty I have of the intentions and judgments of my friend."

Now, this exchange of will is also a reciprocal exchange of regards, so that each man's mind becomes transparent to the other and free of shadows:

> (a) Not one of his actions could be presented to me, whatever appearance it might have, that I could not immediately find the motive for it. Our souls pulled together in such unison, they *regarded* each other with such ardent affection, and with a like affection *revealed* themselves to each other to the very depths of our hearts, that not only did I know his soul as well as mine, but I should certainly have trusted myself to him more readily than to myself.

Along with the "fusion of wills," then, went this exchange of images, so that each friend stood before the other as a true mirror. In this doubling there was unity: a unity that was felt all the more strongly in that it overcame duality, and a doubling that was all the more valued in that it enabled each man to entrust the whole truth about himself to the other—a truth which neither possessed within himself with the same degree of certainty ("I should certainly have trusted myself to him more readily than to myself"). For the self, *effacement* in the will of the friend is also a form of *aggrandizement:* "The secret I have sworn to reveal to no other man, I can impact without perjury to the one who is not another man: he is myself. It is a great enough miracle to be doubled." To be doubled *(se doubler)*: the phrase suggests both *increase,* or redoubling *(redoublement),* of a primary identity and scission, or splitting *(dédoublement),* of a unique substance. My will is redoubled and augmented in the will of my friend; my image is split *(se dédouble)* in the truer image that my friend receives in order to offer it back to me as a gift. Should he die, I am plunged back into my original singularity, as into a *half-life,* as well as shorn of my certainty that the whole truth about me was lodged outside myself, in the severe and fraternal gaze of my friend:

> (a) For in truth, if I compare [all the rest of my life] . . . with the four years which were granted me to enjoy the sweet company and society of that man, it is nothing but smoke, nothing but dark and dreary night. Since the day I lost him . . . I only

drag on a weary life. And the very pleasures that come my way, instead of consoling me, *redouble my grief* for his loss. We went *halves in everything; it seems to me that I am robbing him of his share* . . . I was already so formed and accustomed to being a second self everywhere that only *half of me seems now alive*. . . . There is no action or thought in which I do not miss him, as indeed he would have missed me. For just as he surpassed me infinitely in every other ability and virtue, so he did in the duty of friendship.

The survivor is both guilty (because each time he enjoys a pleasure alone, he is "robbing" his friend of his share) and from now on forced to live a mutilated existence. He feels in himself both a superfluity and a lack. Deprived of his confidant, he must bear unaided life's all too heavy burden. Yet that life is also a mere fragment, nothing but "smoke," now that it has lost the ontological consistency of a doubled existence. It knows only the "redoubling of grief."

To perpetuate the name of La Boétie—"to prolong his existence," to preserve his "living image"—is therefore not merely to discharge a pious obligation to a lost friend. It is also a way, a forever inadequate way, of allowing Montaigne to continue to see (in the fraternal image he carries in his memory) the light of the gaze that La Boétie directed at him, and the image of himself that La Boétie's gaze offered. The place that his dying friend wanted him to secure lies in Montaigne's own consciousness: in this way Montaigne can return a shadow, as it were, of the pleasures robbed from his friend's share and at the same time (through the "curious" process of self-decipherment) perform the duties that his friend is no longer capable of discharging. And so it is that, through *memory* and *reflection*, in a relationship made asymmetrical by death, the pair of fraternal images can be perpetuated by the efforts of a single mind. Having "supported a friend that (he) lost," Montaigne was obliged, by the duty inherited from his friend, to keep a close and vigilant watch on himself, as La Boétie had done previously.

Thus after La Boétie's death, Montaigne continued to feel, and indeed felt even more strongly, what he had felt while his friend was still alive: namely, that being close to one another was superfluous, while being separated enhanced both men's "possession" of life:

(b) We filled and extended our possession of life better by separating: he lived, he enjoyed, he saw for me, and I for him, as fully as if he had been there. One part of us remained idle when

we were fused into one. Separation in space made the conjunction of our wills richer.

Separation, when it had been possible to follow it with reunion, bestowed
fullness; estrangement made possible a more agile exercise of reciprocity.
The friendly dialogue was carried on at a distance. What sort of exercise
was this, if not practice for the definite estrangement? "He *saw* for ME,
and I for HIM." The chiasmus, which is a figure for the crossed glances of
two friends, becomes a resource for the one who is left alone, provided he
keeps alive the image of his departed friend. The reflected gaze or sovereign judgment that Montaigne preserves in his own mind, incorruptible
and solid, somehow replaces the half of himself he is aware of having lost.
In this way La Boétie's friendly, lucid gaze is internalized, or "introjected":
it is the light turned inward, the affectionate vigilance that observes and
"controls" *(contrerolle)* Montaigne's mutable and fantastic existence.
From the abyss of death it continues to watch, in the living eye of self-
consciousness and writing. The inner duality, which divides the act of in-
trospection into an observing subject ("consciousness") and observed
object (variable existence), is a product of death: and it is the observing
subject—in which we normally locate our purest and most independent
act—that takes the place of the dead friend, as his second life and height-
ened absence. Self-consciousness and judgment, in their continuity, fixity,
and incessant desire to establish the truest possible image, carry within
themselves the persistent presence of an other: the experience and denial
of his death. Consciousness escapes change because it belongs not to life
*(la vie)* but to survival *(la survie)*. It is both the most intimate witness and
the spectator from beyond the grave. Thus the writer's solitude is haunted
and traversed by the internalized continuation of a lost "society," just as
it is oriented by the expectation of a future "society," composed of other
friends: the act of writing is intended to link Montaigne and his departed
friend indissolubly in the public mind, in order to put across the living image of an author who himself will soon have no *place* to reside, no *body*,
no "sponsor," other than his own book, offered as a gift to posterity. The
period of studious retirement thus takes on meaning as the interval between two moments of "communication": the exalted communication
with the chosen companion (which precedes the book) and the posthumous communication (achieved through the book) with those who will be
the intimates of Seigneur de Montaigne. Whichever way we face in time,
the essay works in relation to absence, in memory or anticipation of loss.
And all its efforts go toward preserving proximity. What Montaigne has

done for his father and La Boétie (namely, to preserve their living images), his book must do for him. His free intercourse with the authors in his library had shown him how reading might defy space and time: and it is based on this model of survival through the written word that Montaigne, with modesty and audacity (for he claims to be nothing and to have nothing to say), entrusts himself to posterity. Solitary subjectivity keeps itself alive only by means of external society, which it carries over into itself and either protects or foments.

Recall the words that Montaigne used in the dedicatory letter to M. de Mesmes: *"In truth he is still lodged in me so entire and so alive* that I cannot believe he is either so irrevocably buried or so totally removed from communication." And to M. de Foix he wrote: "I indeed, to whom alone *he communicated himself to the life."* The terms are exactly the same as those that he will later use in the introductory note of his book to define, not only for his "relatives and friends" but also for the unknown reader, the intention of the *Essays:* "by this means keep the knowledge they have had of me *more complete and alive.* . . . My defects will here be read *to the life."* The repetition is noteworthy: the book is given the task of securing indirectly ("by this means") the living plenitude that Montaigne's closest friendship had been able to achieve directly, through immediate communication. Now we can more fully understand the place that La Boétie and Montaigne's father occupy in the *Essays:* both are in different ways instigators who justify the act of writing; Montaigne cannot write *about himself* without referring to them, as if he received from *them* both the mandate for his work and the pardon for his imperfections. Though his writing begins with them and with their deaths, however, he does not imitate them or look to them as models: he will never be like them. Unlike his father, he has no male offspring; and he lacks Le Boétie's virtue, all of which went to fulfilling the obligations of friendship. To the friend whom fortune had deprived of works Montaigne offered a work whose author, "deprived of the sweetest of friends," admits that it would have been surpassed by the books that his friend might have written: "And if at the more mature age when I knew him, he had adopted a plan such as mine, of putting his ideas in writing, we should see many rare things which would bring us very close to the glory of antiquity." The only thing that La Boétie *built* was a great friendship ("So many coincidences are needed to build up such a friendship that it is a lot if fortune can do it once in three centuries"), and it is left to Montaigne to "furnish and *build"* himself, for, and by, his book.

The solitude in which Montaigne conversed with himself and, as the humanist expression would have it, became his own crowd *(sibi turba)*, is therefore not sustained solely by the strength of the ego. It bears within itself the needs of the other, the memory or desire of intimate commerce with an alien consciousness. It is the late fruit of the interrupted dialogue with the person who, as Cicero puts it, "est . . . tanquam alter idem" *(De amicitia* 21). It sets the stage for the presentation to the reader of a posthumous self portrait. The requirement of communication fills all temporal dimensions in Montaigne. It looks back to the past:

> (a) For, as I know by too certain experience, there is no consolation so sweet in the loss of our friends as that which comes to us from the knowledge of *not having forgotten to tell them anything* and of having had *perfect and entire communication* with them.

And it also turns toward the future: the friend *with whom* one has fully communicated is also the person *of whom* one will speak, to another audience. It is not enough to have told the friend everything: after his death one must outdo him in benevolence, gratuitously and without hoping for anything in return:

> (b) Those who have deserved friendship and gratitude from me have never lost it through being no longer there; I have paid them better and more carefully in their absence and ignorance. I speak more affectionately of my friends when there is no way left for them to know of it.

### "AT TIBI CERTAMEN MAIUS"

In populating the entire temporal spectrum—the past, taken up by memories of the friend, as well as the future, filled with plans to talk about him "more affectionately" than is possible now, in the present, which is given over to mourning and loss—the writer's consciousness dedicates itself to a project of self-exploration in time that both alters and enhances the exaltation experienced during the friend's lifetime.

Montaigne had read the *Discours de la servitude volontaire* before meeting La Boétie, and this work had aroused in him a desire to know its author:

> (a) And yet I am particularly obliged to this work, since it served as the medium of our first acquaintance. For it was shown to me long before I had seen him, and gave me my first

knowledge of his name, thus starting on its way this friendship which together we fostered, as long as God willed, so entire and so perfect that certainly you will hardly read of the like, and among men of today you see no trace of it in practice.

If Montaigne saw in the *Discours* an invitation to friendship, it was not only because he read in it a denunciation of oppressive monarchs, couched in the form of classical allusions that would have been immediately intelligible to a man of his education, but even more because La Boétie rounded out his definition of tyranny by contrasting it with friendship, which he portrayed as something radically precluded by the omnipotence of the tyrant. Friendship, according to La Boétie (who in this respect adhered to a standard humanist *topos*), is that form of "society" which tyranny makes impossible at every level of collective life:

> It is certain that the tyrant neither loves nor is loved. Friendship is a *sacred name, a holy thing;* it arises only between decent people. It is sustained not so much by profits as by the good life. What makes one friend sure of the other is the knowledge he has of his friend's integrity: the signs he has of this are his friend's natural goodness, faith, and constancy. There can be no friendship where there is cruelty, disloyalty, or injustice. And when wicked men assemble, one has a conspiracy, not a company. They do not love but fear one another. They are not friends but accomplices.
>
> Though tyranny may not prevent sure love, it would be difficult to find such in a tyrant, for, by standing above all others and having no companion, he is already beyond the bounds of friendship, which finds its true quarry in equality, which wants never to stand out and so is always equal.

Friendship, a reciprocal, honest, and disinterested exchange of selves, is diametrically opposed to the self-seeking obsequiousness of the person willing to cast himself into voluntary servitude. Great though the privileges of vice may be, the outcome is certain, the *assentator,* at first pampered and heaped with reward, will sooner or later become the victim of the tyrant's devastating whims. After describing at length the imitative mechanism that causes the relationship of servility to be reproduced from the top to the bottom of any society ruled by tyranny, La Boétie fails to offer any specific model of a free society by way of contrast, other than that of brotherhood among a limited circle of friends. Clearly, for him friendship offers the only possibility of resistance or salvation—and it is limited to "decent people."

The examples cited—Harmodius and Aristogiton, Brutus and Cassius—
raise, on the horizon of legend, the propsect of tyrannicide as the heroic
work to which a great friendship may devote itself. It was certainly not a
work of this sort that would seal the friendship between Montaigne and
La Boétie, however; rather, at a time when power was dispersed among
tyrants great and small (rulers, "parties," anarchic mobs), it was the idea
of seeking, outside power and safe from its arbitrary acts, a secure shelter
in that "sacred name" and "holy thing," friendship. They would devote
themselves to a private commerce and yet be so worthily employed in the
worship of virtue as not to suffer the reproach of having abandoned all
concern for the general welfare.

In the letter in which Montaigne recounts La Boétie's illness and
death, the dying man is described as apostrophizing his "brother" in terms
reminiscent of those just cited from the *Discours de la servitude volontaire:*

> And then, turning his words to me, he said: "My brother,
> whom I love dearly and whom I chose out of so many men in
> order to renew with you that virtuous and sincere friendship,
> the practice of which has for so long been driven from among
> us by our vices that there remain of it only a few old traces in
> the memory of antiquity, I entreat you to accept as a legacy my
> library and my books, which I give you."

Actually, in building up this friendship, La Boétie constantly appealed
to those "old traces," to those exemplary images preserved "in the memory of antiquity." Clearly, he is the link between the admirable past and
the friend he has chosen for himself. He is living proof that the ancient
examples can be brought back to life, just as the two friends revived the
Latin tongue for their own private use. La Boétie used Latin only in the
poems he wrote for his male friends; French was the language of choice
when he addressed himself to ladies. For Latin, as Montaigne would later
say, was endowed with an energy, a density, a moral vigor that outstripped
the feeble powers of the vulgar tongue, the image of a degenerate age.
Latin was the language of virile example, by reason of its higher ontological status. In the three Latin poems addressed to Montaigne, La Boétie assumes the role of guide. His age had put him in the lead (he was three
years older than Montaigne). He took the initiative in discharging one of
the duties Cicero had ascribed to friendship: *monere et moneri,* to admon-
ish and be admonished, "to alert one another." It was he who, with his
eye fixed on virtue's immutable star, scolded the younger man and re-
proached him when he misbehaved or showed weakness with respect to

the temptations of the flesh. It was he (as well as Montaigne's father) who encouraged his young friend to set his course in life by reference to the great men and incorruptible essences. Montaigne was exhorted to follow in the footsteps of his brother, who spoke to him in the language of striving and outdoing. Sometimes the exhortation is to *depart* (along with Belot in a company of three, for another hemisphere, far from the devastation of the civil wars yet without forsaking the melancholy souvenir of the mother country); sometimes it is to *climb* the path of virtue; sometimes it is to shun illusory pleasures, to conquer the *repose* reserved for men of wisdom. At the end of a quest propelled by the energy of refusal and sacrifice awaits legitimate pleasure, tranquil master of all time's horizons:

> Aut nibil est felix usquam, aut praestare beatum
> Sola potest virtus. Sola haec, quo gaudeat, in se
> Semper habet, bene praeteriti sibi conscia, sorti
> Quaecumque est praesenti aequa, et secura futurae.
> Indiga nullius, sibi tota innititur: extra
> Nil cupit aut metuit, nullo violabilis ictu,
> Sublimis, recta, et stabilis, seu pauperiem, seu
> Exilium, mortemve vehit currens rota, rerum
> Insanos spectat, media atque immobilis, aestus.
> Huc atque huc fortuna furens ruit: illa suis se
> Exercet laeta officiis, secum bona vere
> Tuta fruens, ipsoque sui fit ditior usu.
>
> O mihi si liceat tantos decerpere fructus,
> Si liceat, Montane, tibi! Experiamur uterque:
> Quod ni habitis potiemur, at immoriamur habendis!

Translated freely, this reads as follows:

> Either there is no such thing as happiness, or virtue alone can make us happy. It alone always possesses within itself the object of its pleasure, fully conscious of the past, capable of coping today with whatever blows fate may bring, confident in its future destiny. It needs nothing, but relies entirely on itself: outside, it neither desires nor fears anything; nothing can cause it harm; reaching for the heights, erect and stable, it scarcely matters if fortune, by a turn of the wheel, subjects it to poverty, exile, or death: it remains immobile, it occupies the center and contemplates the senseless fury of events. Mad fortune runs to and fro: but serene virtue attends to its duties; keeping its own com-

pany, it enjoys treasures that can never be taken from it, and grows wealthy on the profit it draws from itself.

O, that I may reap such handsome fruits! And that thou too, Montaigne, may reap them as well! *Let us both try it:* and if we do not become the possessors of these fruits, let us die in seeking to possess them!

Here we recognize the voice that Montaigne first heeded and that exhorts him to seek stability, self-possession, self-consistency, and contemplative serenity in the face of mankind's restlessness. The insistence on what is one's "own," on the exclusive relationship to oneself, can encompass two lives in a relationship that subsumes a dual being: "And our free will has no product more properly *its own* than affection and friendship." Admittedly, these are words taken from books (and perhaps transcribed verbatim). But La Boétie, with his affectionate emphasis proves that it is possible not only to repeat the words but also to relive and reincarnate the lesson they set forth. The injunction *experiamur uterque* might also be translated as "let us both undertake the *essay*," and would thus define one sense of the word *essay* (a sense that Montaigne quickly abandoned): an attempt whose object is known in advance, indeed all too well known, since it involves the sovereign good, sovereign in respect of its superiority, uniqueness, and universality—namely, virtue. Virtue is the sacrament of the friendly communion. The invocation of the exemplum, presided over by antique models and formulated *now* in a language of the past, is an exalted modality of the friendship bond. It implies emulation as well as sharing, and the devotion of one's life in its entirety to this unique task: *At immoriamur habendis*! What was the purpose of life becomes the purpose of death: to die in the hope of possessing these marvelous "fruits." This friendship's banner bears the motto "Virtue or Death!"

As we shall have occasion to note more than once in what follows, to sacrifice one's life is the capital act of the exemplary destiny. To proclaim the imperative of virtue is nothing if one does not know how to die for what one has proclaimed. To die according to one's discourse prevents that discourse from dissipating itself in "vain words," in futile rhetoric. Death sets upon judgment the seal of authenticity, which confirms and solidifies what will never achieve a pleasing consistency so long as it is compounded solely of words. The great men of the past live on in memory because they died according to their word. To avoid empty grandiloquence, speech must confront death and appropriate it; it must make death over into the supreme rhetorical effect. Death thus becomes the punctuation that gives meaning, the defining feature, the superlative oratorical act, which does not accompany discourse as a mere gesture but completes it, in the stasis from which there is no return. Only after death has intervened does it become permissible to assert that speech carried within itself a "performative" power, that *doing* began at the same moment as *saying*. An eloquent death retroactively projects its powerful meaning on all the life that precedes it. The exemplum culminates in a monumental death, erected as a column or a trophy, which compels the men of the future to remember, to be amazed, and to strive to imitate the model. Then, nature and fortune permitting, a new exemplum arises in response to the call of the old: thus La Boétie is able, in Montaigne's eyes, to show himself the equal of his ancient models and to die an admirable death, punctuated by a series of maxims. From the first day of his friend's illness, Montaigne collected these maxims with avid fascination. In the minds of contemporaries the *ultima verba* were more than just a spiritual testament; they offered a foretaste of the "direct vision" of the blessed.

> Thus I was as attentive as I could be. . . . For to portray him thus proudly steadfast in his brave demeanor, to make you see that invincible courage in a body struck down and battered by the furious attacks of death and pain, would require, I confess, a far better style than mine. Because although whenever he spoke about weighty and important matters during his life, he spoke about them in such a way that it would have been hard to write them so well, yet at this point it seemed that his mind and tongue were vying in their effort, as if to do him their ultimate service. For without a doubt I never saw him so full of such beautiful ideas or of such eloquence as he was all through this illness.

Throughout his long agony, La Boétie under his friend's watchful eye does an admirable job reciting the role of the dying sage: he dies like a book. Montaigne will remain struck by this for a long time to come. In his memory, his friendship with La Boétie does not merely deserve a place alongside such exemplary friendships as that of Caius Blossius and Tiberius Gracchus ("they were friends more than citizens"), nor is it merely an answer to La Boétie's expectation, as expressed in a letter to Montaigne: "I am not afraid that our nephews will refuse to inscribe our names (provided destiny affords us life) on the list of famous friends." More than this, according to Montaigne, their friendship actually surpassed the examples found in books: "You will hardly *read* of the like." Infused with the hyperbolic enthusiasm to outdo, it surpassed even its models: "Our friendship has no other model than itself, and can be compared only with itself. . . . For the very *discourses* that antiquity has left us on this subject seem to me weak compared with the feeling I have. And in this particular the facts surpass even the precepts of philosophy." La Boétie was possessed of a mind "molded in the pattern of other ages than this," but the friendship that he had "built up" with Montaigne had so fully fused with its ancient models as to have become its own model. Successful imitation had made it unique and inimitable. No longer was it a mere approximation to the fullness of friendship; it was that fullness, achieved and incarnate. The gap between the living reality and the model having vanished, it became possible for existence to confound itself with essence. It was not enough that this friendship should have risen above *"common usage"* and surpassed "other *common* friendships," nor was it enough that it did not "conform to the pattern of mild and regular friendships": in the surpassing of every model that Montaigne describes, a modern reader might decipher aesthetic pride at escaping all norms, the overestimation of a narcissism *à deux* that throws off the initial guidance of the examples by going farther and farther in the direction they indicate. Idealizing, Montaigne concludes that his friendship freed itself of all models to such an extent that its only model was itself: no other could come close.

La Boétie's death plunged Montaigne into "dark and troubling night." The feeling of dizzying superiority that he had achieved at his friend's instigation gave way to self-depreciation, with a melancholic tinge: Montaigne speaks of a black "smoke." Having heard Montaigne haughtily measure the distance that separated him and his friend from the "common" mass (their souls "mingled and blended with each other so completely" as to "efface the seam that joined them"), we find him now, left alone after the loss of La Boétie, declaring more than once that he numbers himself among the *common* crowd: "I consider myself one of the common sort, except in that I consider myself so." Friendship had enabled him to *rise above*, to transcend, the empire of exempla; but the loss of his friend casts Montaigne into *"humble* and inglorious life," a life whose variety, polymorphic abundance, and unstable progress refuse in a different way to conform to the unifying dictates of the models. Montaigne is faced not with the singleness of virtue but with the multiplicity of a "fluctuating and various existence."

What a strange reversal death has brought about! Of the two members of this fraternal couple, La Boétie was the one more advanced in wisdom, better versed in the requirements of virtue, more in control of his passions: the mold that gave shape to his soul subsumed it completely under a single "mark." Fortune (to use the term that Montaigne himself uses indefatigably), having snuffed out La Boétie's life at the age of thirty-two, all at once set upon his immense perfection the sign of incompleteness, of fragmentation. In his sorrow Montaigne sees his friend's incomparable moral grandeur ill served by the acts and works in which that greatness lacked the opportunity to fully objectify itself. La Boétie has left no monument in which the nobility of his soul is fully recognizable. It then becomes clear that the *testimony* of Michel de Montaigne is indispensable as proof that the absence of an important political career and a literary production amounting to no more than a few posthumous pamphlets are at best poor indicators of his friend's true "capacity": mere *sport* that could not possibly reveal to anyone, with the exception of a few keen observers, the true worth of a superior individual. The surviving friend is the only person capable of attesting to the fact of a *disparity* between the limited, heterogeneous nature of the actual work and the great actions and major books of which the author, fortune permitting, would have been capable. By publishing his friend's papers, duplicating his pamphlets, and writing the chapter "Of friendship," Montaigne attempted to demonstrate that the slim legacy actually left by La Boétie was unequal to his miraculous personality. In this connection, the forced imperfection of the work only gives relief to a perfection of spirit that was reduced to remaining almost entirely *internal*. This type of inequality between the outer work and the inner perfection is so closely associated with the assertion of sovereign subjectivity that many "modern" writers (from the Romantics to Valéry and beyond) would later edit themselves as Montaigne edited La Boétie, taking upon themselves the role of the posthumous *sponsor:* the unfinished, the fragmentary, the interrupted text, offered to the reader as a game in which the writer has not fully committed himself or in which he has been unable to lay hold of the infinite object of his desire, all stand as evidence that the writer's unfettered subjectivity surpasses its own products.

But the reversal brought about by La Boétie's death does not end with this aspect of his posthumous fortune. It affects Montaigne as well. After publishing the papers entrusted to him he attempts to continue on his own the work of moral unification in which his friend had tried to enlist him. But this, as we have seen, drags him down into the motley, fragmented world of diversity, to criticize it, to be sure, and yet ultimately to join it, since it is the human condition to live in this world. And whereas La Boétie's admirable unity left as its only external and public record no more than a few brief works, Montaigne's subjective diversity will be collected in a "register" and cast in the form of a book (*livre*) rather than a series of pamphlets (*livrets*), a book incorporating innumerable citations and ornaments in a multifarious whole. The duty of unity, which conscience knows it cannot escape, will be delegated to the book, which will never lack for the *thread* that serves to make of a multitude of "other people's flowers" a single "bunch," a unique bouquet: "Even so someone might say of me that I have here only made a bunch of other people's flowers, having furnished nothing of my own but the thread to tie them. Indeed I have yielded to public opinion in carrying these borrowed ornaments about on me. But I do not intend that they should cover and hide me; that is the opposite of my design, I who wish to make a show only of what is my own, and of what is naturally my own." But what is it to make a show of what is one's own? For Montaigne, it is to incorporate into the very thread of his work an attack on his own propensity to lose the thread: "If in speaking I am emboldened to digress however little from my thread, I never fail to lose it." It is also to declare: "(b) I have little control over myself and my moods. Chance has more power here than I. . . . (c) This also happens to me: that I do not find myself in the place where I look; and I find myself more by chance encounter than by searching and judgment." But just as in the case of the borrowings, or use of "other people's flowers," the text provides the "thread" that enables Montaigne to make a "bunch" of the self's scattered fragments and moments, and even as he says that he has lost the thread of his thought, he never allows the discourse of reflection to be interrupted—indeed, that discourse turns ignorance and forgetfulness to advantage. La Boétie's strength remained bottled up in himself and culminated in a noble death; Montaigne's avowed weakness will transform itself into strength by objectifying itself in his book: a book that moves, that "marches," but with a free and whimsical "step," no longer subject to the injuction to follow the narrow path of virtue.

In the long Latin epistle addressed to Montaigne, La Boétie sees himself as having a mind more limited and stable than that of his friend; Montaigne, whose soul is more complex, seems to him destined to great things but at the same time exposed to the strongest of temptations and the greatest of risks: "But for you there is more to combat, you, our friend, whom we know to be equally suited to impressive vices and impressive virtues." *At tibi certamen maius.* Montaigne, during this time of youth, is subject to contradictory demands and dangerous deviations; he stands in need of "warnings and corrections." Another poem addressed to Montaigne evokes the emblematic situation of Hercules at the crossroads between vice and virtue. Here again, the risk of deviancy and the dangerous attraction of libertinage are the themes of friendly admonition. Indeed, these assertions are true, in a more general and enduring sense, of Montaigne's thought itself. For him there exists no road without a fork, no virtue that does not turn into its opposite, no example that does not call forth a contradictory example.

For Montaigne, the conflict involves more than simply a clash of moral values which, as defined *within* the language of Christianized humanism, are antinomic. Indeed, the conflict challenges the very validity of that language and casts doubt on the obligation to obey its dictates. La Boétie allowed himself to be guided by the precepts of that language to the end of his very brief life, but Montaigne, for his part, puts them to the test, questions them, deviates from them. At first he respects those precepts but eventually he comes to see them as problematic, as one possible set of moral teachings among others. This being the case, it is permissible to choose an independent philosophy, an *"art de vivre"* of one's own.

With the advantage of hindsight, knowing Montaigne's finished work as we do, we may take the liberty of slightly twisting La Boétie's Latin to remark that, for Montaigne, *the greatest combat* lay precisely in his ambiguous relationship—at once attentive and unfaithful—to the lesson he had learned. The *essay,* skeptical and reflective but also full of improvisation, will be obliged to fill the void left by the decision to give up the guidance of exemplary models. La Boétie had been a living example, and his death, before the writing project was even begun, takes on an emblematic meaning: he will never be forgotten, but the virtue that lived in him is now without a representative or a field of action in this world. Whatever he might have done, in which he doubtless would have involved Montaigne, can be done no longer. The only thing left to do, which can and must be done, is to articulate the impossibility of fulfilling the destiny that was La Boétie's; this must be written down and communicated to the reader.

La Boétie left Montaigne with the memory of an exemplary *resolution* in the face of death:

> Because, owing to the unique and brotherly friendship that we
> had borne each other, I had a very certain knowledge of what
> he had intended, judged, and willed during his life, no doubt as
> great as one man can have of another. And because I knew this
> to be lofty, virtuous, full of very certain *resolution,* and in short

admirable, I readily foresaw that if illness left him the power to
express himself, nothing would escape him in such a necessity
but what was great and full of good example.

After La Boétie's death, however, Montaigne finds himself without the person who was the very example of resolution. Even as he makes "room" in
his own conscience for his friend's image and voice, he does not expect
that these will afford him the advice and admonition that formed the sinew
of the living friendship. The role of witness, however deeply internalized,
will have lost much of its pragmatic urgency and efficacy; it will survive in
severe and serene judgment and in self-scrutiny but not in the injunction to
act or in the expectation of future glory. It will not have the disciplinary
but disastrous effects that modern psychology attributes to a tyrannical superego. It is as if La Boétie's death suddenly revealed to Montaigne his
own death, and thus made seem inane any project guided by hope and
turned toward the future. "My plan is everywhere divisible; it is not based
on great hopes; each day's journey forms an end. And the journey of my
life is conducted in the same way." Nothing prevented Montaigne from
falling back into that *irresolution* form which La Boétie had hoped to re-
trieve him; from now on he is willing to let his irresolution show, as a
"scar" in his self-portrait—"irresolution [is] a most harmful failing in ne-
gotiating worldly affairs. I do not know which side to take in doubtful
enterprises. . . . I can easily maintain an opinion, but not choose one."
Choice and resolve were possibilities of shared friendship. The cause of
melancholy is none other than the veil of "smoke" that now clouds the
future and forces consciousness to fall back either on the present or, often
enough as well, on the territory inhabited by retrospective memory. All
that Montaigne has been able to save from the wreckage and incorporate
into himself is the act of vigilant reflection; he will want to secure for that
act an ample field of leisure, from which the need for *combat,* which La
Boétie had foreseen for his friend, will gradually disappear. Happy relax-
ation will supplant bellicose ardor.

Once the anticipation of action ceases to create tension and a need for
efficiency in the use of time, Montaigne's style is free to become sinuous,
to wander endlessly: no urgency hastens his pen. Since the only purpose of
the writing is to make itself manifest, no digression can divert it from its
goal. Its time is the time of pleasure and not that of active life, which imposes a strict economy on persuasive rhetoric: a prelude or postlude to
pragmatic existence, the time of *private* retirement or death. Underlying
the *Essays* is an infinite leisure redolent of both the intimacy of life and the

emptiness of death. To borrow a term favored by Maurice Blanchot, it is *idleness* (*désoeuvrement*) that gives rise to the "work" (*ouvrage*), with all its various forms.

La Boétie, himself a model of resolution, celebrated virtue and addressed the injunction "experiamur uterque" to Montaigne. At the same time, as we have seen, he gave a first definition of the essay: an attempt whose goal is known in advance, though it is not known whether that goal can be attained. La Boétie wanted to take the straightest path to the goal. Montaigne, left alone, will not prohibit himself from *divagating*, circumventing, "swerving aside." Montaigne's irresolution radically transforms the meaning of the essay, whose highly original form can be fully understood only by measuring the distance that separates it from La Boétie's *experiamur:* "If my mind could gain a firm footing, *I would not make essays,* I would make decisions; but it is always in apprenticeship and on trial." What will propel the movement of the essay is the avowal of ineffective effort, constantly starting over only to fail all too quickly, despite the fascination of the great models:

> It happens even to us, who are but abortions of men, sometimes to launch our soul, aroused by the ideas or examples of others, very far beyond her ordinary range; but it is a kind of passion that impels and drives her, and which to some extent tears her out of herself. For when this whirlwind is over, we see that without thinking about it she unbends and relaxes of herself, if not down to the lowest key, at least until she is no longer the same; so that then, for any occasion, for a lost bird or a broken glass, we let ourselves be moved just about like one of the vulgar.

The suspicion is carried to the point of supposing that even "in the lives of the heroes of times past" heroism predominated only "by fits and starts," in "miraculous moments": "But they are indeed mere moments."

Even more, the essay will be the realization of a new type of identification: sympathy of a wholly intellectual sort, comprehension of the great souls of the past, reasoned admiration of models of virtue. But at the same time the writer of the essay is acutely aware of belonging to a different "form," of failing to command the strength necessary to move from intuitive identification to active imitation. The ego perceives itself, then, through its distance and its disparity; and it chooses this very difference as the theme of its discourse. It will articulate the reasons why it chooses to venerate the exemplary figure and, at the same time, the reasons why it cannot hope to live up to the model. At this point it may be useful to re-read the beginning of chapter 1.37, "Of Cato the Younger" (taking care to distinguish the various layers of the text):

(a) I do not share that common error of judging another by my-self. I easily believe that another man may have qualities differ-ent from mine. (c) Because I feel myself tied down to one form, I do not oblige everybody to espouse it, as all others do. I be-lieve in and conceive a thousand contrary ways of life; and in contrast with the common run of men, I more easily admit dif-ference than resemblance between us. I am as ready as you please to acquit another man from sharing my conditions and principles. I consider him simple in himself, without relation to others; I mold him to his own model. I do not fail, just because I am not continent, to acknowledge sincerely the continence of the Feuillants and the Capuchins, and to admire the manner of their life. I can very well insinuate my imagination into their place, and I love and honor them all the more because they are different from me. I have a singular desire that we should each be judged in ourselves apart, and that I may not be measured in conformity with the common patterns.

(a) My weakness in no way alters my necessarily high regard for the strength and vigor of those who deserve it. (c) *There are men who praise nothing except what they are confident they can imitate* [Cicero]. (a) Crawling in the slime of the earth, I do not fail to observe, even in the clouds, the inimitable loftiness of certain heroic souls. It is a great deal for me to have my judg-ment regulated, if my actions cannot be, and to maintain at least this sovereign part free from corruption. It is something to have my will good when my legs fail me. This century in which we live, at least in our part of the world, is so leaden that not only the practice but even the idea of virtue is wanting; and it seems to be nothing else but a piece of school jargon—

(c) They think that virtue's just a word,
And a sacred grove mere sticks

—Horace

—*something they should revere even if they cannot understand it* [Cicero]. It is a trinket to hang in a cabinet, or as an orna-ment on the end of the tongue, like an earring on the tip of the ear.

(a) There are no more virtuous actions to be seen; those that wear virtue's appearance do not for all that have its essence; for profit, glory, fear, habit, and other such extraneous causes lead us to perform them. The justice, the valor, the good nature that we then exercise may be so called in consideration of others and of the appearance they bear in public, but in the doer this is not virtue at all; there is another end proposed, (c) another motivating cause. (a) Now virtue will avow nothing but what is done by and for itself alone.

To write, to exercise one's judgment, does not merely mean to return, via a circuitous path (and with a detour that encompasses the thought of death), to that which was indicted initially and which, as the foregoing shows, continues to be rejected: appearance. It is also to remain in contact—albeit negatively—with what one had sought behind appearances and which had eluded one's grasp: essence, exemplary virtue. The relationship to essence and virtue is from now on devoid of hope and stamped with humility, but it has become the *subject* of an endless discourse. The *ego* that goes "crawling in the slime of the earth" is the same ego that proclaims itself the "subject of [this] book."

The question raised at the outset was that of the self's identity and reasons for writing in a world given over to illusion and hyprocrisy. We have seen Montaigne's answer take shape in stages, marked by encounters with death, aesthetic form, and the problem of relations to others. And we have seen that Montaigne, after a vain attempt to free himself from the prestige of external models, was led to a reflective acceptance of the phenomenal world, as compiled and represented in works of literature.

# Montaigne's Anti-Influential Model of Identity

"I am," Michel de Montaigne imperiously announces in his "Au lec-teur," "myself the matter of my book." Matter is put in the peculiar posi-tion of standing for an equivalency between writer and book, Montaigne the writing self and Montaigne the text. It is through matter, whatever he may mean by it, that man is turned into book. This work of transubstanti-ation is linked to the work of a painter: "for it is myself I am painting." To paint oneself must then be to manipulate one's "matter" in such a way that it becomes a book. When the man Montaigne no longer exists ("hav-ing lost me"), the book, the picture, will remain, on the other side of the "equation," and retain the "shape" of the "matter" that went into them—the "matter" and the "manner" (which I would define for the moment as the changes worked on and in the "matter" as it passes from one side of the equivalency to the other) of Montaigne.

It might be objected that by "matter" he means simply "subject." But subject is an ambiguous word in its own right and this would not simplify matters (*sic*) at all. The word *matière* comes from the Latin *materia, mate-ries,* the first meaning of which was "stuff of which anything is com-posed," lumber for building, or for fuel (*Cassell's Latin Dictionary, Petit Robert*)—either a raw substance from which some finished product is ex-tracted, constructed, or from which energy may be coaxed to some useful end. A thing more or less worthless as is, in itself, which has value only as it fits into a process of shaping or consuming. In one manner or another,

From *Losing the Text: Readings in Literary Desire.* © 1986 by University of Georgia Press.

the concept of matter is always tied to the concept of shape—*manner*. The *Petit Robert,* for instance, cites as one meaning of "matter" the "indeterminate depth of being which form organizes." To say that one is the matter of something outside of oneself is to reduce the self to a kind of raw material, not a form but something susceptible of being formalized and becoming something else. But this shape, this formalized entity in which the matter of the self is invested, is an inanimate object, ink and paper. Then matter in the sense of *res, chose,* thing, a material substance, but one which retains the characteristics of that other primary matter, "dough" of the self, that "stuff" which was animate and only in part a physical phenomenon. And, in fact, the essential "matter" of a book is not tangible either—the meaning, I mean, and not the ink and the paper. The two meanings of matter are bound up with each other on each side of the equation, as much in Montaigne the man/writer as in the book. If we consider these two faces of "matter" more closely, it becomes apparent that what I have called the "meaning" of the book, analogous to the "mind" of Montaigne, is really no more than the organization, the form imposed on the ink and the paper. It is only the manner to which the matter has been subjected. In the "Au lecteur," the word *manner* does not appear. Perhaps because it is already there, within the word *matter.* Matter connotes manner, above all when we are talking about texts, in which the two are indistinguishable. And we may find that, for Montaigne, body and mind/spirit are just as mutually involved as matter and manner, and in just the same way. If this dialectical quaternity (mind is to body as meaning is to writing) implicit in the idea of "matter" retains some connotation of utility, of serving some useful end apart from its own being—what would that end be, what sort of construction might Montaigne mean?

He is nearest to answering this question in the essay "Du pédantisme [On teaching]." To deal with the transmission of ideas and information, Montaigne formulates his own model of the self, of its transactions with itself and with other selves. What emerges in his answer is a remarkable contradiction of Freudian psychology, an ingenious and impenetrable defense against all those who would read Montaigne the book. The real sense of "Au lecteur," as not welcome, not counsel, but *warning,* a sentinel's shrill "Who goes there?" emerges, as if Montaigne sensed that he was to become the literary fountainhead and paterfamilias to four centuries of French prose writers—*his* readers—as if, in the paradox of his "Au lecteur," at once beckoning to and denying its audience, Montaigne were already worried about what the future might make of him.

FEEDING THE MIND

To Montaigne, the word *pedant* would not have born the connotation of bookish affectation which it does for us. It meant simply teacher, profess-or, from the Greek *paideuin,* to educate or teach. The issue in the essay "Du pédantisme" is pedagogy, the inverse of Montaigne's own activity as writer: the transfer of bookish matter into the minds (manner) of the young. Same equation, worked backward.

Montaigne approaches the issue by wondering how it can be that "a soul rich in the knowledge of so many things does not become more lively and attentive for knowing, and that a rude and commonplace mind can shelter within itself, without being any better for it, speeches and judgments of the most excellent intellects." Answering his own question, he returns to the idea of knowledge as *stuff:* "To receive so many other brains," he says—brains, grey matter, mental acuity—". . . it is necessary . . . that one's own be beaten down." Then the mind, the self as mind, occupies a limited space and can accommodate only so much "stuff." By this matter, Montaigne says he means food, fuel—"just as too much liquid chokes a plant, or too much oil smothers a lamp; so also is the action of the mind stifled by too much study and *matter.*" But this rule does not always apply. Sometimes foreign matter does not stanch the soul but rather fills it. These are the two possible outcomes of education. Either the soul is mashed in or it is filled out, crushed or created. How to avoid the former and achieve the latter?

Montaigne seems to finesse the problem by passing over it to a consideration of the "utility" of philosophy. He praises those philosophers who, "just as they were great in knowledge, so were they still greater, in every act."

> Thus was it said of that geometrist of Syracuse who, having been diverted from study so as to put something in practice for the defense of his country, that of a sudden he displayed frightful engines and effects surpassing all human credence, all the while disdaining his own manufactures, and thinking by them to have corrupted the dignity of his art, for which his palpable works were only an apprenticeship and a plaything; thus, when occasionally put to tests of action, they have been seen to soar on so high a wing that their souls and hearts seemed to have been enlarged and enriched by intelligence of things.

What he is praising are souls *enlarged* and enriched, that is, filled up, *bien remplies,* but the essential aspect of this virtue is the act of translation, from idea to thing, thought to act, manner to matter. Montaigne appears to assume that this is best done by only a well-ballasted soul, a full and fulgent spirit, as if to force the idea through the substantiating flume required a certain critical mass.

## MEMORY IS NOT EQUAL TO MIND

Memory can contribute little to this mass. The distinction between memory and mind, or memory and soul, is one on which Montaigne manically insists—as he must, for memory is the plasma of influence, the link between the self and what it has read. The difference between memory and mind is that the former has no digestive tract. One cannot be nourished, filled, enriched, by memory. Memory can serve as a reservoir, a silo, for storing "grey matter," but it cannot absorb it. It is a kind of baggage compartment and not part of the organic self. "We work only to *fill* the memory, and leave the understanding and the consciousness empty. Just as birds sometimes go in search of grain and *carry it in their beaks without eating it,* so as to feed it to their young, so our teachers go about picking up knowledge out of books, and holding it just on the end of their lips, so as only to disgorge it on the wind." He wonders if he might not be guilty of comparable error: "pilfering here and there from books sayings which suit me, not to keep them, for I have no keeping-places, but to transport them into this one where, in truth, they are no more mine than they were where I got them." Interesting indeed that Montaigne, endowed as he was with a prodigious memory, should say that he has no "keeping-places." With what he has already said about memory, wouldn't this mean that he wishes to make his book into a surrogate for the memory (keeping-place) he claims to lack? And doesn't he imply that this "writerly" transfer of knowledge is very different from the one enacted by teachers, disgorging their memories? The answer to both questions must be yes, though for the time being Montaigne is content to leave them unresolved.

Now he is concerned about the malnourishment of students subjected to an "education" which is no more than ceaseless transfer, retention and disgorgement, back and forth between teacher and student. In this system, knowledge is just a "useless coin" which neither purchases nor enriches, but is simply passed from hand to hand. "We merely repeat"—"A parrot could easily say as much." Again, Montaigne implies his own complicity with what he is criticizing, with those who take up "matter" only to spit it out. He seems to confirm his culpability ("pilfering") by telling the story of the wealthy Roman who thought he could hire the learning of others whom he made to speak in his place, "each according to his *game*" (*gibier*).

Leaving the issue of his own "malnourishment" and repetitiveness completely ambiguous, Montaigne abruptly repeats the opposition between that which is only carried, and that which is consumed: "What good does it do us to have our bellies full of meat if it is not digested?" Here for the first time "matter" is described as "meat," flesh. The meat of what animal, what sort of "game"? For the sake of analysis, let us stick as nearly as possible to the figurations Montaigne has given us, keeping in mind that it is tropes we are dealing with, not facts: since he is talking about "grey matter," the learning of men, this can only mean human "meat." Montaigne is proposing a theory of pedagogy based on an analogy with cannibalism—a subject to which he devoted an entire essay (the thirty-first of the first book). Firstly, it is necessary to *dismember* the body of matter, the material corpus, but Montaigne believes that one ought to go further. We ought not simply to put the game in the bag and forget about it. This way starvation lies. We ought to eat it, chew it up, and digest it—*alter* it organically and chemically so that it disappears into us. The meat must "transform itself into ourselves," "augment and fortify us."

Montaigne complains that, instead of the alimentary destruction of classical authors and works, teacher and pupil prefer simply to lay out these "bookish corpses" piecemeal. The metaphorical comparison with real flesh, the bodily self, is so protracted and confused in this rhetoric, comparison always approaching equation, that we have to wonder if, on the rhetorical level, Montaigne still recognizes a difference between mental matter and substantial matter. Instead of improving their own bodies, growing stronger and more lively ("allègres"), the bad pedants give themselves up to the display and adoration of bits and pieces of the dead, a bookish idolatry, whereas he and his students ought to make of the carrion, not gods, but meals.

The student "ought to bring back a full soul," while, taught as he is, "he brings it back merely swollen, having only puffed it up instead of enlarging it." Fullness: still mental "matter" which occupies space, opposed to "puffing-up," "unpleasant, morbid swelling"—that is, *solid* plenitude (enlargement) versus hollow and illusory plenitude (puffiness). So, says Montaigne, do teachers "worsen" what is committed to them instead of "improving it" (it is worth drawing attention to the fact that *amender* can mean to fertilize, as in *amender une terre,* to manure a field), "as a carpen-

ter and a mason do." As carpenter and mason do: to improve means to
fashion, manipulate, a raw material.

Montaigne hurls a derisive pun after these quack-teachers: "My
Perigourdean vernacular most agreeably calls these knowledgeables 'letterstruck' (*lettreférits*), as you would say 'taken with letters' (*lettreférus*),
those whom letters have, so to speak, struck with a hammer." They love
"letters" of passion, but this passion makes the letters master of the peda-
gogues and not the other way around, as it should be. Passion and violence: the comparison is based on a physical conception of the link binding
teacher and literature, learning. The teacher is so madly in love that he lets
the beloved make a fool of him. He does not "possess" the beloved, never
attains to fructification or coupling (read: digestion, alimentary absorption, nourishment) because he loves too much, adores in the fashion of the
Provencal troubadours, as Dante adored Beatrice. The object of desire is
placed on a pedestal and never touched. Such worshipful treatment makes
"literature" coy and unyielding. Thus Montaigne might not, had he written the *Inferno*, have put Paolo and Francesca in hell for consummating
the desire that a *reading* suscitated (see *Inferno*, canto 5)—he might have
put them in Paradise instead. These "letterstruck" teachers teach students
to suffer letters passively, *to be influenced by them*, not how to "enjoy,"
to "possess" them, to transcend their influence. In this rhetorical context,
the idea of the gamesack full of game which is never eaten, of comestible
ballast, suggests sperm, chastity, the retention of fluid leading to swelling,
an unhealthy and "hollow" overfullness. The idea of plenitude becomes
sexually charged by the figurative language used to describe it. The ideal
is to *possess* "letters," "enjoy" them, by filling them with oneself. The text
is no longer simply a gamesack but an alimentary and sexual apparatus
which forms a complement to the reader's and plugs into it, becoming a
part of his own (mental) matter, corpus. The reader fecundates himself,
empties himself into himself, makes himself "full" (*gros*, pregnant). Montaigne is building an auto-erotic model for the transfer of learning as it
*ought* to occur. Masturbation is not an appropriate simile for this idea; it
is more akin to the practice of teachers whose knowledge is "as a useless
coinage good for no other use and employ than to be counted and thrown
away." The ideal advocated by Montaigne is autofecundation, a kind of
sublime narcissism, not masturbation. The dead writer makes this possible
by providing a "matter," a text, which is hollow and may be hooked up
to the reader and "filled" by him.

Whether writing or reading, one ought to be involved in a discourse
with oneself, then. The readerly or writerly self ought to constitute a self-

contained world of desire and requital. *So far* this looks like the purest so-lipsism, but Montaigne seems to have thought it the only alternative to be-ing partial, dependent, passive, dominated not only by texts and learning but by other humans (texts also in their own fashion) and the world. The pedants he criticizes have only a partial knowledge; they know their "mat-ter" intellectually, but they are not intimate with it, do not practice it. They know nothing of the other face of "grey matter," its substantial side. "They know the theoretical side of everything, but try to find one who puts it into practice." Their passion for letters is platonic, abstract, not car-nal, and never attains to procreation. They never "give birth." They do not even make a distinction between the whole and the part, the complete and the partial: "I saw a friend of mine in my house by way of passing the time, conversing with one of this type, counterfeit a jargon of nonsense, words without order, *a fabric of bits and pieces picked up at random,* ex-cept that it was often interspersed with words suited to their argument, and so amuse this idiot all of an afternoon at debating, the latter thinking all the while to be answering objections put to him; and yet he was a man of learning and reputation, and wore a handsome robe." So in fact, Mon-taigne sees nothing in anyone, any text, but himself, speaks only of him-self, whether he says so or not. When, in "Advice to the Reader," he refers to "friends," readers, he is speaking firstly to himself, of himself. It is Mon-taigne and only Montaigne on both sides of the equation, matter equals matter. If he hopes that the reader/friend will be able to take nourishment from "the knowledge they have had of me," this is because he proposes that every reader, himself included, *possess* this text and through it nourish his own knowledge of himself. Every reader, holding the book open before him, ought to say, "I am myself the matter of my (this) book."

## READER AS AUTHOR

Montaigne insists that no one need write a book to *possess* one, in fact to have written one. This is what he proposes as the end of education, to teach the young to read every book as if they were writing it. Montaigne is advocating the abolition of the concept of author as we understand it, of the book as something belonging to, springing from, a single source. He proposes reading and learning as dismemberment (willful distortion, breaking apart) and digestion (absorption and reconstruction)—the two movements of reading described by Harold Bloom, borrowing kabbalistic terminology, as *shevirat ha-kelim* and *tikkum:* the "breaking of the ves-sels" and "restitution." [Harold Bloom, *Kabbalah and Criticism.*] Also like

Bloom, Montaigne insists on a physical metaphor for this process; his is digestion while Bloom's is a jar of wine. Montaigne's is more solid and substantial, and more gruesome. Montaigne's theory of reading is very different in nature and coloration, if not so much in detail, from Bloom's: dismemberment and digestion, alimentary annihilation of every self ever to have written a book, in order that the reader become whole, nourish himself. Yet it is impossible not to recognize Montaigne's "voice" in every line of the *Essais*. What we must do, he says himself, is not look on this "presence" as the presence of Montaigne, who is in every sense absent, but as the presence of the self to itself. He tells us this by formally excluding himself, withdrawing himself (the first of Bloom's movements of interpretation is "contraction," *zimzum*) from the book at its beginning: "Goodbye, then, from Montaigne." Do not expect to encounter in these pages the Montaigne who nourished and completed himself by writing, Montaigne the writerly self. You the reader must invent your own Montaigne, one which has nothing but the most arbitrary and superficial connection with the one telling you "Goodbye."

He cites Adrian Turnèbe as a pedant who had risen above the practice of his peers. The example shows us that, when Montaigne uses the word *matter*, he is speaking firstly of mental "matter." He reverses the usual priority of signification, saying that it is the "outward shape" which is "a thing of emptiness." He is denouncing the idealism which is the basis for all realism. His dialectic of materiality does not begin on the plane of substance, but begins in and always rebounds toward the level of spirit, mind, mental "matter." But this latter is still matter. The "natures" which he calls admirable are "beautiful and strong," adjectives usually applied to "outward shape," which he has just called "emptiness." He cites a verse from Juvenal to underline the essentially material quality of virtue: "queis arte benigna / Et meliore luto finxit praecordia Titan [those whose hearts the titan Prometheus, by a particular grace, has fashioned from a superior *mud*.]" This virtue comprises knowledge, but it also, and this is more important, comprises what Montaigne calls "meaning [le sens]."

*Sensus* in Latin can mean sensation, emotion, or judgment, perception. The important connotation in either meaning is *sense*, the aspect of knowing which is rather corporeal than abstract. "Knowledge" ("science"), on the one hand, corresponds to "the outward shape," which is secondary, and on the other, understanding and consciousness are defined as material, part of the soul, of the spiritual, of the noncorporeal. And again Montaigne repeats the opposition of the "carried" and the "eaten": "Now we must not attach knowing to the soul, but rather incorporate it in the soul; we must not simply pour it over the soul, but color the soul with it; and if it does not change the soul, and improve its imperfect state, certainly it would be better to leave things as they are."

Here Montaigne intercalates the thematic of sexuality. A confirmed chauvinist, he insists that women can have nothing to do with the assimilation and transfer of knowledge. Learning is for him always a masculine phenomenon, "active," "positive" sexuality. A woman must know nothing of herself, concern herself only with that which is carried, with outward shape, with her husband, with "completing" him, bearing his children. So that she knows nothing of the essential "matter," spiritual "matter," and remains dependent, passive, accessory, comparable to the pedant who is excessively enamored of "letters," and lets them "beat him up."

Following this digression, he returns to the central issue of knowledge, in particular that knowledge which does not make men good servants of the state, but only good businessmen, makers of money. Without this utility, "you would undoubtedly see them [letters] as pitiful as they ever were." Interesting that Montaigne should use a feminine plural noun (*lettres*) for knowledge immediately after discussing women. It is the "femininity" of "letters" and of bad teachers which he is condemning here. And he points out that it is money which suports this femininity. Knowledge corrupts these pedants because they sprang from an innately and *economically* inferior matter: "Our studies in France having hardly any other goal than profit, except for those whom nature has made to be born to generous, rather than lucrative, positions, giving themselves over to letters, for such a short while (retired, before having acquired a taste for them, to a profession which has nothing to do with books), the only ones left to engage themselves solely in study are persons of base fortune who seek only to make a living by it." These latter are dependent on letters, while those born to more generous positions have no need of them. These dependents are no more than "gamesacks," cases for their learning, hunters who never eat their game but carry it and finally sell it, to make a living. The bad teacher uses his knowledge to turn a profit while virtuous persons profit by making knowledge a part of themselves. The virtuous may destroy, decompose what they know without fear of consequences. The bad pedant must take care to keep it intact for his buyers. Knowledge, says Montaigne, is a drug which must be partaken of only with the utmost prudence and strength of character. Pedants, because they are "vitiated sheaths," easily addict themselves.

The custom in Persia, according to Montaigne, was to teach virtue rather than letters per se. Before giving "matter" (solid food) to the schoolboy, he was taught to digest it properly ("these took on the burden of making his body handsome and healthy"). And the essential part of this process was that the business of teaching was not trusted to women, but to eunuchs, "because of their virtue." What sort of virtue can this be? It consists precisely in being needless, not depending: a eunuch would (one supposes) be free from sexual impulse, not depend on femininity (or masculinity, for that mater). Consider, says Montaigne, the government of Lycurgus, his concern for "the nourishment of children," his teaching which "formed and molded them vigorously." Hippias, on the other hand, an example of those who have to peddle what they know for pennies, found that such a virtuous people as the Spartans had no interest in his product. Virtue refuses to consider knowledge as merchandise. The mere exchange of it does not educate. It must be torn to pieces, turned into living flesh. Insofar as one knows how to tear and digest, one does not need to "know." Inasmuch as study signifies "exchange," "the study of knowledge softens and *effeminizes* courage."

Virtuous knowledge is finally defined as a destructive, digestive force which does not respect distinctions among the kinds of matter, a skill at transubstantiation. It can turn any and all matter into one: the self. This "knowing," then, is rather a "manner" than a matter. What the young must be taught, Montaigne repeats incessantly in this essay, is how to be themselves: how to dismember, cut up, chew up, devour, desecrate, digest, the carrion of books, and above all how not to keep it intact. In this way, they learn to "contain" everything, to need nothing, and so they learn how not to be passive, dependent, accessory. The student is himself both master and slave, as Hegel puts it in *The Phenomenology of Mind;* or even, he becomes his own father—he fructifies and gives birth to himself, at once precursor and successor to himself.

## THE FORMULA OF THE SELF

Montaigne begins his book, and I began this essay, by sketching an equivalency between the text and the self. This alchemical equation is the emblem of transubstantiation, of the para-chemical process of resolving all matter into one, and it also reveals the "digestive" genealogy of precursors which the self, any writing or reading self, must drag like a tail, becoming finally a "precursor" to others. The end of every self, having learned how to manipulate "matter," having decomposed some of it, is to put it back together. First it recomposes it as "flesh," the substance of the mind, but the writer takes the process a step further. He devours himself, decomposes his own "body," reshaping it into a text. Why? So that it may serve as nourishment, first to himself, and then to others—not as his flesh, but as *theirs*.

Reading and writing are then metaphorically cannibalistic (filling the "shapes" left by others with one's own flesh and "eating" it). We should not be surprised to read this passage in essay thirty-one:

> I have a song made up by a prisoner, in which there is this touch: that they all boldly come and assemble themselves to dine on him; for they will be eating piece for piece their fathers and their forebears, who have served as food and nourishment to his own body. "These muscles, he says, this flesh and these veins, they are yours, poor fools that you are; you do not recognize that the substance of the members of your ancestors is still there; savor them well, you will discover in them the taste of your own flesh." Invention which in no wise smacks of barbarism.

This idea cannot really be solipsistic at all, because it denies the self as a distinct entity, as any kind of entity. It is nothing but a force, a hunger, a consuming, a digestion, which is its own end and object, engulfing all ends and all objects, all identities past, present *and possible*—future ones included. There is no self, as we (Freud) conceive it, Montaigne is saying, no self that may be positively conceived and described. The reading self, devouring its own stuff in the shape of the other (the text), by writing in its turn is merely preparing a sumptuous repast for other cannibals/readers to come.

So we are not dealing here with a simple linear equation but rather with a circular tautology. Montaigne's model is like the ancient alchemists', which depicted the process of transubstantiation as a dragon swallowing the tail of his image, his double. By denying the very concept of a distinct identity and self, Montaigne means to withdraw himself from the linear succession of readers and writers by embracing it, restating it so that it disappears. He cannot be "influenced" by precursors but simply feeds on himself in their shapes. The book itself is only that, a shape, a "gamesack," until it is read, while for the writer the book is the excrescence of digestion, the skin which he leaves behind when he has eaten himself all up.

What Montaigne proposes here is a powerful alternative to the Freudian model of the self. What we must understand about both models is that there is nothing inevitable about either one. Both are elaborate, painstakingly, desperately articulated *defenses,* personal justifications, primers for living and knowing. We all construct such walls, more or less crudely, with doors in them, so that there are points of entry and exit. There is nothing inevitable, "true," about any of them. Montaigne's model is instructive because it so ingeniously overrides Freud's, anticipates and undoes it, and by doing so exposes itself and Freudian psychology for what they really are: hollow "shapes," fascinating for their meticulous emptiness.

Implicitly, Montaigne is saying that the primary object-choice, the object of primary identification, which is the model for the superego and for every subsequent object of desire (see Freud, *Three Essays on the Theory of Sexuality* and *Totem and Taboo*), is neither the mother nor the father but the primordial, unconstituted, un-self, which is only expressing its hunger for itself, its own substance, by biting its mother's breast, loving others, reading books. So the "un-self" can neither influence nor be influenced, never reads or writes anything but itself.

Freud, on the other hand, insists that cannibalism is secondary—that is, derives from the desire to incorporate the other, the desired object—and primitive. "By incorporating parts of a person's body through the act of eating," he says, "one at the same time acquires the qualities possessed by him." By devouring their father the sons "accomplished their identification with him, and each one of them acquired a portion of his strength" (Jean Laplanche and J. B. Pontalis, *The Language of Psychoanalysis*). Not at all, replies Montaigne. The son only devours his father because he has projected his own person into the form and image of his father in order to recognize himself, to nourish himself (his un-self). Influence is a meaningless concept because every "self" begets itself, is constituted negatively, consumes itself, shapes and reshapes itself, leaving only the notation, the calculus of the circular equation, the skin of the dragon who has swallowed himself, waste, fecal matter, so to speak (fecal matter, substantial emblem of the transubstantiative powers of digestion, was one of the primary ingredients in alchemical recipes), which serves only as "fertilizer" for the flowers which grow nearby, and which will in their turn "fecal-date" themselves.

# Chronology

| | |
|---|---|
| 1533 | Michel Eyquem is born at Montaigne, son of Pierre Eyquem. |
| 1534–39 | Montaigne is tutored exclusively in Latin; no French is spoken in his presence. |
| 1539–46 | Studies at the Collège de Guyenne in Bordeaux. |
| 1547–59 | Studies philosophy at Bordeaux and law at Toulouse. |
| 1554 | Montaigne's father, Pierre Eyquem, is elected mayor of Bordeaux. Montaigne assumes the position of Counselor in the Cour des Aides of Périgueux. |
| 1557 | Montaigne becomes a Counselor in the Bordeaux Parlement. |
| 1559 | His friendship with La Boétie begins. |
| 1563 | La Boétie dies. |
| 1565 | Montaigne marries Françoise de la Chassaigne. |
| 1568 | Pierre Eyquem dies. |
| 1569 | Montaigne's translation of Raymond Sebond's *Theologia Naturalis* published. |
| 1570 | Montaigne retires from the Bordeaux Parlement, has La Boétie's *Discours de la servitude volontaire* published, and begins to write the *Essais*. |
| 1580 | First edition of the *Essais* published (two books). Montaigne goes on a voyage to Germany, Switzerland, and Italy. |
| 1581–85 | Montaigne serves as mayor of Bordeux. |
| 1588 | New edition of the *Essais*, with a third book and additions to the first two. |

1592    Montaigne dies.

1595    Posthumous edition of the *Essais* published, based on the additions to the Bordeaux copy.

# Contributors

HAROLD BLOOM, Sterling Professor of the Humanities at Yale University, is the author of *The Anxiety of Influence, Poetry and Repression,* and many other volumes of literary criticism. His forthcoming study, *Freud: Transference and Authority,* attempts a full-scale reading of all of Freud's major writings. A MacArthur Prize Fellow, he is general editor of five series of literary criticism published by Chelsea House. During 1987–88, he was appointed Charles Eliot Norton Professor of Poetry at Harvard University.

HERBERT LÜTHY is a Swiss historian. He has translated Montaigne into German and is the author of *France against Herself, La Banque Protestante en France,* and *Wozu Geschichte?*

DONALD M. FRAME, Professor Emeritus of French at Columbia University, is the leading American figure in Montaigne scholarship. He is the translator of Montaigne's complete works and the author of a biography on Montaigne, as well as numerous works of criticism concerning Montaigne.

MAURICE MERLEAU-PONTY was one of France's most prominent post–World War II philosophers along with Sartre. He is perhaps best known for his revision of Husserl's phenomenology in works such as *The Phenomenology of Perception* and *The Visible and the Invisible,* although he is also known for politically committed works such as *Humanism and Terror.*

LOUIS MARIN is Professor at the Ecole des Hautes Etudes in Paris, and visiting Professor at the Johns Hopkins University. He is the author of numerous books, among which are, *Semiotique de la passion, topiques et figures; Le Récit est un piège; La Critique du discours: sur la "Logique" de Port-Royal et les "Pensées" de Pascal,* and *Utopics: Spatial Play.*

233

TERENCE CAVE is a Tutor in Modern Languages and a Lecturer in French at St. Johns College, Oxford. He has edited two books on Ronsard, and is the author of *The Cornucopian Text: Problems of Writing in the French Renaissance*.

IRMA S. MAJER is Assistant Professor of French at Mount Holyoke College.

CATHERINE DEMURE teaches philosophy at the University of Aix-Marseilles and has written several articles on Montaigne.

THOMAS M. GREENE is Professor of Renaissance Studies and Comparative Literature at Yale University. His critical works include *The Descent from Heaven, Rabelais: A Study in Comic Courage, The Light in Troy: Imitation and Discovery in Renaissance Poetry*, and *The Vulnerable Text*.

JEAN STAROBINSKI is Professor of French at the University of Geneva and the recipient of the 1984 Balzan Prize. A major contemporary critic of French literature, his works include *Jean-Jacques Rousseau: La transparence et l'obstacle, L'Oeil vivant, La Relation critique, 1789: The Emblems of Reason*, and *Words upon Words: The Anagrams of Ferdinand de Saussure*.

JEFFERSON HUMPHRIES is Assistant Professor of French and Italian at Louisiana State University and A & M College—Baton Rouge. He is the author of *The Otherness Within: Gnostic Readings in Marcel Proust, Flannery O'Connor, and François Villon; Metamorphoses of the Raven: Literary Overdeterminedness in France and the South since Poe;* and *The Puritan and the Cynic: The Literary Moralist in America and France*.

# Bibliography

Auerbach, Erich. "L'humaine condition." In *Mimesis: The Representation of Reality in Western Literature,* translated by Willard R. Trask, 285–311. Princeton: Princeton University Press, 1953.

Baraz, Michael. *L'être et la connaissance selon Montaigne.* Paris: J. Corti, 1968.

Barnett, Richard. *Dynamics of Detour: Codes of Indirection in Montaigne, Pascal, Racine, and Guilleragues.* Tübingen: Neu C., 1983.

Bauschatz, Cathleen M. "Montaigne's Conception of Reading in the Context of Renaissance Poetics and Modern Criticism." In *The Reader in the Text: Essays on Audience and Interpretation,* edited by Susan R. Suleiman and Inge Crosman, 264–91. Princeton: Princeton University Press, 1980.

Beaujour, Michel. *Miroirs d'Encre.* Paris; Seuil, 1980.

———. "Speculum, Method, and Self-Portrayal: Some Epistemological Problems." In *Mimesis: From Mirror to Method, Augustine to Descartes,* edited by John D. Lyons and Stephen G. Nichols, Jr., 188–96. Hanover, N.H.: University Press of New England for Dartmouth College, 1982.

Blanchard, Jean Marc. "Of Cannibalism and Autobiography." *MLN* 93 (1978): 654–76.

Bloom, Harold, ed. *Modern Critical Interpretations: Montaigne's* Essays. New Haven, Conn.: Chelsea House, 1987.

Boase, Alan M. *The Fortunes of Montaigne: A History of the* Essais *in France, 1580–1669.* London: Methuen, 1935.

Bowen, Barbara C. *The Age of Bluff: Paradox and Ambiguity in Rabelais and Montaigne.* Urbana: University of Illinois Press, 1972.

———. "Montaigne's Anti-*Phaedrus*: 'Sur des vers de Virgile' (*Essais,* III, v)." *Journal of Medieval and Renaissance Studies* 5, no. 1 (1975): 107–21.

Brody, Jules. "From Teeth to Text in 'De l'experience': A Philological Reading." *L'Esprit créateur* 20 (Spring 1980): 7–22.

———. *Lectures de Montaigne.* Lexington, Ky.: French Forum, 1982.

Brown, Frieda S. " 'De la solitude': A Re-examination of Montaigne's Retreat from Public Life." In *From Marot to Montaigne: Essays on French Renaissance Literature,* edited by Raymond C. La Charite, 137–46. *Kentucky Romance Quarterly* 19, supplement no. 1, 1972.

————. *Religious and Political Conservatism in the* Essais *of Montaigne.* Geneva: Droz, 1963.

Brunschvicg, Léon. *Descartes et Pascal, Lecteurs de Montaigne.* New York and Paris: Brentano's, 1944.

Brush, Craig B. "The Essayist Is Learned: Montaigne's *Journal de voyage* and the *Essais.*" *Romantic Review* 62 (1971): 16–27.

————. "Reflections on Montaigne's Concept of Being." In *From Marot to Montaigne: Essays on French Renaissance Literature,* edited by Raymond C. La Charite, 147–66. *Kentucky Romance Quarterly* 19, suppl. no. 1, 1972. .

Buffum, Imbrie. *L'Influence du voyage de Montaigne sur les* Essais. Princeton: Princeton University Press, 1946.

*Bulletin de la Société des amis de Montaigne* 1– (1913–).

Burke, Peter. *Montaigne.* Oxford: Oxford University Press, 1981.

Butor, Michel. *Essais sur les* Essais. Paris: Gallimard, 1968.

Cameron, Keith, ed. *Montaigne and His Age.* Exeter: University of Exeter, 1981.

Cave, Terence. "The Mimesis of Reading in the Renaissance." In *Mimesis: From Mirror to Method, Augustine to Descartes,* edited by John D. Lyons and Stephen G. Nichols, Jr., 149–65. Hanover, N.H.: University Press of New England, 1982.

————. "Montaigne." In *The Cornucopian Text: Problems of Writing in the French Renaissance,* 271–321. Oxford: Clarendon, 1979.

Clark, Carol. *The Web of Metaphor: Studies in the Imagery of Montaigne's* Essais. Lexington, Ky.: French Forum, 1978.

Coleman, D. G. "Montaigne's 'Sur des vers de Virgile': Taboo Subject, Taboo Author." In *Classical Influences on European Culture,* A.D. 1500–1700, edited by R. R. Bolgar, 135–40. Cambridge, Cambridge University Press, 1976.

Compagnon, Antoine. *Nous, Michel de Montaigne.* Paris: Seuil, 1980.

————. *La Seconde main ou le travail de la citation.* Paris: Seuil, 1979.

Conley, Tom. "Cataparalysis." *Diacritics* 8, no. 3 (Fall 1978): 41–59.

————. "Montaigne's *Gascoingne:* Textual Regionalism in 'Des Boiteux.' " *MLN* 92 (1977): 710–23.

————. "The Page's Hidden Dimension: Surface and Emblem in Montaigne's *Essais.*" *Bulletin of the Midwestern Modern Language Association* 7, no. 1 (1974): 13–25.

Cottrell, Robert D. *Sexuality/Textuality: A Study of the Fabric of Montaigne's* Essais. Columbus: Ohio State University Press, 1981.

de Man, Paul. "Montaigne and Transcendence." In *Fugitive Essays,* edited by Lindsay Waters. Minneapolis: University of Minnesota Press, forthcoming 1987.

Dow, Neal. *The Concept and Term "Nature" in Montaigne's* Essais. Philadelphia: University of Pennsylvania Press, 1940.

Duval, Edwin M. "Montaigne's Conversions: Compositional Strategies in the *Essais.*" *French Forum* 7 (1982): 5–22.

Emerson, Ralph Waldo. "Montaigne; or, the Skeptic." In *Representative Men: Seven Lectures,* 149–84. Boston: Phillips, Sampson, 1850.

*L'Esprit créateur* 8, no. 3 (Fall 1968). Special Montaigne Issue.

*L'Esprit créateur* 20, no. 1 (Spring 1980). Montaigne: A Quadricentennial Celebration.

Frame, Donald M. "Did Montaigne Betray Sebond?" *Romanic Review* 38 (1947): 297–329.

———. *Montaigne: A Biography*. New York: Harcourt, Brace & World, 1965.

———. *Montaigne in France, 1812–1852*. New York: Columbia University Press, 1940.

———. *Montaigne's Discovery of Man: The Humanization of a Humanist*. New York: Columbia University Press, 1955.

———. *Montaigne's* Essais: *A Study*. Englewood Cliffs, N.J.: Prentice-Hall, 1969.

Frame, Donald M., and Mary B. McKinley, eds. *Columbia Montaigne Conference Papers*. Lexington, Ky.: French Forum, 1981.

Friedrich, Hugo. *Montaigne*. Bern: Franke, 1949.

Gide, André. "Montaigne." *The Yale Review* 28 (1939): 572–93.

Glauser, Alfred. *Montaigne paradoxal*. Paris: A.-G. Nizet, 1972.

Gray, Floyd. *La balance de Montaigne: exagium/essai*. Paris: A.-G. Nizet, 1972.

———. "Montaigne and Sebond: The Rhetoric of Paradox." *French Studies* 28 (1974): 134–45.

———. "The Unity of Montaigne in the Essays." *Modern Language Quarterly* 22 (1961): 79–86.

Greenberg, Mitchell. "Montaigne at the Crossroads: Textual Conundrums in the *Essais*." *Stanford French Review* 6 (1982): 21–34.

Hallie, Philip P. *The Scar of Montaigne: An Essay in Personal Philosophy*. Middletown, Conn.: Wesleyan University Press, 1966.

Harth, Erica. " 'Sur des vers de Virgile' (III, 5): Antinomy and Totality in Montaigne." *French Forum* 2 (1977): 3–21.

Henry, Patrick. "Recognition of the Other and Avoidance of the Double: The Self and the Other in the *Essais* of Montaigne." *Stanford French Review* 6 (1982): 175–88.

Holyoake, John. *Montaigne:* Essais (Critical Guides to French Texts). London: Grant & Cutler, 1983.

Horkheimer, Max. "Montaigne und die Funktion der Skepsis." In *Kritische Theorie. Eine Dokumentation,* edited by Alfred Schmidt, vol. 2, 201–59. Frankfurt am Main: S. Fischer Verlag, 1968.

Hunt, R. N. Carew. "Montaigne and the State." *Edinburgh Review* 246, no. 502 (October 1927): 259–72.

Kritzman, Lawrence D. *Destruction/decouverte: Le fonctionnement de la rhétorique dans les* Essais *de Montaigne*. Lexington, Ky.: French Forum, 1980.

La Charite, Raymond C. *The Concept of Judgement in Montaigne*. The Hague: Martinus Nijhoff, 1968.

———, ed. *O un amy! Essays on Montaigne in Honor of Donald M. Frame*. Lexington, Ky.: French Forum, 1977.

Lanson, Gustave. *Les* Essais *de Montaigne: étude et analyse*. Paris: Mellotée, 1930.

Lapp, John C. "Montaigne's 'Negligence' and Some Lines from Virgil." *Romanic Review* 61 (1970): 167–81.

Larkin, Neil M. "Montaigne's Last Words." *L'Esprit créateur* 15, nos. 1–2 (Spring-Summer 1975): 21–38.

Locher, Caroline. "Primary and Secondary Themes in Montaigne's 'Des cannibales.' " *French Forum* 1 (1976): 119–26.

McFarlane, Ian D. "Montaigne and the Concept of the Imagination." In *The*

*French Renaissance and Its Heritage, Essays Presented to Alan M. Boase,* edited by D. R. Haggis et al., 117–37. London: Methuen, 1968.

McFarlane, Ian D., and Ian Maclean, eds. *Montaigne: Essays in Memory of Richard Sayce.* Oxford: Clarendon, 1982.

McGowan, Margaret. *Montaigne's Deceits: The Art of Persuasion in the* Essais. London: University of London Press, 1974.

McKinley, Mary B. *Words in a Corner: Studies in Montaigne's Latin Quotations.* Lexington, Ky.: French Forum, 1981.

Mehlman, Geoffrey. "La Boétie's Montaigne." *Oxford Literary Review* 4, no. 1 (1981): 45–61.

Moore, W. G. "Montaigne's Notion of Experience." In *The French Mind: Studies in Honour of Gustave Radler,* edited by W. G. Moore, 34–52. Oxford: Clarendon, 1952.

Norton, Glyn P. *Montaigne and the Introspective Mind.* The Hague: Mouton, 1975.

Norton, Grace. *Studies in Montaigne.* New York: Macmillan, 1904.

*Oeuvres et critiques.* 8, nos. 1–2 (1983). "Montaigne" (Special Issue).

O'Neill, John. *Essaying Montaigne: A Study of the Renaissance Institution of Reading and Writing.* London: Routledge & Kegan Paul, 1982.

Papic, Marko. *L'Expression et la place du sujet dans les* Essais *de Montaigne.* Paris: Presses universitaires de France, 1970.

Pouilloux, Jean-Yves. *Lire les* Essais *de Montaigne.* Paris: Maspero, 1969.

Poulet, Georges. "Montaigne." In *Studies in Human Time,* translated by Elliot Coleman, 39–49. Baltimore: Johns Hopkins University Press, 1956.

Raymond, Marcel. "L'Attitude religieuse de Montaigne." In his *Génies de France:* 50–67. Neuchâtel: Éditions de la Baconnière, 1942.

Regosin, Richard L. *The Matter of My Book: Montaigne's* Essais *as the Book of the Self.* Berkeley: University of California Press, 1977.

———. " 'Le Miroitier vague': Reflections on the Example in Montaigne's *Essais.*" *Oeuvres et critiques* 8, nos. 1–2 (1983): 73–86.

———. "Recent Trends in Montaigne Scholarship: A Post-Structuralist Perspective." *Renaissance Quarterly* 37 (1984): 34–54.

———. "Sources and Resources: The Pretexts of Originality in Montaigne's *Essais.*" *Sub-Stance* 21 (1978): 103–15.

Rendall, Steven. "In Disjointed Parts/Par articles décousus." In *Fragments: Incompletion and Discontinuity,* edited by Lawrence D. Kritzman. New York: New York Literary Forum, 1981.

———. "*Mus in pice:* Montaigne and Interpretation." *MLN* 94 (1979): 1056–71.

———. "Reading Montaigne." *Diacritics* 15, no. 2 (Summer 1985): 44–53.

———. "On Reading the *Essais* Differently." *MLN* 100 (1985): 1080–85.

———. "The Rhetoric of Montaigne's Self-Portrait." *Studies in Philology* 73 (1976): 285–301.

Rider, Frederick. *The Dialectic of Selfhood in Montaigne.* Stanford: Stanford University Press, 1973.

Rigolot, François. "Montaigne's Maxims: From a Discourse of the Other to the Expression of Self." *L'Esprit créateur* 22, no. 3 (Fall 1982): 8–18.

Russell, Daniel. "Montaigne's Emblems." *French Forum* 9 (1984): 261–75.

Samaras, Zoe. *The Comic Element in Montaigne's Style*. Paris: A.-G. Nizet, 1970.

Sayce, Richard A. *The Essays of Montaigne: A Critical Exploration*. London: Weidenfield & Nicolson, 1972.

Screech, M. A. *Montaigne and Melancholy: The Wisdom of the* Essays. London: Duckworth, 1983.

Starobinski, Jean. "Dire l'amour: Remarques sur l'érotique de Montaigne." "Dire": *Nouvelle revue de psychanalyse* 23, (1981): 299–323.

———. *Montaigne in Motion*. Translated by Arthur Goldhammer. Chicago: University of Chicago Press, 1985.

Strowski, Fortunat. *Montaigne*. 2d ed. Paris: F. Alcan, 1931.

Supple, James J. *Arms versus Letters: The Military and Literary Ideals in the* Essais *of Montaigne*. New York: Oxford University Press, 1984.

Tetel, Marcel, ed. *Actes du colloque international: Montaigne (1580–1980)*. Paris: A.-G. Nizet, 1983.

Thibaudet, Albert. *Montaigne*. Edited by Floyd Gray. Paris: Gallimard, 1963.

Villey, Pierre. *Les Sources et l'évolution des* Essais de Montaigne. 2 vols. Paris: Hachette, 1908.

Weller, Barry. "The Rhetoric of Friendship in Montaigne's *Essais*." *New Literary History* 9 (1978): 503–23.

Wilden, Anthony. "Montaigne on the Paradoxes of Individualism: A Communication About Communication." In *System and Structure: Essays in Communication and Exchange*, 88–105. London: Tavistock, 1972.

———. "Montaigne's *Essays* in the Context of Communication." *MLN* 85 (1970): 454–78.

———. " 'Par divers moyens on arrive à pareille fin': A Reading of Montaigne." *MLN* 83 (1968): 577–97.

Winter, Ian J. *Montaigne's Self-Portrait and Its Influence in France, 1580–1630*. Lexington, Ky.: French Forum, 1976.

*Yale French Studies* 64 (1983). Special Montaigne Issue.

Zweig, Stefan. *Montaigne*. Translated into French by Jean-Jacques Lafaye and François Brugier and revised by Jean-Louis Bandet. Paris: Presses universitaires de France, 1982.

# Acknowledgments

"Montaigne, or the Art of Being Truthful" by Herbert Luthy from *The Proper Study: Essays on Western Classics,* edited by Quentin Anderson and Joseph A. Mazzeo, © 1962 by St. Martin's Press, Inc. Reprinted by permission. This essay originally appeared in *Encounter* 1, no. 2 (November 1953), © 1953 by Encounter Ltd. Reprinted by permission.

"The Whole Man, 1586–1592" by Donald M. Frame from *Montaigne's Discovery of Man: The Humanization of a Humanist* by Donald M. Frame, © 1955 by Columbia University Press. Reprinted by permission of Columbia University Press.

"Reading Montaigne" by Maurice Merleau-Ponty from *Signs* by Maurice Merleau-Ponty, © 1964 by Northwestern University Press. Reprinted by permission of Northwestern University Press. This essay originally appeared in *Signes,* © 1960 by Editions Gallimard. Reprinted by permission of Editions Gallimard.

"Montaigne's Tomb, or Autobiographical Discourse" by Louis Marin from *The Oxford Literary Review* 4, no. 3 (1981), © 1981 by the *The Oxford Literary Review*. Reprinted by permission. All rights reserved.

"Problems of Reading in the *Essais*" by Terence Cave from *Montaigne: Essays in Memory of Richard Sayce,* edited by Ian D. McFarlane and Ian Maclean, © 1982 by Oxford University Press. Reprinted by permission of Oxford University Press.

"Montaigne's Cure: Stones and Roman Ruins" by Irma S. Majer from *MLN* 97, no. 4 (May 1982), © 1982 by the Johns Hopkins University Press, Baltimore/London. Reprinted by permission of the Johns Hopkins University Press.

"The Paradox and the Miracle: Structure and Meaning in 'The Apology for Raymond Sebond' [*Essais* 2.12]" (originally entitled "Montaigne: The Paradox and the Miracle: Structure and meaning in 'The Apology for Raymond Sebond' [*Essais* 2.12]") by Catherine Demure from *Yale French Studies* 64 (1983), © 1983 by Yale University. Reprinted by permission of *Yale French Studies*.

"Dangerous Parleys—*Essais* 1.5 and 6" by Thomas M. Greene from *Yale French Studies* 64 (1983), © 1983 by Yale University. Reprinted by permission of *Yale French Studies*.

" 'And Then, for Whom Are You Writing?' " by Jean Starobinski from *Montaigne in Motion*, translated by Arthur Goldhammer, © 1985 by the University of Chicago. Reprinted by permission of the University of Chicago Press.

"Montaigne's Anti-Influential Model of Identity" by Jefferson Humphries from *Losing the Text: Readings in Literary Desire* by Jefferson Humphries, © 1986 by the University of Georgia Press. This essay originally appeared in *Sub-Stance* 11, no. 2 (1982), © 1982 by the Board of Regents of the University of Wisconsin System. Reprinted by permission of the University of Wisconsin Press.

# Index

# Modern Critical Views

*Continued from front of book*

Gabriel García Márquez
Andrew Marvell
Carson McCullers
Herman Melville
George Meredith
James Merrill
John Stuart Mill
Arthur Miller
Henry Miller
John Milton
Yukio Mishima
Molière
Michel de Montaigne
Eugenio Montale
Marianne Moore
Alberto Moravia
Toni Morrison
Alice Munro
Iris Murdoch
Robert Musil
Vladimir Nabokov
V. S. Naipaul
R. K. Narayan
Pablo Neruda
John Henry, Cardinal
  Newman
Friedrich Nietzsche
Frank Norris
Joyce Carol Oates
Sean O'Casey
Flannery O'Connor
Christopher Okigbo
Charles Olson
Eugene O'Neill
José Ortega y Gasset
Joe Orton
George Orwell
Ovid
Wilfred Owen
Amos Oz
Cynthia Ozick
Grace Paley
Blaise Pascal
Walter Pater
Octavio Paz
Walker Percy
Petrarch
Pindar
Harold Pinter
Luigi Pirandello
Sylvia Plath
Plato

Plautus
Edgar Allan Poe
Poets of Sensibility & the
  Sublime
Poets of the Nineties
Alexander Pope
Katherine Anne Porter
Ezra Pound
Anthony Powell
Pre-Raphaelite Poets
Marcel Proust
Manuel Puig
Alexander Pushkin
Thomas Pynchon
Francisco de Quevedo
François Rabelais
Jean Racine
Ishmael Reed
Adrienne Rich
Samuel Richardson
Mordecai Richler
Rainer Maria Rilke
Arthur Rimbaud
Edwin Arlington Robinson
Theodore Roethke
Philip Roth
Jean-Jacques Rousseau
John Ruskin
J. D. Salinger
Jean-Paul Sartre
Gershom Scholem
Sir Walter Scott
William Shakespeare
  (3 vols.)
  Histories & Poems
  Comedies & Romances
  Tragedies
George Bernard Shaw
Mary Wollstonecraft
  Shelley
Percy Bysshe Shelley
Sam Shepard
Richard Brinsley Sheridan
Sir Philip Sidney
Isaac Bashevis Singer
Tobias Smollett
Alexander Solzhenitsyn
Sophocles
Wole Soyinka
Edmund Spenser
Gertrude Stein
John Steinbeck

Stendhal
Laurence Sterne
Wallace Stevens
Robert Louis Stevenson
Tom Stoppard
August Strindberg
Jonathan Swift
John Millington Synge
Alfred, Lord Tennyson
William Makepeace
  Thackeray
Dylan Thomas
Henry David Thoreau
James Thurber and S. J.
  Perelman
J. R. R. Tolkien
Leo Tolstoy
Jean Toomer
Lionel Trilling
Anthony Trollope
Ivan Turgenev
Mark Twain
Miguel de Unamuno
John Updike
Paul Valéry
Cesar Vallejo
Lope de Vega
Gore Vidal
Virgil
Voltaire
Kurt Vonnegut
Derek Walcott
Alice Walker
Robert Penn Warren
Evelyn Waugh
H. G. Wells
Eudora Welty
Nathanael West
Edith Wharton
Patrick White
Walt Whitman
Oscar Wilde
Tennessee Williams
William Carlos Williams
Thomas Wolfe
Virginia Woolf
William Wordsworth
Jay Wright
Richard Wright
William Butler Yeats
A. B. Yehoshua
Emile Zola